Monograph No. 2

# FUNGI OF PAKISTAN

SULTAN AHMAD
Bilal Chaudhry
Imran A Chaudhry
Maaria Chaudhry

*Second Edition*                    2014

# INTRODUCTION

The present Monograph deals with 1219 species of Fungi recorded from the area now comprising the Province of West Pakistan. Up to 1947 this area was a part of the British India and its mycoflora was listed by Butler & Bisby (1931) and Mundkur (1938). These Monographs recorded no more than 198 species from this region; an unusually low record for so vast an area (over 300,000 sq. miles).

Most of the 1,000 new records added since 1938 are by the present author himself, but he feels convinced that he has been able to list only a small fraction of the entire mycoflora of this region. The Divisions of Kalat, Hyderabad, Khairpur, Quetta and Dera Ismail Khan have either remained totally unexplored, or only a few sporadic records have been made from there. All ·that is wanted is a Pioneer, and he will find hundreds if not thousands of species of Fungi not recorded previously.

Despite all this, the author feels justified in presenting this list of 1219 species : Butler & Bisby and Mundkur listed no more than 3000 species of Fungi from the whole of British India and Burma covering an area five times as large again as West Pakistan. It is the fervent hope of the author that the present Monograph will serve to stimulate further research on systematic Mycology.

15th July,

,

Sultan Ahmad

# Class : **MYXOMYCETES**

Order : MYXOGASTRALES

Family : CERATIOMYXACEAE

## Ceratiomyxa Schroet.

C. fruticulosa (Mull.) Macbr.; Lister, p. 4 ; Martin, p. *7 ;* Lodhi, p. 375. On rotting logs, Kagan Valley : Mahandri ; on stumps of *Abies pind row,* Murree.

Family : AMAUROCHAETACEAE

## Amaurochaete Rost.

A. ferruginea Macbr. & Martin *;* Martin, p. 68 *;* Lodhi, p. 378. On dead wood, Balakot.

Family : ARCYRIACEAE

## Arcyria \Viggers.

A. cinerea (Bull.) Pers.; Sacc. Sy!!. Fung. VII : 427 ; Lister, p. 231 ; Martin, p. 45 ; Lodhi, p. 377. On dead wood, Murree.

A. denudata (L.) Wettst.; Lister, p. *235 ;* Martin, p. 46 ; Lodhi, p. 377. On dead wood, Murree.

A. insignis Kalchbr. & Cke.; Sacc. Syll. Fung. VII : 432 ; Martin, p. 46 *;* Lodhi, p. 377 ; Lister, p. 236. On dead wood, Murree ; Kagan.

A. nutans (Bull.) Grev.; Sacc. Syll. Fung. VII : 429 ; Lister, 239 ; Martin, p. 45, Lodhi, p. 377. On wood, Murree ; Kagan.

Family : CRIBRARIACEAE

## Cribraria Pers.

C. argillacea (Pers.) Pers.; Sacc. Sy!!. Fung. VII : 416 ; Lister, p. 170 ; Martin, p. 26 ; Lodhi, p. 377. On dead wood, Kagan.

C. aurantiaca Schrad.; Sacc. Sy!!. Fung. VII : 413 ; Martin, p. 30 ; Lodhi, p. 377. On dead wood, Murree.

## Dictydium Schr::i d.

D. cancellatum (Batsch) Macbr.; Lister, p. 179 ; Martin, p. 32 ; Lodhi, p. 377. On dead wood, Murree.

Family : DIDYMIACEAE

## Didymium Schrad.

D. dubium Rost. ; Sacc. Syll. Fung. VI : 376 ; Lister, p. 112 ; Martin, p. 143 ; Lodhi, p. 383. On mossy bark, Murree.

D. minus (Lister) Morgan ; Martin, p. 146 ; Lodhi, p. 383 ; Lister, p. 115 as D. *melanospermum* var. *minus.*   On fallen leaves, Murree.

D. squamulosum (Alb. & Schw.) Fr.; Sacc. Syll. Fung. VII : 377 ; Lister, p. 117 ; Martin, p. 144 ; Lodhi, p. 383.   On living leaves of *Sarcococca saligna* and fallen leaves of *Quercus dilatata,* Murree.

### Family : LYCOGALACEAE
### Lycogala Mich.

L. epidendrum (L.) Fr.; Sacc. Syll. Fung. VII : 435 ; Lister, p. 199 ; Martin, p. 20 ; Lodhi, p. 376.   On dead wood, Kagan.

L. exiguum Morgan ; Martin, p. 21 ; Lodhi, p. 376 ; Lister, p. 199 as *L. epidendrum* var. *exiguum.*   On fallen log of *Pinus excelsa,* Murree.

### Family : PHYSARACEAE
### Badhamia Berk.

B. capsulifera (Bull.) Berk.; Sacc. Syll. Fung. VII : 333 ; Lister, p. 10 ; Martin, p. 97 ; Lodhi, p. 381.   On fallen twigs of *Rosa* sp., Murree.

B. macrocarpa (Ces.) Rost.; Sacc. Syll. Fung. VII : 330 ; Lister, p. 16 ; Martin, p. 99 ; Lodhi, p. 381.   On mossy bark, Murree.

### Craterium Trent.

C. aureum (Schum.) Rost ; Sacc. Syll. Fung. VII : 357 ; Lister, p. 79 ; Martin, p. 127 ; Lodhi, p. 382.   On fallen leaves, Murree.

C. leucocephalum (Pers.) Ditmar ; Sacc. Syll. Fung. VII : 356 ; Lister, p. 77 ; Martin, p. 126 ; Lodhi, p. 382.   On living shoots of *Sarcococca saligna* and *Hedera himalaicus,* Murree.

### Diachea Fr.

D. splendens Peck ; Sacc. Syll. Fung. VII : 388 ; Martin, p. 71 ; Lodhi, p. 379 ; Lister, p. 102 as D. *bulbillosa* var. *splendens.*   On fallen twigs and leaves, Sangla Hill.

D. subsessilis Peck ; Sacc. Syll. Fung. VII : 388 ; Lister, p. 104 ; Martin, p. 71 ; Lodhi, p. 379.   On fallen leaves of *Quercus dilatata,* Murree.

### Diderma Pers.

D. chondrioderma (de By. & Rost.) Lister ; Lister, p. 258 ; Martin, p. 134 ; Lodhi, p. 382.   On dead and living leaves of grasses, Lahore.

D. effusum (Schw.) Morgan ; Lister, p. 85 ; Martin, p. 134 ; Lodhi, p. 382.   On dead branches, Sangla Hill ; on living leaves of *Hedera himalaicus,* Murree ; on plant debris, Ladhar, Sheikhupura Dist.

D. hemisphaericum (Bull.) Hornem.; Lister, p. 84 ; Martin, p. 135 ; Lodhi, p. 383. On fallen leaves, Kagan.

D. niveum (Rost.) Macbr.; Lister, p. 88 ; Martin, p. 134 ; Lodhi, p. 382. On dead leaves, Murree.

### Fuligo Haller

F. cinerea (Schw.) Morgan ; Lister, p. 69 ; Martin, p. 94 ; Lodhi, p. 380. On straw and dead leaves, Ladhar, Sheikhupura Dist.

F. intermedia Macbr.; Martin, p. 95 ; Lodhi, p. 380 ; Lister, p. 69 under F. *cinerea*. On grass culms and dead leaves, Ladhar, Sheikhupura Dist.

F. megaspora Sturg.; Lister, p. 70 ; Martin, p. 95 ; Lodhi, p. 380. On the ground amongst fallen needles of *Pinus excelsa*, Nathia Gali.

F. septica (L.) Weber ; Martin, p. 93 ; Lister, p. 66 ; Lodhi, p. 380. On grass leaves, Sangla Hill ; on trunk of *Azad irachta indica*, Balakot ; on dead wood, Murree ; on bark of *Marus alba*, Changa Manga.

### Physarella von Hoeh.

P. oblonga (B. & C.) Morgan; Martin, p. 128; Lister, p. 72; Lodhi, p. 382. On bark of *Marus alba*, Sangla Hill.

### Physarum Pers.

P. bivalve Pers.; Lister, p. 58 ; Martin, p. 108 ; Lodhi, p. 381 ; Sacc. Syll. Fung. VII : 347 as P. *sinuosum*. On fallen pine needles, Balakot ; on fallen branches of *Rosa* sp. & *Rumex* sp., Murree ; on old culms of *Saccharum munja*, Ladhar, Sheikhupura Dist.

P. cinereum (Batsch) Pers.; Sacc. Syll. Fung. VII : 344 ; Lister, P. 53 ; Martin, p. 105 ; Lodhi, p. 381. On living leaves of grasses etc., Ladhar, Sheikhupura Dist.

P. contextum (Pers.) Pers.; Sacc. Syll. Fung. VII : 342 ; Lister, p. 60 ; Martin, p. 110 ; Lodhi, p. 381. On fallen branches of *Quercus dilatata.*, Murree; on fallen needles and cones of *Pinus excelsa*, Murree.

P. nutans Pers.; Lister, p. 46 ; Martin, p. 124 ; Lodhi, p. 382. On dead wood, Murree.

P. polycephalum Schw.; Sacc. Syll. Fung. VII : 352 ; Listei-, p. 37 ; Martin, p. 123 ; Lodhi, p. 381. On bark, Lahore.

P. pusillum (B. & C.) Lister ; Martin, p. 117 ; Lister, p. 44 ; Lodhi, p. 381. On bark, dead wood and manure heaps, Lahore ; Kagan ; Ladhar, Sheikhupura Dist.

Family : RETICULARIACEAE

## Enteridium Ehrenb.

E. rozcanum (Rost.) Wingate ; .Lister, p. 194 ; Martin, p. 23 ; Lodhi, p. 376. On logs, Kagan.

## Reticularia Bull.

**R**. lycoperdon Bull.; Sacc. Syll. Fung. VII :418 ; Lister, p. 195 ; Martin, p. 22 ; Lodhi, p. 376. In a hollow trunk of *Marus alba,* Balakot.

Family : STEMONITIDACEAE

## Comatricha Preuss.

C. typhoides (Bull.) Rost.; Lister, p. 145 ; Martin, p. 84 ;· Lodhi, p. 379. On rotten stumps of *Abies pind row,* Murree.

## Lamproderma Rost.

L. scintillans (Berk. & Br.) Morgan ; Lister, p. 153 ; Martin, p. 90 ; Lodhi, p. 380. On fallen needles of *Pinus excelsa,* Murree.

## Stemonitis Gleditsch

S. axifera (Bull.) Macbr.; Lister, p. 137 ; Martin, p. 76 ; Lodhi, p. 379. On fallen logs of *Pinus excelsa,* Murree.

S. sp]endens Rost.; Sacc. Sy!!. Fung. VII :398 ; Lister, p. 135 ; Martin, p. 76 ; Lodhi, p. 379. On dead wood, Murree ; Lahore.

Family : TRICHIACEAE

## Hemitrichia Rost.

**H.** clavata (Pers.) Rost.; Lister, p. 221 ; Martin, p. 58 ; Lodhi p. 378. On dead wood, Murree.

**H.** stipitata (Mass.) Macbr7; Martin, p. 58 ; Lodhi, p. 378 ; Lister, p. 221 under *H. clavata.* On dead wood, Murree.

H. vesparium (Batsch) Macbr.; Lister, p. 218 ; Martin, p. 59 ; Lodhi, p. 378. On dead wood, Murree ; Changa Manga.

F<imily : TUBULINACEAE

## Tubifera Gmel.

T. ferruginosa (Batsch) **J.** F. Gmel.; Lister, p. 187 ; Martin, p. 17 ; Lodhi, p. 376. On rotting wood and mossy bark, Murree.

Order : PLASMODIOPHORALES

## Sorosphaera Schroet.

S. veronicae Schroeter ; Sacc. Syll. Fung. VII : 466 ; Cook, p. 197 ; Mundkur & Ahmad, p. 1. On leaves and stems of *Veronica agrestis,* Lahore ; Ladhar, Sheikhupura Dist.

Tetramyxa Goebel

T. parasitica Goebel ; Sacc. Syll. Fung. VII : 465 ; Cook, p. 217 : Mund-kur & Ahmad, p. 1. On leaves and nodes of *Z anichel lia palustris* var. *pedicell ata,* Ladhar, Sheikhu pu ra Dist.

# Class : **PHYCOMYCETES**

## Order : CHYTRIDIALES

### Family : SYNCHYTRIACEAE

Synchytrium de Bary &·Woronin

S. marsiliae Lodhi apud Ahmad & Lodhi in Sydowia 7 : 266, 19;>3.    On *M arsilia minuta,* Chuharkana ; Kalashah Kaku.

### family : CLADOCHYTRIACEAE

Physoderma Wallr.

P. alfalfae (Lagerh.) Kading in Lloydia 13 : 44, 1950 ; Sacc. Syll. Fung. XXII : 515 as *Urophl yctis alfa.l fae ;* Sydow & Ahmad, p. 439. On *Vicia hirsut a,* Lahore.

P. maydis Miyabe ; Kading, p. 55 ; Sacc. Syll. Fung. XXIV : 20 as *Physo-d erma zeae-mayd is* Shaw; Malik & Khan, p. 522. On *Zea mays,* Hazara.

P. schroeteri Krieger ; Sacc. Syll. Fung. XIV: 447 ; Kading, p. 46 ; Butler & Bisby, p. 1.  On leaves of *Scirpus* sp., Lahore (B. Dass).

P. trifolii (Passer.) Kading, in Lloydia 13 : 50 ; Sacc. Syll. Fung. XVII : 515; Sydow & Ahmad, p. 439. On *Trifolium resupinatum,* Chillianwala.

### Family : RHIZIDIACEAE

Rhizidiomyces z.opf

R. apophysatus Zopf ; Sacc. Syll. Fung. VII : 816.  Parasitic on *Achl ya k lebsiana,* Lahore.

## Order : SAPROLEGNIA LES

### Family : SAPROLEGNIACEAE

Achlya Nees ex Pringsh.

A. americana Humphrey ; Sacc. Syll. Fung. IX : 245 ; Chaud huri & Kochhar, p. 31 ; Chaudh uri *et al,* p. 31 ; Coker, p. 11. In ponds, Lahore.

A. androcomposita Hamid in Proc. Ind. Acad. Sci. 15 : 209, 1942 ; Chaud huri *et al,* p. 34. In ponds, Lahore.

A. aplanes Maurizo ; Sacc. Syll. Fung. XI : 245 ; Chaud huri & Kochhar, p. 148 ; Chaud huri *et al,* p. 34 ; Coker, p. 143. In ponds, Lahore ; Gujranwala.

A. conspicua  Coker ; Chaudhuri  &  Kochhar,  p. 146 ; Chaudhuri *et al,* p. 35 ; Coker, p. 131.  In ponds, Lahore.

A. de Baryana Humphrey ;  Chaudhuri & Kochhar,  p. 147 ; Chaudhuri *et al,* p. 37.  In tap water, Lahore.

A. dubia Coker ; Chaudhuri & Kochhar,  p. 146 ;  Chaudhuri *et al,* p. 38 ; Coker, p. 135.  In ponds, Lahore ; Gujranwala.

——var. pigmenta Chaudhuri & Kochhar in Proc. Ind. Acad. Sci. 2 : 147, 1935 ; Chaudhuri *et al,* p. 39.  In ponds, Lahore ; Gujranwala.

A. flagellata Coker ; Chaudhuri & Kochhar, p. 144 ; Chaudhuri  *et al,* p. 41 ; Coker, p. 116.  In ponds, Lahore.

A. imperfecta Coker ; Chaudhuri & Kochhar,  p. 144 ;  Chaudhuri  *et al,* p. 42 ; Coker, p. 188.  In ponds, Lahore.

A. klebsiana Pieters ;  Sacc. Syll. Fung. XXIV : 27 ;  Chaud huri & Kochhar, p. 145 ; Chaudhuri *et al,* p. 43 ; Coker p. 120.  In ponds, Lahore.

——var. indica Chaudhuri & Lotus  in Proc.  Ind. Acad. Sci. 3 : 328, 1935 ; Chaudhuri *et al,* p. 46.  In ponds, Lahore.

——var. kashyapia Chaudhuri apud Chaudhuri *et al,* p. 46. Syn. *Achlya kashyapia* Chaudhuri.  In ponds, Lahore.

A. oblongata de Bary ; Hamid, p. 209 ; Chaudhuri *et al,* p. 50  ;  Coker, p. 132.  In ponds, Lahore.

A. prolifera (Nees) de Bary ; Sacc. Syll. Fung. VII : 274 ; Chaudhu ri & Lotus, p. 328 ; Chaudh uri *et al,* p. 52 ; Coker, p. 143. In ponds, Lahore ; Sheikhupura.

A. proliferoides Coker ; Chaudhuri & Kochhar, p. 143 ; Chaudhuri *et al,* p. 52 ; Coker, p. 115.  In ponds, Lahore.

### Isoachlya  Kaufmann

I. monilifera (de Bary) Kauffman ; Chaudhuri & Kochhar, p. 141 Chaudhuri *et al,* p. 29 ; Coker, p. 88.  In ponds, Lahore.

### Protoachlya Coker

P. paradoxa Coker ; Chaudhuri & Banerjee, p. 216 t Chaudhuri *et al,* p. 58 ; Coker, p. 91.  In drains and ponds, Lahore ; Sheikhupura.

### Pythiopsis de Bary

P. intermedia Chaudhuri & Banerjee in Proc. Ind. Acad. Sci. 15 221, 1942 ; Chaudhuri *et al,* p. 24.                    In ponds and drains, Lahore.

### Saprolegnia  Nees ex Pringsh.

S. parasitica Coker ; Chaudhuri & Kochhar, p. 139 ; Chaud huri  *et al,* p. 25 ; Coker, p. 57.  In tap water, Lahore.

————**var.** kochhari Chaudhuri in Proc. Ind. Acad. Sci. 2 : 139, 1935 , Chaudhuri *et al*, p. 26. Parasitic on *Belone cancinula* and other fishes, Hiran Minar (Sheikhupura).

S. rhaetica Maurizio ; Chaudhuri & Banerjee, p. 224 ; Chaudhuri *et al*, p. 27 ; Coker, p. 67.   On dead house flies lying in tap water, Lahore.

Order : PERONOSPORALES

Family : ALBUGINACEAE

Albugo Pers. ex S. F. Gray

A. bliti (Biv.) Kuntze. -Syn. *Cystopus bliti* (Biv.) de Bary ; Sacc. Syll. Fung. VII : 236 ; Malik & Khan, p. 522. On leaves of *Amarantus blitum*, Peshawar (S. A. Malik) ; of *A. paniculatus*, Swat : Kulali ; of *Digera arvensis*, Ladhar, Sheikhupura Dist.; Lyallpur.

A. candida (Gmel.) Kuntze. -Syn. *Cystopus candidus* (Gmel.) Leveille ; Sacc. Syll. Fung. VII : 234 ; Sydow & Ahmad, p. 439. On leaves of *Cleome viscosa*, Rawalpindi ; of *Capsella bursa-pastoris*, Dargai ; of *Eucladium syriacum*, Dargai ; of *Eruca sativa*, Lyallpur ; Swat : Mingora ; of *Neslia paniculata*, Swat ; of *Notoceros canariense*, Dargai ; of *Malcolmia africana*, Dargai ; of *Sisymbrium irio*, Sargodha ; Dargai.

A. impomoeae-panduratae (Schw.) Swingle. -Syn. *Cystopus ipomoeae-panduratae* (ScJ:iw.) Stev. & Swing.; Sacc. Syll. Fung. XI : 341 ; Sydow & Ahmad, p. 439.   On leaves and branches of *lpomoea aquatica*, Sialkot ; of *I. hederacea*, Swat : Madian.

A. platensis (Speg.) Swingle. -Syn. *Cystopus platensis* Speg.; Sacc. Syll. Fung. XI : 212. On leaves of *Boerhaavia diffusa*, Ladhar, Sheikhupura Dist.

A. portulacae (DC.) Kuntze. -Syn. *Cystopus portulacae* (DC.) Lev.; Sacc. Syll. Fung. VII : 235. On leaves of *Portulaca oleracea*, very common in Swat.

A. tragopogi (Pers.) Schroeter. -Syn. *Cystopus tragopogonis* Schroeter ; Sacc. Syll. Fung. VII : 234.   On leaves of *Cnicus arvensis*, Lyallpur ; „ of *Cousinia minuta*, Dargai ; of *Serratula pallida*, Cangla Gali.

Family : PERONOSPORACEAE

Bremia Regel

B. lactucae Regel ; Sacc. Syll. Fung. VII : 244 ; Sydow & Ahmad, p. 439 ; Shaw, Mycologia 41 : 326. as *B. ganglioniformis* (Casp.) Shaw. On leaves of *Lactuca scariola*, Ladhar, Sheikhupura Dist.; of *Launea nudicaulis*, Lyallpur.

B. sonchi Sawada ; Sacc. SyU. Fung. XXIV : 62 ; Sydow & Ahmad, p. 439 ; Malik & Khan, p. 522. On leaves of *Sonchus oleraceus*, Ladhar ; Lahore ; Kagan Valley.

## Peronospora Corda

**P.** aestivalis Sydow ; Gaeumann, p. 200 ; Thind, p. 200. On leaves of *Medicago sativa*, Shahdara ; of M. *denticulata*, Lahore ; Gakkhar ; Lyallpur ; Sargodha.

**P.** affinis Rossm.; Sacc. Syll. Fung. VII : 251 ; Gaeumann, p. 304. On leaves of *Fumaria indica,* Changa Manga.

**P.** alta Fuckel ; Sacc. Syll. Fung. VII :262 ; Gaeumann, p. 307 ; Sydow & Ahmad, p. 439 ; Thind, p. 213 as *P. plantaginis.* On leaves of *Plantago amplexicaulis,* Lahore ; Sargodha.

**P.** aparines (de Bary) Gaeumann ; Sacc. Syll. Fung. XXIV: 58 ; Gaeumann, p. 246 ; Thind, p. 208. On leaves of *Galium aparine,* Lahore ; Changa Manga.

**P.** arborescens (Berk.) de Bary ; Sacc. Syll. Fung. VII :251 : Gaeumann, p. 69 ; Thind, p. 207. On leaves of *Papaver rhoeas* and *P. somniferum,* Lahore.

**P.** astragalina Sydow ; Gaeumann, p. 188 ; Thind, p. 203. On leaves of *Astragalus tribuloides,* Lahore.

**P.** brassicae Gaeumann ; Sacc. Syll. Fung. XXIV : 45 ; Gaeumann, p. 260 ; Thind, p. 209. On leaves of *Brassica campestris, B. napus* and *B. juncea,* Lahore ; of *Goldbachia laevigata,* Jhang; of *Malcolmia africana,* Lahore : Sargodha ; Lyallpur ; Sangla Hill ; of *Raphanus sativus,* Lahore.

**P.** cannabina Otth ; Sacc. Syll. Fung. XIV : 458 ; Gaeumann, p. 315. On leaves of *Cannabis sativus,* Lahore.

**P.** effusa (Grev.) Rabenhorst ; Sacc. Syll. Fung. VII : 256 : Gaeumann, p. 227 ; Thind, p. 204. On leaves of *Chenopodium album,* Lahore; Changa Manga ; Lyallpur ; Sangla Hill ; Peshawar.

**P.** gaeumannii Mundkur in Sci. Monogr. Imp. Counc. Agric. Res. No: 12, p. 8, 1938. On leaves of *Argemone mexicana,* Lahore.

**P.** kochiae Gaeumann .; Sacc. Syll. Fung. XXIV :41 ; Gaeumann, p. 231 ; Thind, p. *20?·* On leaves of *Kochia indica,* Changa Manga.

**P.** lathyri-palustris Gaeumann ; Gaeumann, p. 192 ; Thind, p. 198. On leaves of *Lathyrus sativus,* Shahdara ; Lyallpur.

**P.** littoralis Gaeumann ; Gaeumann, p. 224 ; Sacc. Syll. Fung. XXIV : 39. On leaves of *Atriplex laciniata,* Changa Manga.

**P.** meliloti Sydow ; Gaeumann, p. 203 ; Thind, p. 202. On leaves of *Melilotus alba* and M. *parviflora,* Lahore ; Gakkhar ; Jhang ; Lyallpur; Gujranwala.

**P.** muralis Gaeumann ; Sacc. SylL Fung. XXIV : 41; Gaeumann, p. 223 ; Sydow & Ahmad, p. 439. On leaves of *Chenopodium murale ,* Sargodha.

**P.** parasitica (Pers.) de Bary ; Sacc. Syll. Fung. VII : 249 ; Gaeumann, p. 263 ; Thind, p. 211. On leaves of *Eruca sativa,* Lahore, Sheikhupura Dist.

**P.** sisymbrii-officinalis Gaeumann; Sacc. Syll. Fung. XXIV : 51; Gaeumann, p. 276 ; Thind, p. 212. On leaves of *Sisymbrium irio,* Gujranwala ; Changa Manga.

**P.** swinglei Ell. & Kellerman ; Sacc. Syll. Fung. IX : 344 ; Gaeumann, p. 138. On leaves of *Salvia pi ebeid ,* Changa Manga.

**P.** trifolii-repentis Sydow ; Gaeumann, p. 215 ; Thind, p. 201. On leaves of *Trifolium resupinatum,* Lahore.

**P.** trigonellae Gaeumann ; Gaeumann, p. 216 ; Sydow & Ahmad , p. 439 ; Thind, p. 199. On leaves of *Trigonella foenum-graecum,* Shahdara ; of *T. polycerata,* Jallo ; Sangla Hill.

**P.** variabilis Gaeumann ; Sacc. Syil. Fung. XXIV : 39 ; Gaeumann, p. 226 ; Thind, p. -205. On leaves of *Chenopodium album ,* Kagan; Lahore ; Lad har, Sheikhupura Dist.

**P.** vicia:e-sativae daeumann ; Sacc. Syll. Fung. XXIV : 56 ; Gaeuinann, p. 219 ; Thind, p. 197. On leaves of *Vicia sativa ,* Lahore ; Lyallpur.

### Plasmopara Schroet.

**P.** obducens Schroeter ; Sacc. Syll. Fung. VII : 242. On leaves of *Impatiens royfei ,* Swat : Kalam.

**P.** pusilla (de Bary) Schroeter ; Sacc. Syll. Fung. Vil : 241; Malik & Khan, p. 522. *bn* leaves of *Geranium wallichianum,* Hazara (S. A. Malik).

### Pseudoperonospora Rostov.

Ps. cubensis (Berk. & Curtis) Rostov. ; Sacc. Syll. Fung. XVI : 520. On leaves of *Cucumis melo,* Lyallpur.

### Sclerospora Schroet.

S. graminicola (Sacc.)'Schroeter ; Sacc. Syll. Fung. VII : 238. On leaves and ears of *Pennisetum typhoid es,* very common throughout the area.

## Family : PYTHIACEAE

### Phytophthora de Bary

P. infestans (Mont.) de Bary ; Sacc. Syll. Fung. VII : 237. On *Solanum tuberosum*, Murree.

### Pythiogeton Minden

P. sterilis Hamid in Proc. Ind. Acad. Sci. 15 : 212, 1942 ; Chaudhuri *et al*, p. 63. On decaying twigs lying in water, Lahore.

### Pythium Pringsh.

P. aphanidermatum (Edsm.) Fitzp. ; Malik & Khan, p. 522. On *Capsicum annuum*, Tarnab Farm, Peshawar (S. A;Malik).

## Order : MUCORALES

## Family : MUCORACEAE

### Mucor Mich. ex Fr.

M. repens Schostakowitsch ; Zycha, p. 104 ; Hukam Chand, Proc. Ind. Acad. Sci. 5 : 325 as M. *botryoid es* Lendner. Isolated from the soil, Lahore.

M. microsporus Namyslowski ; Zycha, p. 81. On dung, Lahore.

M. mucedo Linn. ex Fries ; Sacc. Syll. Fung. VII : 191 ; Zycha, p. 85 ; Ginai, J. Ind. Bot. Soc. 15 : 271 as M. *griseosporus* Povah. On dung, Lahore (Ginai ; Mahju).

### Pilobolus Tode ex Fr.

P. crystallinus (Wigg.) Tode ; Sacc. Syll. Fung. VII : 185 ; Zycha,, p. 157; Mahju, J. Ind. Bot. Soc. 12 : 157. On dung, Lahore.

P. kleinii van Tieghem ; Sacc. Syll. Fung. VII: 185; Zycha, p. 152 ; Ginai, J. Ind. Bot. Soc. 15 :273. On dung, Lahore.

P. longipes van Tieghem ; Sacc. Syll. Fung. VII : 185 ; Zycha, p. 148 ; Mahju, J. Ind. Bot. Soc. 12 : 157. On dung, Lahore (Mahju).

P. nanus van Tieghem; Sacc. Syll. Fung. VII : 186 ; Zycha, p. 149; Ginai, J. Ind. Bot. Soc. 15 :272. On dung, Lahore (Ginai).

P. oedipus Mont. ; Sacc. Syll. Fung. VII : 186 ; Zycha, p. 150 ; Mahju, p. 157 as *P. minutus* Speg. On dung, Lahore.

P. sphaerosporus (Grove) Palla ; Zycha, p. 149. On dung, Lahore.

### Rhizopus Ehrenb. ex Cda.

R. arrhizus Fischer ; Sacc. Syll. Fung. XI :240 ; Zycha, p. 112. -Syn. R. *nodosus* Namys. Isolated from soil, Lahore.

R. microsporus van Tieghem ; Sacc. Syll. Fung. VII :213 ; Zycha, p. 110. Isolated from air, Lahore.

R. oligosporus Saito ; Zycha, p. 111.  Isolated from soil, Lahore.

R. nigricans Ehrenb. ; Sacc. Syll. Fung. VII : 212 ; Zycha, p. 116.  On bread, Lahore.

### Family : CEPHALIDACEAE

### Cunni.nghamella  Matr.

C. echinulata Thaxter ; Sacc. Syll. Fung. XVII : 508 ; Zycha, p. 169 ; Chaudhuri & Sachar *in* Ann. Myc. 32, p. 92 as C. *verticillata* Paine. Isolated from soil, Lahore.

### Dicranophora  Schroet.

D. fulva Schroet. ; Zycha, p. 157.  On dung, Lahore.

### Piptocephalis de Bary

P. fresniana de Bary ; Sacc. Syll. Fung. VII : 226.  Parasitic on *Mucof'* sp., Lahore.

### Syncephalus van Tiegh.

S. sphaerica van Tiegh. ; Sacc. Syll. VII : 228 ; Ginai, p. 272 ; Zycha, p. 179.  Parasitic on *Mucof'* sp., Lahore.

### Family : THAMNIDIACEAE

### Chaetocladium  Fres.

C. jonesii (Berk. & Br.) Fres. ; Sacc. Syll. Fung. VII : 220.  Parasitic on *Mucof'* sp., Lahore.

### Family : MORTIERELLACEAE

### Mortierella Coemans

M. nigrescens van Tiegh. ; Sacc. Syll. Fung. VII  223.  On a rotting fungus, Murree.

### Family : ENDOGONACEAE

### Endogone Link ex Fr.

E. fulva (Berk.) Pat. ; Zycha, p. 219.  On the ground, Ladhar, Sheikhupura Dist.

### Order : ENTOMOPHTHORALES

### Empusa Cohn,

E. muscae (Fr.) Cohn ; Sacc. Syll.,Fung. VII: 281.  On house flies, Lahore.

### Entomoph thora  Fres.

E. aphidis Hoffm. ; Sacc. Syll. Fung. VII : 283.  On *Aphis* sp., Lahore.

# Class : **ASCOMYCETES**

Subclass I. SYNASCOMYCETES

Order : PROTOMYCETALES

## Protomyces Unger

**P.** macrosporus Unger ; Sacc. Syll. Fung. VII : 319. On leaves and stems of *Coriandrum sativum,* Lahore ; Lyallpur ; Sangla Hill ; Gujranwala ; Sheikhupura.

**P.** pachydermus Thuem. ; Sacc. Syll. Fung. VII : 319. On peduncles and leaves of *Taraxacum officinale,* Swat : Mingora.

Subclass II. HEMIASCOMYCETES

Order : TAPHRINALES

## Taphrina Fr.

T. aurea Pers. ex Fr. ; Sacc. Syll. Fung. VIII : 812. On leaves of *Populus ciliata,* Murree.

T. deformans (Berk.) Tul. ; Sacc. Syll. Fung. VIII : 812 as *Exoascus deformans.* On leaves of *Prunus persica ,* Peshawar ; of *P. eburnea,* Baluchistan : Ziarat.

T. pruni (Fckl.) Tul. ; Sacc. Syll. Fung. VIII : 817 as *Exoascus pruni.* On fruits of *Prunus padus,* Murree.

Subclass III. EUASCOMYCETES

Series A. ASCOLOCUL.t\RES (BITUNICATAE)

Order : PSEUDOSPHAERIALES

## Amphididymella Petr.

A. ahmadii Mueller in Sydowia 9 : 256, 1955. On dead branches of *Smilax parvifolia,* Murree ; of *Berberis* sp., Rawalpindi.

## Amphisphaeria Ces. & de Not.

A. fallax de Not. ; Sacc. Syll. Fung. II : 719 ; Ahmad & Lodhi, Sydowia 7 : 267. On the bark of *Quercus dilatata,* Murree.

A. striata Niessl ; Sacc. Syll. Fung. II : 721. On *Quercus Ilex,* Swat : Kulali.

## Botryosphaeria Ces. & de Not.

B. dothidea (Moug.) Ces. & de Not. ; Sacc. Syll. Fung. I : 460. On dead branhes of *Pyrus* sp., Swat : Miana ; of *Morus alba,* Changa Manga.

B. quercum (Schw.) Sacc. ; Sacc. Syll. Fung. I : 4%. On dead braqches of *Viburnum grandifiorum,* Patriata, Murree Hills.

## Cucurbitaria S. F. Gray

C. astragali Karst. & Hariot ; Sacc. Syll. Fung. JX :918. On dead branches of *Astragal us* sp., Chitral.

C. b_erberidis (Pers.) Gray ; Sacc. Syll. Fung. II : 308 ; Ahmad & Lod hi, Sydowia 7 : 267. On dead branches of *Berberis lycium*, Murree ; Kagan Valley : Shogran ; Swat : Mingora, Kul ali.

C. confluens Plowr. ; Sacc. Syll. Fung. II : 32]. On dead branches of *Quercus Il ex,* Swat : Kalam.

C. pakistanica Petr. in Sydowia 8: 165, 1954. On dead branches of *Acacia modest a,* Choa Sa_idan Shah, Salt Range.

C. sorbi Karst. ; Sacc. Syll. Fung. II : 314. On dead branches, Changla Gali.

## Didymella Sacc.

D. cadubriae Sacc. ; Sacc. Syll. Fu ng. I : 550. On dea d branches of *Berberis* sp., Murree.

D. olearum H. Fabr. ; Sacc. Syll. Fung. IX : 669. On dead branches of *Olea cuspid ata,* Swat : Khaza Khela.

## Didymosphae'ria Fuck.

D. brunneola Niessl ; Sacc. Syll. Fung. I : 709. On dead branches of *P!ectrant hus rugostts,* Swat : Ba hrain.

D. conoidea Niessl ; Sacc. Syll. Fung. I : 702. On dead branches of *S enecio chrysanthemoid es,* Changla Gali.

D. verrucispora Ahmad in Sydowia 2 : 74, 1948. On dead branches of *Gossypium* sp., Ladhar, Sheikhupura Dist.

## Dothidea Fr.

D. collecta (Schw.) Ell. & Ev. ; N. Am. Pyren. p. 613, 1892 ; Ahmad & Lod hi, Sydowia 7 : 267. On dead branches of *S arcococca sa /igna ,* Murree ; Patriata.

D. tetraspora Berk. & Br. ; Sacc. Syll. Fung. XIV: 578 ; Ahmad & Lodhi, Sydowia 7 :267. On dead branches of *H ed era nepal ensis,* Murree.

## Euryachora Fuck.

E. paeoniae Mueller & Ahmad in Sydowia 9 : 236, 1955. On dead branches of *Pa eonia* sp., Swat : Kalam.

## Gibberidea Fuck.

G. pithyophila (Fr.) v. Arx·; Sacc. Syll. Fung. II : 311 as *Cucurbit aria pithyo phil a.* On living branches of *Abies pindrow ,* Changla Gali ; Kagan Valley : Shogran.

## Guignardia Via la & Ravaz

G. bidwelli (Ellis) Viala & Ravaz ; v. Arx & Mueller, Bietr. z. Krypto-
gamenfl. der Schweiz 11 : 45, 1954 ; Malik & Khan, p. 523; Sacc.
Syll. Fung. I : 441 as *Physalospora euganea* ; Ahmad, Sydowia 2 : 74 as
*Phomatospora salvadorina.* On dead branches of *S al vadora oleoid es,*
Lad har, Sheikh u pura Dist.

## Karstenula Speg.

K. capparidis Petr. in Sydowia 8 : 106, 1954. On dead branches of
*Cap paris aphyll a,* Lad har, Sheikhupura Dist.

## Lasiobotrys Kze. ex Fr.

L. lonicerae Kuntze; Sacc. Syll. Fung. XXIV: 252. Syn. -L. *butl eri* Theiss.
& Syd.; Ahmad & Lodhi, Sydowia 7 : 267. On living leaves of *Lonicera*
sp., Baluchistan : Ziarat.

## Lasiosphaeria Ces. & de Not.

L. hirsuta (Pers. ex Fr.) Ces. & de Not. ; Sacc. Syll. Fung. II : 191 ;
Ahmad & Lodhi, Sydowia 7 : 267. On decayed wood and old
sporophores of *Lenzites betulina,* Murree.

L. ovina (Pers. ex Fr.) Ces & de Not. ; Sacc. Syll. Fung. II : 199.- Syn.
*Lasiosord ariel l a ovina* (Pers. ex Fr.) Chenant. On dead wood,
Murree ; Kagan Valley.

## Leptomassaria Petr.

L. capparidis Ahmad in Sydowia 7 : 268, 1953.    On dead branches of
*Capparis aphyl la,* Changa Manga.

## Leptosphaeria Ces. & de Not.

L. artemisiae (Fuck.) Auersw.; Sacc. Syll. Fung. II :33 ; Mueller, Sydowia
4 : 287, 1950. On dead branches of *Artemisia* sp., Swat : Khaza
Khela.

L. capparidicola Mund k. & Ahmad in Mycol. Pap. Imp. Myc. Inst.,
no. 18, p. 4, 1946.- Syn. *L. ahma d ii* Petr. in Sydowia 8 : 167, 1954.
On dead branches of *Capparis aph ylla ,* Ladhar, Sheikhu pura Dist.

L. dearsa (Berk. & Br.) Auersw.; Sacc. Syll. Fung. II :41 ; Mueller,
Sydowia 4 : 297, 1950. On dead branches of *Senecio chrysanthemoid es,*
Changla Gali.

L. dolioloides Auersw. ; Sacc. Syll. Fung. II : 44 ; Mueller, Sydowia
4 :295, 1950. On dead branches of *Senecio chrysanthemoid es,* Kagan
Valley : Sharhan.

L. doliolum (Pers. ex Fr.) Ces. & de Not. ; Sacc. Syll. Fung. II : 44 ;
Mueller, Sydowia 4 : 234, 1950. On dead branches of *Phytolacca*

*acinosa,* Kagan Valley : Shogran; of *Calamintha umbrosa,* Swat : Khaza Khela ; of *Echinops* sp., Changla Gali.

L. gallicola Sacc. ; Sacc. Syll. Fung. II : 213. On dead branches of *Cheno· podium album,* Changa Manga.

L. modesta (Desm.) Auersw. ; Sacc. Syll. Fung. II : 39 ; Mueller, Sydowia 4 : 292, 1950. On dead branches of *S crophularia* sp., Kagan Valley : Sharhan.

L. nitschkei Rehm ; Sacc. Syll. Fung. II : 26 ; Mueller, Sydowia 4 : 236, 1950. On dead branches of *Senecio chrysant hemoid es,* Changla Gali.

L. ogilviensis (Berk. & Br.) Ces. & de Not.; Sacc. Sy!!. Fung. II : 34 ; Mueller, Sydowia 4 : 240, 1950. On dead branches of *Echinops* sp., Changla Gali ; of *Senecio chrysanthemoides,* Changla Gali.

L. sepincola (Berk. & Br ) Winter ; Mueller, Sydowia 4 : 284 1950 ; Sacc. Syll. Fung. II : 164 as *M etasphaeria sepincol a.* On dead branches of *Rubus* sp., Swat : Mingora.

L. spegazinii Sacc. & Syd. ; Sacc. Syll. Fung. XIV : 570.   On culms of *S accharum munja ,* Ladhar, Sheikhupura Dist.

## Massaria de Not.

M. epileuca Berk. & Curt. ; Sacc. Syll. Fung. II : 6. On dead  branches of *M orus al ba,* Ladhar, Sheikhupura Dist.; Changa Manga, Lahore.

## Massarina Sacc.

M. graminicola Mundk. & Ahmad in Mycol. Pap. Imp. Myc. Inst., no. 18, p. 4, 1946.   On dead runners of *Eleusine fiagel lifera,* and *Cynodon d actyl on,* Ladhar, Sheikhupura Dist.

## Metasphaeria Sacc.

M. ambigua Berl. & Bres. ; Sacc. Syll. Fung. IX : 827. On dead branches of *Chenopod ium album,* Changa Manga.

M. helvetica Sacc. & Berl. ; Sacc. Syll. Fung. IX : 835. On dead branches of *Lonicera* sp., Murree.

M. scalaris (Dur. & Mont.) Sacc.; Syll. Fung. II : 168. On dead branches of *Olea cuspidata,* Swat : Khaza Khela.

## Mycosphaerella Johansan

M. dalbergiae Mueller & Ahmad in Sydowia 9 : 243, 1955. On overwinter- ed leaves of *Dalber gia sissoo,* Ladhar, Sheikhupura ; Lahore.

M. hedericola (Desm.) Lindau ; Sacc. Syll. Fung. I : 481 as *Sphaerel la* On overwintered leaves of *H ed era nepal ensis,* Murree.

M. fragariae (Tu!.) Lindau ; Sacc. Syll. Fung. I : 505.   On leaves of *Fragaria vesca*, Hazara (S. A. Malik).

M. killiani Petr. in Ann. Myc. 39 : 324, 1941 .- Syn. *Dotliidel la trifolii* ; *Cymadot hia trifolii* Wolf in Mycologia 27 : 71, 1935. On leaves of *Trifolium resupinatum*, Peshawar.

M. rabiei Korachevski, in Min. Agr. and Nat. Domains, Sofia 1916. The imperfect stage, *Ascochyta rabiei* occurs on leaves and pods of *Cicer arietinum*, Sargodha ; Sangla Hill ; Campbellpur.

M. tassiana (de Not.) Johansan ; Sacc. Syll. Fung. 1 : *50*.  On stems of *Aquilegia vulgaris*, Chitral (Chaudbri).

## Ophiobolus Riess

O. acuminatus (Sw.) Duby ; Sacc. Syll. Fung. II : 340 ; Mueller in Ber. Schw. Bot. Ges. 62 : 323. On dead stems of *Echinops* sp., Cbangla Gali.

O. indigoferae Mueller & Ahmad in Sydowia 9 : 235, 1955. On dead branches of *Indigofera* sp., Swat : K.alam.

**O.** penicillus (Schw.) Sacc. ; Sacc. Syll. Fung. II : 352 ; Mueller in Ber. Schw. Bot. Ges. 62 : 331. On dead stems of *Cnicus argyracanthus* & *Echinops sp.,* Changla Gali.

O. spirosporus Ahmad in Sydowia *2* : 75, 1948.   On dead culms of *Saccharum spontaneum*, Lahore.

**O.** tenellus (Auersw.) Sacc.; Sacc. Syll. Fung. II : 346. On dead branches of *Scrophularia* sp., Kagan Valley : Sharhan.

## Otthia Nitsch.

O. lisae (de Not.) Sacc. ; Sacc. Syll. Fung. I : 739.   On dead branches of *Berberis* sp., Swat : Mingora, Miana, Bahrain.

## Pleospora Rab.

**P.** heleocharidis Karst.; Sacc. Syll. Fung. II : 271. On *Heleocharis palustris*, Labore ; Choa Saidan Shah.

**P.** herbarum (Pers.) Rabenh.; Sacc. Syll. Fung. II : 239 ; Ahmad, Sydowia 2 : 76 ; Mueller, Sydowil *5 :* 277, 1951. On leaves of *Citrus* sp., Lahore ; on spines of *Acacia arabica*, Ladhar, Sheikhupura Dist.; on dead branches of *Otostegia limbata*, Barikot ; Rawalpindi ; on dead branches of *Berberis* sp., Swat : Mingora.

**P.** hispida Niess!; Sacc. Syll. Fung. II : 214 as *Pyrenoph-0ra hispida(Niessl)* Sacc.   On dead branches of *Artemisia* sp., Swat : Mingora.

P. leca nora (Fabre) Rehm ; Mueller, Sydowia 5 : 304, 1951. On dead branches of *Saccharum spont aneum,* Lahore.

P. orbicularis Auersw.; Sacc. Syll. Fung. II : 255; Mueller, Sydowia 5 : 271, 1951. On dead branches of *Berberis vul garis,* Murree.

P. pachyasca {Syd.) Petr.; Sacc. Syll. Fu ng. XXII : 378 as *Pyreno phora pach yasca* Syd. On leaves of *Astragalus* sp., Chitral.

P. passerianus Berl.; Sacc. Syll. Fung. IX : 885. On dead branches, Barum Valley, Chitral (Chaudhri).

P. pegani Bubak ; Sacc. Syll. Fung. XXIV: 243 ; Mueller, Sydowia 5 : 292, 1951. On dead branches of *Peganum harmal a,* Ladhar, Sheikhupura. Dist.

P. permunda (Cke.) Sacc.; Sacc. Syll. Fung. II : 243 ; Mueller, Sydowia 5 : 294, 1951. On dead branches of *Boerhaavia d iffusa,* Bahrain ;. on *Art emisia* sp., Swat : Mingora ; of *Aquil egia vul garis,* Chitral.

P. planispora Ell.; Mueller, Sydowia 5 : 294, 1951 ; Sacc. Syll. Fung. IX : 894 as *Cl athrospora pl anispora.* On dead stems of *Tricholepis stewartii ,* Murree.

P. rudis Berl. On dead branches of *Lantana indica,* Rawalpindi.

P. scrophulariae (Desm.) v. Hoehn.; Mueller, Sydowia 5 · 288, 1951; Sacc. Syll. Fung. II : 57 as *Leptos phaeria.* On dead branches of *Abutilon indicum,* Changa Manga ; of *Peristro phe bicalycul at a,* Rawalpinc;li ; of *Ind igofera* sp., Changla Gali.

P. vulgaris Niess! ; Sacc. Syll. Fung. II : 243. On culms of *Saccharum munja ,* Ladhar, Sheikhupura Dist.

## Plowrightia Sacc.

P. berberidis (Wahl.) Sacc.; Sacc. Syll. Fung. II : 637. On dead branches of *Berberis* sp., Mingora.

## Pringsheimia Schuzer.'

P. sepincola (Fr.) v. Hoehn.; on dead branches of *Rubus* sp., Swat : Mi an a.

## Rechingeriella Pet r.

R. eutypoides Petr. in Sydowia 8 : 170, 1954. On dead roots, Ladhar, Sheikhupura Dist.

## Sporormia de Not.

S. disjuncta (Ahma d) Petr. in Sydowia 9 : 489, 1955.- Syn. *Lasiosphaeria disjunct a* Ahmad in Sydowia 7 : 267, 1953. On dead wood., Changa Manga, Lahore.

S. minima Auersw.; Sacc. Syll. Fung. II : 124 ; Ginai. Ind. Bot. $oc. Jour. 15 : 275.   On rabbit dung, Lahore.

### Teichospora Fuck.

**T.** ignavis Karst.; Sacc. Syll. Fung. II : 296 & IX : 905. On dead branches of *Lonicera* sp., Kagan Valley : Shogran.

**T.** interstitialis (C. & P.) Sacc. ; Sacc. Syll. Fung. II : 293. On dead branches, Chitral (Chaudhri).

T. oleicola Pass. & Beltr.; Sacc. Syll. Fung. II : 291.   On dead branches of *Olea cuspidata,* Swat : Khaza Khela.

**T.** patellarioides Sacc. ; Sacc. Syll. Fung. II : 305; Ahmad, Sydowia 2 : 76. On a log of *Albizzia lebbek,* Ladhar, Sheikhupura.

### Thyridium Sacc.

**T.** americanum Ell. & Ev. ; Sacc. Syll. Fung. XI : 348 ; Petrak, Sydowia 4 : 18 as *Xylosphaeria.* On dead wood of *Dalbergia sissoo,* Ladhar, Sheikhupura Dist.

**T.** rousselianum Sacc. & Sp. ; Sacc. Syll. Fung. II : 323 ; Petrak, Sydowia 4 : 19 as *Xylosphaeria.* On dead branches of *Indigofera* sp., Changla Gali.

### Trabutia Sacc. & Roum.

**T.** quercina (Fr. & Rud.) Sacc. & Roum. ; Sacc. Syll. Fung. I : 449 ; v. Arx & Mueller, Beitr. z. Kryptogamenfl. d. Schweiz 11 : 86, 1954. On living leaves of *Quercus dilatata,* Murree ; of **Q.** *I {ex,* Swat : Bahrain.

### Valsaria De Not.

V. insitiva Ces. & de Not. ; Sacc. Syll. Fung. I : 746.   On dead branches of *Pyrus* sp., Swat : Miana, of *Zizyphus oxyphylla,* Poonch (Arshad).

V. salvadorina Mundk. & Ahmad in Mycol. Pap., Imp. Mycol. Inst., p. 6. 1946. On the bark of *Salvadora oleoides,* Changa Manga ; Ladhar, Sheikhupura Dist.

V. tamaricis Mundk. & Ahmad in Mycol. Pap. Imp. Myc. Inst., p. 7, 1946. On fallen branches of *Tamarix articulata,* Bahawalpur State : Panjnad.

### Venturia de Not.

V. geranii (Fr.) Winter ; Sacc. Syll. Fung. I : 541 as *Stigmatea geranii* ;' Ahmad & Lodhi in Sydowia 7 : 267 as *Spilosticta geranii.* on leaves of *Geranium* sp., Kagan Valley : Shogran.

V. rumicis Desm. -Syn. *Spilosticta rumicis* (Desm.) Petr.; Ahmad & Lod hi, in Sydowia 7 : 268. On *Rumex nepalensis,* Kagan Valley : Shogran.

## Xylosphaeria Otth

X. ahmadii Petr. in Sydowia 8 : 170, 1954. On *Dal bergia sissoo , Ficus religiosa, Aerua javanica , S uaeda fruticosa, Punica granatum* and *Zizy phus jujuba ,* Ladhar, Sheikhu pu ra Dist.

[*Pleospora diaporthoid es* (Ellis & Everh.) Sacc. reported by Wehmeyer (Mycologia 41 : 581, 1949) is probably this species].

### Order : HYSTERIALES

### Family : HYSTERIACEAE

## Dichaena Fr.

D. quercina (Pers. ex Fr.) Fr.; Sacc. Syll. Fung. II : 771. On dead branches of *Quercus dil atata,* Murree ; of Q. *Ilex,* Swat : Bahrain.

## Gloniopsis de Not.

G. levantica Rehm ; Sacc. Syll. Fu ng. XVII : 910. On dead wood, Shogran.

## Glonium Muehl.

G. clavisporum Seaver in Mycologia 17 : 4, 1925. On dead wood of *Prunus cornuta,* Shogran.

G. lineare. (Fr.) de Not.; Sacc. Syll. Fung. II : 732. On dead pieces of wood, Murree.

## Hysteriu m Tode ex Fr.

**H.** macrosporu m Peck ; Sacc. Syll. Fung. 11 : 748. On dead wood of *Pinus excel sa ,* Charehan.

**H.** pulicare Pers. ex Fr.; Sacc. Syll. Fu ng. II : 743. On dead branches of *Lonicera* sp., Patriata.

## Hysterographium Corda

**H.** dalbergiae Ahmad in Sydowia 4 : 82, 1950. On dead wood of *Dal bergia sissoo,* Lahore ; Ladhar, Sheikhu pu ra Dist.

**H.** fraxini (Pers. ex Fr.) de Not.; Sacc. Syll. II : 776. On dead branches of *Olea cuspid ata,* Choa Saidan Shah ; Swat : K haza Khela.

H. mori {Schw.) Rehm ; Sacc. Syll. Fung. II : 783. On dead branches, Swat : Kalam.

### Order : LOPHIOSTOMAT ALES

### Family : LOPHIOSTOMATACEAE

## Khekia Petr.

K. mutabilis (Pers.) Pet r. On dead branches of *Viburnum grand ifiorum ,* Murree.

Lophiostoma (Fr.) Ces. & de Not.

L. insidiosum (Desm.) Ces. & de Not.; Sacc. Syll. Fung. II : 70 & IX : 1090.  On culms of *Saccharum munja*, Ladhar, Sheikhupura Dist.; on dead branches of *Rumex hastatus,* Swat : Bahrain.

L. mai:rostomoides de Not., Sacc. Syll. Fung. II : 644 ; Ahmad & Lodhi, p. 267.  On dead branches of *Berberis* sp., Murree.

L. simillimum Karst.; Sacc. Syll. Fung. II : 707 & IX : 1090.  On dead branches of *Indigofera gerardiana,* Swat : Kulali.

Platystomum Trev.

P. compressum (Pers. ex Fr.) Trev. ; Sacc. Syll. Fqng. XVII : 889 ; Ahmad & Lodhi, Sydowia 7 : 267. On dead branches of *Desmodium* Kagan Valley : Sharhan.

Series B.  ASCOHYMENIALFS  (UNITUNICATAE)
Subseries A. *PLECTOMYCETES*
Order : ASPERGILLALES
Family : GYMNOASCACEAE

Gymnoascus Baran.

G. bourquelotii Baud.; Sacc. Syll. Fung. XI : 437 ; Lodhi & Naeem, T. B. M. S. 38 : 240.  Isolated from cotton seeds, Lahore.

Myxotrichum Kez. ex Fr.

M. aeruginosum (Mont.) Sacc.; Sacc. Syll. Fung. IV : 319 ; Mahju, Ind. Bot. Soc. Jour. 12 : 158.  On dung, Lahore.

M. chartarum (Kze.) Sacc.; Sacc. Syll. Fung. IV : 317 ; Mahju, 1. c., p. 158.  On dung, Lahore.

Family : ASPERGILLACEAE

Magnusia Sacc.

M. bartlettii Mass. & Salm.; Sacc. Syll. Fung. XVI : 1123 ; Ginai, Ind. Bot. Soc. Jour. 15 : 273.  On dung, Lahore.

Thielavia Zapf

T. basicola Zapf in Sitz. Bot. Prov. Brandenb. 18 : 101-105, 1876 ; Sacc. Syll. Fung. I : 39 ; Butler & Bisby, p. 39.  On roots of *Viola odorata,* Lahore.

Subseries B. *PYRENOMYCETES*
Order : XYLARIALES
Family : CHAETOMIACEAE

Ascotricha Berk.

A. pusilla (Ell. & Ev.) Chivers ; Sacc. Syll. Fung. XXIV : 240 · Ahmad in Sydowia 4 : 83.  On paper and card board, Lahore.

## Chaetomium Kze. ex Fr.

C. aureum Chivers ; Sacc. Syll. Fung. XXIV : 840 ; Lodhi & Naeem, T. B. M. S. 38 : 241. Isolated from cotton seeds, Lahore.

C. brasiliense Bat. & Pont.?; Lodhi & Naeem, T. B. M. S. 38 : 241. Isolated from seeds of *Spinacea oleracea,* Lahore.

C. gangligerum Ames in Mycologia 41 : 640, 1949 ; Lodhi & Naeern, T. B. M. S. 38 : 24L Isolated from seeds of *Verbena* sp. & *Cheiranthes cheiri,* Lahore.

C. globosum Kze.; Sacc. Syll. Fung. I : *222* ; Ginai, Ind. Bot. Soc. Jour. 15 : 275 ; Ahmad, Sydowia 4 : 83 ; Lodhi & Naeem, T. B, M. S. 38 : 240. Isolated from seeds of *Pastinacea sativa,* Lahore ; on decayed leaves and branches, Ladhar (Sheikhupura) ; Lahore.

C. indicum Cda.; Sacc. Syll. Fung. I : 222 ; Lodhi & Naeem, T. B. M. S. 38 : 240. Isolated from seeds of *Spinacea oleracea,* Lahore.

C. spirale Zopf ; Sacc. Syll. Fung. I : 224 ; Mahju, Ind. Bot. Soc. Jour.. 12 : 159. On dung, Lahore.

## Melanospora Corda

M. theleboloides (Fckl.) Winter ; von Arx & Mueller, Amer. Pyren., p. 145 ; Lodhi & Naeem, T. B. M. S. 38 : 241. Isolated from seeds of *Spinacea oleracea* and *Beta vulgaris,* Lahore.

M. zamiae Cda.; Sacc. Syll. Fung. II : 463 ; von Arx & Mueller, Amer. Pyren. p. 141 ; Lodhi & Naeem, T. B. M. S. 38 : 241. Isolated from cotton seeds, Lahore.

Order : XYLARIALES

Family : XYLARIACEAE

## Acanthostigma de Not.

A. lahorense Ahmad in Sydowia 8 : 164, 1955. On dead wood, Lahore.

## Amphisphaerella (Sacc.) Kirschst.

A. xylostei (Pers.) Munk in Dansk Bot. Arkiv. 15 : 89, 1953 ; Sacc. Sy!!. Fung. I : 300 as *Anthostoma xyl ostei.* On dead branches of *Lonicera* sp., Kagan Valley : Sharhan.

## Anthostomella Sacc.

A. Iodhii Ahmad in Sydowia 2 : 72, 1948. On petioles of a palm, Botanic Garden, Lahore.

## Bombardia Fr.

B. arachnoid ea (Niessl) Cain in Univ. Toronto Stud. Biol. Ser. No. 38,

p. 73. -Syn. *Podospora arachnoidea* Niessl ; *Sordaria arachnoidea* Sacc.; *Pleurage arachnoidea* Griff.-    On dung, Patriata, Murree Hills.

## Coniochaeta  (Sacc.) Cke.

C. pulveracea (Ehrenb.) Munk in Dansk  Bot.  Ark.  12  :  11, 1948 ; Sacc. Syll. Fung. I : 264 as *Rosellinia pulveracea* ; Ahmad in Sydowia 2: 73. On culms of *Saccharum munja* & *S. officinarum*, Ladhar, Sheikhupura  Dist.

C. ligniaria (Grev.) Mass. in Grevillea  16 : 37,  1887 ;  Sacc.  Syll.  Fung. I : 269 as *Rosellinia ligniaria.* On dead wood , Gakkhar ;   Choa Saidan Shah.

## Daldinia de Not.

D.  albozonata Lloyd, Myc. Writ. 5 : 822, 1919.  On  burnt  rhizomes of *Saccharum munja*, Ladhar, Sheikhupura Dist.; Lahore; Sargodha.

D. concentrica (Bolt. ex Fr.) Ces. & de Not. ; Sacc. Syll. Fung. I : 393. On  old  stumps of deciduous trees, Kagan Valley : Shogran ; Swat : Bahrain.

D. eschscholzii (Ehrenb.) Rehm ; Sacc. Syll.  Fung.  XVII : 617.  On *Citrus aurantium, Dalbergia sissoo* and *Morus alba,* Lahore ; Changa Manga ; Sangla Hill.

## Hypoxylon Bull. ex Fr.

H. glomeratum Cke.; Sacc. Syll.  Fung. II : xxviii & IX : 559.   On  dead wood of *Citrus* sp., Lahore ; of *Morus alba,* Lahore ;  Changa  Manga.

H. hypomiltum Mont.; Sacc. Syll. Fung, I : 354.  On branches of *Marus alba* and *Dalbergia sissoo,* Changa Manga ; of *Viburnum grandifiorum*, Patriata.

H. latissimum Speg.; Sacc. Syll. Fung. IX : 557 ; Ahmad -in Sydowia 2 : 73. On dead branches of *Capparis aphylla* and *Gossypium* sp.; Ladhar, Sheikhupura  Dist.

H. rubiginosum Pers. ex Fr.; Sacc. Syll. Fung. I : 376.   On branches of *Viburnum grandifiorum,*  Murree.

H. serpens Pers. ex Fr.; Sacc. Syll. Fung. I : 378.  On dead wood , Murree.

H. ustulatum Bull. ex Fr.; Sacc. Syll. Fung. I : 351 as  *Ustulina vulgaris* Tul.    On dead wood, Changla Gali.

## Nummularia  Tul.

N. bulliardi Tul.; Sacc. Syll. Fung. I : 396.   On *Quercus incana* and *Q. dilatata,* Murree ; Ghora Gali ; Kagan Valley : Kund.

## Penzigia Sacc.

P. capparidis (Mundk. & Ahmad) Ahmad in Sydowia 2 : 73, 1948. On dead branches of *Capparis aphyl' a*, Ladhar (Sheikhupura).

P. quercum Mueller & Ahmad in Sydowia 9 : 244, 1955. On the bark of *Quercus dilatata*, Murree.

## Poronia Willd. ex Fr.

P. indica Ahmad in Lloydia 9 : 142, 1946. On dead roots of *Cenchrus biflorus* and buried pieces of wood, Ladhar (Sheikhupura) ; Gakkhar.

P. kurziana (Curr.) Lloyd in Myc. Writ. 6: 939, 1919; Ahmad in Lloydia 9 : 141, 1946 ; Sacc. Syll. Fung. II (Addenda ad vol.) : 29 as *Kretschmaria kurziana*. On dead leaves and rhizomes of *Saccharum munja*, Sargodha ; Ladhar (Sheikhupura).

## Rosellinia de Not.

R. aquila (Fr.) de Not.; Sacc. Syll. Fung. I : 252 ; Ahmad, Sydowia 2 : 73. On dead branches of *Dalbergia sissoo*, *Zizyphus jujuba* and *Ficus palmata*, Ladhar (Sheikhupura) ; Lahore.

R. corticium (Schw.) Sacc.; Sacc. Syll. Fung. I : 253. On fallen branches, Patriata, Murree Hills.

## Sordaria Ces. & de Not.

S. coprophila (Fr.) Ces. & de Not.; Sacc. Syll. Fung. I : 230 ; Ginai, Ind. Bot. Soc. Jour. 15 : 273. On dung, Lahore.

S. curvula de Bary ; Sacc. Syll. Fung. I : 234 ; Mahju, Ind. Bot. Soc. Jour. 12 : 158. On dung, Lahore.

S. decipiens Wint.; Sacc. Syll. Fung. I : 235 ; Ginai, 1. c. p. 274. On dung, Lahore.

S. fimicola Ces. & de Not.; Sacc. Syll. Fung. I : 240 as Hypocopra fimicola. On dung, Lahore.

S. macrospora Auersw.; Sacc. Syll. Fung. I : 241 as *Hypocopra macrospora* ; Mahju, 1. c. p. 158. On dung, Lahore.

S. winteri Karst:; Sacc. Syll. Fung. I : 234 ; Ginai, 1. c. p. 274. On dung, Lahore.

## Xylaria Hill ex Grev.

X. hypoxylon Linn. ex Fr.; Sacc. Syll. Fung. I : 339 ; Ahmad, Sydowia 2 : 76. On stones of *Zizyphus jujuba*, Gujranwala ; Ladhar (Sheikhupura) ; On stumps of *Morus alba*, Changa Manga ; on old stumps, Murree ; Patriata ; Changla Gali.

X. nigripes (Klotzsch) Sacc.; Sacc Syll. Fung. IX : 527.    On the ground,
Gujranwala ; on termite nests, Lahore.

X. polymorpha (Pers.) Grev.; Sacc. Syll. Fung. I : 309.    On decayed
stumps, Murree ; Patriata.

### Zignrella Sacc.

Z. herbana Pass.; Sacc. Syll. Fung. IX : 861.    On branches of *Pyrus* sp.,
Swat.

### Family : DIATRYPACEAE

### Diatrype Fr.

D. berberidis Cke.; Sacc. Syll. Fung. IX : 476.    On dead branches of
*Berberis* sp., Swat : Mingora.

D. stigma (Hoff.) de Not.; Sacc. Syll. Fung. I : 193 ; Ah mad & Lod hi ,
Sydowia 7 : 267. On dead branches of *Viburnum gra1 1 difiorum ,*
Murree ; Patria ta ; Changla Gali.

### Diatrypella Ces. & de Not.

D. barlerire Syd. in Ann. Myc. 14 : 361 ; Sacc. Syll. Fu ng. XXIV : 741.
On dead branches of *Capparis a phylla ,* Changa Manga.

### Eutypa Tul.

E. lata (Pers.) Tul.; Sacc. Syll. Fung. I : 170. On dead bra nches of
*Viburnum grandifiorum ,* Patriata ; Murree.

E. lundibunda Sacc.; Sacc. Syll. Fung. I : 167. On branches of *M elia*
*azed arach* & *Citrus aurantium ,* Lahore ; Changa Manga.

### Eutypella (Nitsch.) Sacc.

E. stellulata (Fr.) Sacc.; Sacc. Syll. Fung. I : 149 ; Ahmad, Sydowia
2 : 76. On dead branches of *Suaed a fruticosa ,* Lad har, Sheikhupura
Dist.

E. zizyphi Syd. & Butl.; Sacc. Syll. Fung. XIV : 721 ; Ahmad, Sydowia
2 : 76. On dead branches of *Zizy phus ju juba ,* Lahore ; Changa
Manga ; Lad har, Sheikhupu ra Dist.

### Family : PHYLLACHORACE.1£

### · Phyllachora Nits.

P. cynodontis (Sacc.) Niessl ; Sacc. Syll. Fung. II : 602.    On lea ves of
*Cynodon dactyl on,* Lahore ; Quetta ; Sangla Hill ; Rawalpindi.

P. desmodii P. Henn.; Sacc. Syll. Fung. XIV : 664 ; Petr. & Ahmad,
Sydowia 8.: 168. On leaves of *Desmod ium tiliaefol ium,* Swa t : Kulali ;
Hazara.

P. fallax Sacc.; Petr. & A hmad *in* Sydowia 8 : 168; Sacc. Syll. Fung. II : 628 as *Dothid ell a fal l ax* Sacc. On leaves of *Chrysopogon monticol a,* Salt Range : Choa Saidan Shah.

P. lespedezae (Schw.) Sacc.; Sacc. Syll. Fung. II : 614 ; Petr. & Ahmad, Sydowia 8 : 169. On leaves of *Lespedeza Jalconeri,* Murree ; Changla Gali ; of *L. sericea,* Poonch (Arshad).

P. poae (Fckl.) Sacc.; Sacc. Syll. Fung. II : 603. On leaves of *Poa bul - bosa,* Chakdara.

P. penniseti Syd. ; Sacc. Syll. Fung. XXIV : 584. On leaves of *Pennise- tum orientale,* Swat : Madian.

P. sacchari-spontanei Syd.; Sacc. Syll. Fung. XXIV : 586. On leaves of *S accharum spontaneum,* Lahore.

### Family : CLAVICIPITACEAE

### Epichloe (Fr.) Tu!.

E. typhina (Pers. ex Fr.) Tu!.; Sacc. Syll. Fung. II : 578. On *Oryzo psis lateral* is, Murree ; Swat : Madian ; on *Brachypodlum syl vaticum,* Kagan Valley : Sharhan.

### Order : DI A PORTHALES

### Family : DIAPORTHACEAE

### Diaporthe Nitsch.

D. arctii (Lasch) Nitsch. ; Sacc. Syll. Fung. I : 653 ; Wehmeyer, p. 22. On dead branches of *Cynanchum* sp., Lahore.

D. decorticans (Lib.) Sacc. & Roum. ; Sacc. Sy!!. Fung. I : 619 ; Ahmad & Lodhi, Sydowia. 7 : 266 ; Wehmeyer, p. 136 as *D. padi* Otth. On fallen branches of *Prunus cornuta,* Kagan Valley : Shogran.

### Diaporthopsis Fabre

D. spiraeae Mueller & Ahmad in Sydowia 9 : 210, 1955. On dead branches of *Spiraea lindleyana,* Swat : Kulali.

### Dictyoporthe Pet r_

D. ahmadii Petr. in Sydowia 9 : 557, 1955. On dead branches of *S piraea* sp., Kagan Valley : Shogran.

### Family : GNOMONIACEAE

### Gnomonia Ces. & de Not.

G. cerastis (Riess) Ces. & de Not. ; Sacc. Syll. Fung. I : 569. On petioles of *Acer pictus,* Dunga Gali, M urree Hills.

## Linospora Fckl.

L. populina (Pers.) Schroet.; Sacc. Syll. Fung. II : 357.   On fallen leaves of *Populus* sp., Murree.

### Family : VALSACEAE

## Valsa Fr.

V. abicties Fr.; Sacc. Syll. Fung. I : 111.   On dead branches of *Abies pindrow*, Kagan Valley : Shogran.

V. ceratosperma (Fr.) Maire ; Sacc. Syll. Fung. I : 108 as *V. ceratophora*. On fallen branches of *Prosopis julifiora* , Changa Manga.

V. pini (Alb. & Schw.) Fr.; Sacc. Syll. Fung. 1 : 113.   On dead branches of *Cedrus deodara*, Kagan Valley : Shogran.

## Valsella Fckl.

V. moricola Ahmad in Sydowia 2 : 72, 1948.   On dead branches of *Marus alba*, Changa Manga.

### Order : HYPOCREALES

### Family : HYPOCREACEAE

## Broomella Sacc.

B. montaniensis (Ell. & Ev.) Muell. & Ahmad in Sydowia 9 : 233, 1955. On dead branches of *Clematis* sp., Changla Gali.

## Glomerella Sp. & v. Schrenk

G. cingulata (Stonem.) Spaulding & v. Schrenk in U. S. Dept. Agric. Bureau of Pl. Ind. Bull. 44 : 29, 1903. This is the perfect stage of *Colletotrichum lindemuthianum.*

G. tucumanensis (Speg.) v. Arx & Muell., Amer. Pyren., p. 195. On leaves of *Saccharum spontaneum,* Lahore. This is the perfect stage of *Colletotrichum graminicol um.*

## Hypocrea F.r.

l-l. citrina ( Pers.) Fr.; Sacc. Syll. Fung. II : 528. On dead' branches and on rocks, Murree.

H. gelatinosa (Tode ex Fr.) Fr.; Sacc. Syll. Fung. II : 524 ; Seaver, My-cologia 2 : 58 as *Chromocrea gelatinosa*. On dead branches, Murree ; Patriata.

H. rufa (Pers.) Fr.; Sacc. Syll. Fung. II : 520. On logs, Patria ta ; Muzaffarabad ; Lun Bagla.

## Hypomyces Fr.

H. aurantium (Pers.) Fckl.; Sacc. Syll. Fung. II : 470. On *Polystictus versicolor,* Murree ; Charehan.

H. chrysospermum (Bull.) Tul.; Sacc. Syll. Fung. II : 467. On *Boletus* sp., Swat : Kalam ; Murree.

H. hyalinus (Schw.} Tul. ; Sacc. Syll. Fung. III : 474. On dead branches of *Viburnum grand ifiorum,* Pat riata.

### Nectria Fr.

N. cinnabarina Fr.; Sacc. Syll. Fung. II : 479. On dead branches of *Skimmia laureola.* Changla Gali.

N. coccinea Fr.; Sacc. Syll. Fung. II : 481. On dead branches of *Berberis* sp., Swat : Mingora ; Changla Gali.

N. episphaeria Tode ex Fr. ; Sacc. Syll. Fung. II : 497. On *Diaporthe berberidis,* Murree ; on *Hypoxylon rubiginosum,* Patriata.

N. sanguinea Pers. ex Fr.; Sacc. Syll. Fung. II : 493. On fallen branches of *Dalbergia sissoo, Morus alba* and *Prosopis julifiora,* Changa Manga ; of *Cedrus deodar<i.;* Kagan Valley : Shogran.

### Neocosmospora E. F. Smith

N. vasinfecta E. F. Smith ; Sacc. -Syll. Fung. XVI : 562. On roots of *Gossypium* sp., Mirpur Khas.

### Podocrea Sacc.

P. cordiceps Penz. & Sacc.; Sacc. Syll. Fung, XVII : 799. On rotten cones of *Pinus excelsa,* Patriata, Murree Hills.

### Polystigma DC. ex Chev.

P. ochraceum (\Vahlenb.) Sacc.; Sacc. Syll. Fung. II : 458. On leaves of *Prunus cornuta,* Swat : Kalam ; Kagan Valley : Sharhan.

### Order : ERYSIPHALES
### Family : ERYSIPHACEAE

### Erysiphe Hedw. f. ex Fr.

E. cichoracearum (DC.} Salmon ; Blumer, Beitr. Krypt. Fl. Schweiz 7 : 246. On leaves of *Plantago ovata* and *Galium* sp., Kagan Valley : Batakundi, Sharhan.

E. convolvuli DC.; Blumer, p. 205. On leaves of *Convolvulus arvensis,* Quetta.

E. graminis DC.; Sacc. Syll. Fung. I : 19 ; Blumer, p. 160. On leaves of *Triticum vulgare,* Peshawar ; Gilgit.

E. horridula (Wallr.} Lev.; Sacc. Syll. Fung. I : 17 ; Blumer. p. 235. On leaves of *Cynoglossum wallichii,* Kagan Valley : Batakundi.

E. pisi DC.; Blumer, p. 187. On leaves of *Pisum sativum,* Chillianwala ; Peshawar.

E. polygoni DC.; Blumer, p. 201.   On leaves of *Polygonum avicul are,*
Swat : Kalam ; of *Chenopodium botrys,* ⸱ azara (S. A. Malik).

E. umbelliferarum de Bary ; Sacc. Syll. Fung. I : 17 ; Blumer, p. 195.
On dead overwintered stems of *H eracleum thomsoni* var. *gl abior,*
Chitral : Barum Valley ; of *Bunium* sp., Swat : Kalam.

### Leveillula  Arnaud

**L**. taurica (Lev.) Arn.; Sacc. Syll. Fung. XXIV : 226 ; Blumer, p. 404.
On leaves of *Peganum harmala,* Hasanabdal ; ;:)angla Hill.

### Microsphaera  Lev.

M. astragali (DC.) Trev.; Sacc. Syll. Fung. I : 12 ; Blumer, p. 234. On
leaves of *Oxytropis* sp., Kagan Valley : Batakundi ; of *Astra galus* sp.,
Chitral (I. I. Chaudhri).

### Phyllactinia Lev.

P. mespili (Cast.) Blumer, p. 396.   On leaves of *Cotoneaster bacillaris,*
Murree.

P. salmonii Blumer, p. 401.    On leaves of *Prunus amygd alus.* Quetta.

P. subspiralis (Salm.) Blumer ; Sacc. Syll. Fung. XXII : *20* ; Blumer, p.
399.   On leaves of *Dal bergia sissoo,* Lahore ; Hasanabdal ; Sangla
Hill.

P. suffulta (Rabent.) Sacc. Sy!!. Fung. I : 5 ; Blumer, p. 391.  On  leaves
of *S alix tetrasperma,* Quetta.

### Podosphaera Kzc. ex Lev.

P. leucotricha (Ell. & Ev.) Salm.; Blumer, p. l48 ; Sacc. Syll. Fung. IX :
365 as *Sphaerotheca l eucotricha.* On  leaves of *Pyrus malus* Lahore ;
Murree.

### Sphaerotheca  Lev.

S. fuliginea (Schlech.) Salmon ; Sacc. Syll. Fung. XXII : 20 ; Blumer, p.
l20. On leaves *of Taraxacum officinale,* Kagan  Valley : Batakundi ;
of *C ucurbita pepo,* Swat : Kulali.

### Uncinula Lev.

U. polychaeta (Berk. & Curt.) Ellis ; Sacc. Syll. Fung. IX : 367.- Syn.
*Uncinulopsis pol ychaet a* (B. & C.)  Wei  in  Nanking J. 11 : 112, 1942.
On  leaves of *Celtis a ustralis,* Abbottabad ; of C. *erioca'Ypa ,* Swat ;
K ulali.

U. salicis (DC.) Winter ; Blumer, p. 363. On leaves of *S atix* sp., Changla
Gali ; Quetta ; of *Populus ciliat a,* Murree.

Order : CORONOPHORALES

Family : CORONOPHORACEAE

Tympanopsis Starb.

T. euomphala (Berk. & Cur t.) Starb.; Sacc. Syll. Fung. XI : 383 ; Fitzpatrick, Mycologia 15 : 54 ; v. Arx & Mueller, Beitr. Krypt. Fl. Schweiz. 11 : 380 as *Scortechinia euomphal a* ; Sacc. Syll. Fung. I 462 as *Botryosphaeria.* On dead branches of *Viburnum grandifiorum,* Patriata : Murree Hills.

Family : NITSCHKIACEAE

Fracchia Sacc.

F. heterogenea Sacc.; Sacc. Syll. Fung. I : 93 ; Fitzpatrick, Mycologia 16 : 104. On dead branches of *M angifera indica,* Lahore.

Nitschkia Otth

N. cupularis (Pers. ex Fr.) Karst.; Fitzpa trick, Mycologia 15: 32 ; Ahmad, Sydowia 2 : 72. On dead branches of *Viburnum grandifiorum* , Murree.

N. salvadorae Ahmad in Sydowia 8 : 167, 1954. On dead branches of *S al vadora ol eoides,* Ladhar, Sheikhupura Dist.

Subseries· C. *DI SCOM YCET ES*

Group 1. OPERCULATAE

Order : PEZIZALES

Family : PEZIZACEAE

Aleuria Fuck.

A. aurantia (Pers. ex Fr.) Fuck.; Seaver Operculate cup-fu ngi, p. 97 ; Ahmad, Biologia 1 : 5 ; Sacc. Syll. Fung. VIII : 74 as *Peziza aurantia* Pers. On the ground, Murree ; Changla Gali.

A. murreeana Ahmad in Biologia 1 : 5, 1955. On the ground, Patriata, Murree Hills.

Aleurina Sacc. & Syd.

A. pakistanica Ahmad in Biologia 1 : 5, 1955. On the ground, Nathia Gali.

Ascobolus Pers. ex Fr.

A. glaber Pers. ex Fr.; Sacc. Syll. Fung. VIII : 517 ; Seaver, Operculate cup-fungi, p. 83 ; Ahmad, Biologia 1 : 7. On dung, Ladhar, Sheikhupura Dist.

A. immersus Pers. ex Fr.; Sacc. Syll. Fung. VIII : 523 ; Seaver, Operculate cup-fungi, p. 83 ; Ahmad, Biologia 1 : 6. On dung, .Lahore.

A. magnificus B. O. Dodge in Mycologia 4 : 21 8 ; Seaver, Opercu late cup-fungi, p. 87 ; Ahmad , Biologia 1 : 7. On dung, Lahore ; Sialkot ; Ladhar, Sheikhupu ra Dist.

A. stercorarius (Bull. ex Fr.) Schroet.; Sacc. Syll. Fung. XVI : 1149 ; Seaver, Operculate cup-fungi, p. 82 ; Ahmad, Biologia 1 : 7. On the ground, Lahore ; on dung, Nathia Gali.

### Ascodesmis van Tiegh.

A. microscopica (Crouan) Seaver in Mycologia 8 : 3, 1916 ; Ahmad, Biologia 1 :4. On dung of rabbit.

### Ascophanus Boud.

A. carneus (Pers. ex Fr.) Boud.; Sacc. Syll. Fung. VIII : 534 ; Seaver, Operculate cup-fungi, p. 115 ; Ahm ad , Biologia 1 : 8. On dung, Lahore.

A. granulatus (Bull. ex Fr.) Speg.; Seaver, Operculate cup-fungi, p. 116 ; Ahmad , Biologia 1 : 10 ; Sacc. Syll. Fung. VIII : 129 as *H umaria granul ata* Bull. ex Fr. On dung, Mu rree ; Patriata.

A. ochraceus (Crouan) Boud.; Sacc. Syll. Fung. VIII : 531 ; Seaver, Operculate cup-fungi, p. 117 ; Ahmad , Biologia 1 : 10. On dung, Nathia Gali ; Pat riata.

### Geopyxis (Pers.) Sacc.

G. bronca (Peck) Seaver ; Seaver, Operculate cup-fungi, p. 213 ; Ahmad , Biologia 1 : 19 ; Sacc. SylL Fung. VII : 92 as *Peziza bronca.* On the ground, Murree ; Nathia Gali ; Kagan Valley : Shogran ; Patriata ; Swat : Mt. llam.

G. cupularis (L. ex Fr.) Sacc.; Sacc. Syll. Fung. VIII : 72 ; Seaver, Operculate cup-fungi, p. 212 ; Ahmad, Biologia 1 : 19. Among need-les of *Cedrus deod ara,* Patriata.

### Humaria Fuck.

H. ahmadii Cash in Mycologia , 40 : 725, 1948 ; Ahmad , Biologia I : l4. On the ground, Lahore ; Changla Gali ; Kagan Valley : Shogran ; Swat : Kalam.

H. albospadicea (Grev.) Cash a pud Ahmad in Biologia 1 : l6.- Syn. *Patell a al bospadicea* (Grev.) Seaver, Operculate cup-fungi, p. 178. On the ground, Patriata ; Nathia Gali ; Murree.

H. gregaria Rehm ; Ahmad, Biologia 1 : l5 ; Sacc. Syll. Fung. VIII : l70 as *Lachnea gregaria* Phill.; Seaver, Operculate cup-fungi, p. 176 as *Patel la gregaria* (Rehm). On the ground, Swat : Kalam.

**H.** hemisphaerica (Wigg. ex Fr.) Fuck.; Ahmad, Biologia 1 : 15; Sacc. Syll. Fung. VIII : 166 as *Lachnea hemisphaerica.* On the ground, Swat : Mt. Ilam.

**H.** pulcherrima Speg.; Ahmad, Biologia 1 : 15 ; Sacc. Syll. Fung. VIII : 181 as *Lachnea pul cherrima ;* Seaver, Opercui ate cup-fungi, p. 172 as *Patell a pulchenima_* (Crouan) Seaver., On dung, Shahdara, Lahore.

**H.** scutellata (L. ex Fr.) Fuck.; Ahmad, Biologia 1 : 14 ; Sacc. Syll. Fung. VIII : 173 as *Lachnea scutellata ;* Seaver, Operculate cup-fungi, p. 159 as *Patell a scutel lat a* (L.) Morgan. On rotten wood, Murree ; Na thia Gali ; Kagan Valley : Shogran , Batakundi ; Swat : Kalam, Miana.

## Humarina Seaver

**H.** gerardii (Cke.) Seaver in Operculate cup-fungi, p. 138; Ahmad, Biologia 1: 12 ; Sacc. Syll. Fung. VIII : 150 as *H umaria gerardii.* On the ground, Patriata, Murree Hills.

**H.** luteola (Torrend) Cash apud Ahmad in Sydowia 4 : 83 ; Ahmad, Biologia 1 : 11. On the ground, Lahore.

**H.** plumbeoatra Cash in Mycologia 40 : 736 ; Ahmad, Biologia 1: 12. On the ground, Ladhar, Sheikhupura Dist.

**H.** semiimmersa (Karst.) Seaver in Operculate cup-fungi, p. 130 ; Ahmad, Biologia 1 : 11 ; Sacc. Syll. Fung. VIII : 143 as *H umaria semiimmersa.* On the ground, Ladhar, Sheikhupura Dist.

**H.** tetraspora (Fuck.) Seaver in Operculate cup-fungi, p. 134 ; Ahmad, Biologia 1 : 11 ; Sacc. Syll. Fung. VIII : 121 as *H umaria tetraspora.* On the ground, Lahore.

**H.** umbrina Cash in Mycologia 40 : 726 ; Ahmad, Biologia 1 : 12. On the ground, Lahore.

**H.** zizyphi Cash in Mycologia 40 : 727 ; Ahmad , Biologia : 11. On stones of *Zizyphus jujuba ,* Ladhar, Sheikhupura Dist.

## Lamprospora de Not.

**L.** trachycarpa (Curr.) Seaver in Operculate cup-fungi, p. 71 ; Ahmad, Biologia 1 : 4 ; Sacc. Syll. Fung. VIII : 105 as *Detonia trachycar pa.* On the ground , Nathia Gali.

## Lasiobolus Sacc.

**L.** equinus (Muell.) Karst.; Seaver, Operculate cup-fungi, p. 155 *i* Ahmad, Biologia 1 : 44. On richly manured soil, Charehan, Murree Hills.

## Otidea Fuck.

**O.** leporina (Batsch ex Fr.) Fuck.; Sacc. Syll. Fung. VIII : 94 ; Ahmad ,
Biologia 1 : 16 ; Seaver, Operculate cup-fungi, p. 185 as *Scodellina leporina* (Batsch) S. F. Gray. On the ground, Murree; Kagan Valley : Sharhan.

## Paxina Kze.

**P.** acetabuLum (L. ex Fr.) Kze.; Seaver, Operculate cup-fungi, p. :w2 ;
Ahmad, Biologia 1 : 18 ; Sacc. Syll. Fung. VIII : 59 as *Acetabula vulgaris.* On the ground, Murree ; Patriata ; Swat : Bahrain.

**P.** hispida (Schaeff. ex Fr.) Seaver in Operculate cup-fungi, p. 205; Ahmad,
Biologia 1 : 18 : ; Sacc. Syll. Fung. VIII : 28 as *H el uella macropus*
(Pers.) Karst. On the ground, Kagan Valley : Shogran ; Changla Gali.

**P.** sulcata {Pers. ex Fr.) Kze.; Seaver, Operculate cup-fungi, p. 204 ;
Ahmad, Biologia 1 : 18 ; Sacc. Syll. Fung. VIII : 62 as *Acetabula sulcata.* On the ground, Murree ; Nathia Gali ; Patriata.

## Peziza Dill. ex Fr.

**P.** badia Pers. ex Fr.; Sacc. Syll. Fung. VIII : 82 ; Seaver, Operculate cup-
fungi, p. 221 ; Ahmad, Biologia 1 : 19. Oo the ground, Nathia Gali ;
Murree ; Patriata ; Shogran ; Swat ; Ladhar, Sheikhupura Dist.

**P.** repanda Wahl. ex Fr.; Seaver in Operculate cup-fungi, p. 231; Ahmad,
Biologia 1 : 19 ; Sacc. Syll. Fung. VIII : 100 as *Discina repand a.* On
rotten coniferous wood, Shogran ; Dunga Gali ; Murree Hills.

## Plectania Fuck.

**P.** coccinea (Scop. ex Fr.) Fuck.; Seaver, Operculate cup-fungi, p. 191 ;
Ahmad, Biologia 1 : 17 ; Sacc. Syll. Fung. VIII : l54 as *Sarcoscypha coccmea.* Attached to buried sticks, Swat : Bahrain.

**P.** occidentalis (Schw.) Seaver in Operculate cup-fangi, p. 193 ; Ahmad,
Biologia 1: 17 ; Sacc. Syll. Fung. VIII : 154 as *Sarcoscypha occidentalis.*
On sticks lying on or buried in the ground, Murree ; Patriata.

## Pyronema Carus

**P.** confluens (Pers. ex Fr.) Tul.; Sacc. Syll. Fung. VIII : 107 ; Ahmad,
Biologia 1 : 8 ; Seaver, Operculate cup-fungi, p. 109 as *Pyronema omphalod es* (Bull.) Fuck. On burnt ground, Lahore; Ladhar, Sheikhupura Dist.

## Rhyparobius Boud.

**R.** crustaceus (Fuck.) Rehm ; Sacc. Syll. Fung. VIII : 539 ; Seaver, Operculate cup-fungi, p. 145 ; Ahmad, Biolog_ia 1 : 13. On dung, Lahore.

## Saccobolus Boud.

S. depauperatus (Berk. & Br.) Reh m ; Sacc. Syll. Fung. VIII : 525 ; Seaver, Operculate cu p-fungi, p. 95 ; Ahmad, Biologia 1 : 8. On mud plaster of wall, Ladhar, Sheikhupura Dist.

S. kerverni (Crou an) Boud.; Sacc. Syll. Fung. VIII : 524 ; Seaver, Operculate cup-fungi, p. 93 ; Ahmad, Biologia 1 : 8. On dung, Lahore ; Murree ; Sialkot.

## Sepultaria Mass.

S. arenicola ( Lev.) Mass.; Seaver, Operculate cup-fungi, p. 149 ; Ahmad, BiOlogia 1 : 13 ; Sacc. Sy11. Fung. VIII : 170 as *Laehn ea sepulta.* On the ground, Swat : Bahrain.

## Family : HELVELLACEAE

## Helvella L. ex Fr.

H. crispa Scop. ex Fr. ; Sacc. Syll. Fung. VIII : 18 ; Seaver, Operculate cup-fungi, p. 247 ; Ahmad, Biologia 1 : 23. On the ground, Murree; Patriata ; Shogran ; Kalam.

H. elastica Bu ll. ex Fr.; Sacc. Syll. Fung. VIII : 24 ; Seaver, Operculate cup-fungi, p. 249 ; Ahmad, Biologia 1 : 23. On the ground, Murree ; Swat ; Shogran.

H. ephippium Lev.; Sacc. Sy!!. Fung. VIII : 28 ; Ahmad, Biologia 1 : 23. On the ground, Murree ; Patriata ; Charehan ; Kagan Valley ; Swat.

H. mitra Schaeff. ex Fr.; Seaver, Operculate cup-fungi, p. 246 ; Ahmad, Biologia 1 : 22 ; Sacc. Sy!!. Fung. VIII : 19-as *Helvella lacunosa.* On the ground, Murree ; Patriata ; Nathia Gali ; Kagan Valley ; Swat.

## Morchella Dill. ex Fr.

M. conica Pers. ex Fr.; Sacc. Syll. Fung. VIII : 9 ; Seaver, Operculate cup-fungi, p. 239 ; Ahmad, Biologia 1 : 21. On the ground, Kagan Valley :Shogran.

M. crassipes Vent. ex Fr.; Sacc. Syll. Fung. VIII : 12 ; Seaver, Operculate cup-fungi, p. 237 ; Ahmad, Biologia 1 : 21. On the ground, Murree.

M. deliciosa Fr.; Sacc. Sy!!. Fung. VIII : 10 ; Seaver, Operculate cup-fungi, p. 240 ; Ahmad, Biologia 1 : 21. On the ground, Murree.

M. esculenta (L. ex Fr.) Fr.; Sacc. Sy!!. Fung. VIII : 3 ; Seaver, Operculate cup-fungi, p. 238 ; Ahmad, Biologia 1 : 21. On the ground, Murree.

## Verpa Sw<irtz ex Fr.

V. bohcmica (Krombh.) Schroeter ; Seaver, Operculate cup-fungi, p. 244 ; Ahmad, Biologia 1 : 22 ; Sacc. Syll. Fung. VIII : 14 as *Morchella bohemica.* On the ground, Murree.

### Order : TUBERALES
### Family : TERFEZIACEAE

## Terfezia Tul.

T. leonis Tul.; Sacc. Syll. Fung. VIII : 903. In sandy soil, Shorkot ; Panjnad ; Pallah, Bahawalpur.

### Group 2. INOPERCULATAE
### Order : OSTROPALES
### Family : OSTROPACEAE

## Schizoxylon Pers. emend. Tul.

S. insigne (de Not.) Rehm in Rabh. Krypt. Fl. Deutsch. p. 125:3, 1896.- Syn. *Oomyces insignis* de Not.; *Schizoxylon alboatrum* Rehm ; S. *occidentale* Ell. & Ev. On dead branches of *Punica granatum* and *Nerium odorum*, Ladhar, Sheikhupura Dist.; Lahore ; of *Olea ci:spidata*, Salt Range : Choa Sa!dan Shah ; of *Bignonia* sp., Lahore. On dead branch, Swat : Kalam ; on decorticated branches of *Pinus excelsa*, Kagan Valley : Shogran.

## Stictis Pers. ex Fr.

S. radiata Pers. ex Fr.; Sacc. Syll. Fung. VIII : 682. On dead branches of *Sarcococca saligna*, Murree ; Charehan.

### Order : HELOTIALES
### Family : PHACIDIACEAE

## Colpoma Wallr.

C..quercina Wallr.; Sacc. Syll. Fung. II : 803.- Syn. *Clithris quercina* (Pers. ex Fr.) Rehm. On branches of *Quercus dilatata*, Murree ; Changla Gali.

## Lophodermium Chev.

L. paeoniae Rehm ; Sacc. Syll. Fung. XIV: 720 ; Tehan, Ill. Biol. Monogr. 27 : 104 as *Lophodermina paeoniae.* On dead branches· of *Paeonia emodi*, Swat : Kalam ; Kagan Valley : Shogran.

L. pini-excelsae Ahmad in Sydowia 8 : 172, 1954. On leaves of *Pinus excelsa*, Kagan Valley : Shogran.

### Rhytisma Fr.

**R.** acerinum Pers. ex Fr.; Sapc. Syll. Fung. VIII : 753. On leaves of *Acer pictum*, Hazara (S. A. Malik).

**R**. punctatum Pers. ex Fr.; Sacc. Syll. Fung. VIII : 753. On leaves of *Acer oblongum,* Dunga Gali, Murree Hills.

### Therrya Sacc.

T. cembrae (Rehm) Cash cor_nb. nov. -Syn. *Coccomyces cembrae* Rehm in Hedwigia 24 : 232, 1885 ; Sacc. Syll. Fung. VIII : 749. On dead branches of *Pinus excelsa,* Kagan Valley : Shogran ; Swat : Kalam.

### Family : DERMATEACEAE

### Ascocalyx Naumov

A. abieties Naumov; Groves, Mycologia 28 : 458 ; Sacc. Syll. Fung. VIII : 569 as *Scleroderris pitya* ; Seaver, Inoperculate cup-fungi, p. 331 as *Godronia abieties.* On dead branches of *Abies pindrow,* Kagan Valley : Shogran.

### Mollisia Karst.

M. cinerea (Batsch ex Fr.) Karst.; Sacc. Syll. Fung. VIII : 336 ; Seaver, Inoperculate cup-fungi, p. 301. On dead wood , Murree ; Patriat a ; Kagan Valley : Shogran.

### Pezicula Tu!.

**P.** brenckleana Seaver, in Inoperculate cup-fungi, p. 341. On dead branches of *Rosa* sp., Kagan Valley : Shogran.

### Pseudopeziza Fuck.

**P.** medicaginis (Lib.) Sacc.; Sacc. Syll. Fung. VIII : 724 ; Seaver, Inoperculate cup-fungi, p. 186. ·On leaves of *Medicago lupulina* , Kagan Valley.

**P.** repanda (Fr.) Karst.; Sacc. Syll. Fung. VIII : 724 ; Seaver, Inoperculate cup-fungi, p. 187. On leaves of *Galium* sp., Kagan Valley : Shogran.

**P.** trifolii (Biv. ex Fr.) Fuck.; Sacc. Syll. Fung. VIII : 723 ; Seaver., Inoperculate cup-fungi, p. 185. On leaves of *Trifolium pratense,* Kagan Valley : Shogran.

### Pyrenopeziza Fuck.

**P.** lavaterae Mueller & Ahmad in Sydowia 9 : 239, 1955. Gn dead branches of *Lavatera kashmiriana,* Kagan Valley : Sharhan.

**P.** mollisioides (Sacc. & Briard) Petr.; Sacc. Syll. Fung. VIII : 717 as *Phacidium mollisioides..* On dead stems of *Euphrbia cornigera,* Kagan. Valley : Shogran.

## Tapesia (Pers. ex Fr.) Fuck.

T. rosae (Pers. ex Fr.) Fuck.; Sacc. Syll. Fung. VIII : 374 ; Seaver, In-operculate cup-fu ngi, p. 195. On dead branches of *Rosa* sp.-, Kagan Valley : Shogran ; Changla Gali.

## Tympanis Tode ex Fr.

T. abietina Groves in Canad. Jour. Bot. 30 : 599, 1952. On fallen branch-es of *Abies pindrow*, Kagan Valley : Shogran.

T. mallicola Groves in Canad. Jour. Bot. 30 : 637, 1952. On dead branch-es of *Prunus cornuta,* Kagan Valley : Shogran.

### Family : ORBILIACEAE

## Orbilia Fr.

O. inflatula Karst.; Sacc. Syll. Fung. VIII : 627 ; Seaver, Inoperculate cup-fungi, p. 154. On dead wood, Kagan Valley.

O leucostigma Fr.; Sacc. Syll. Fung. VIII : 629 ; Seaver, Inopercula te cup-fungi, p. 154. On rotten wood, Patriata, Murree Hills.

### Family : HELOTIACEAE

## Cyathicula de Not.

C. coronata (Bull. ex Fr.) de Not.; Sacc. Syll. Fung. VIII : 394 ; Seaver, Inopercula te cup-fungi, p. 112. On dead herbaceous stt!ms, Dunga Gali, Murree Hills ; Kagan Valley : Batak undi.

## Durella Tul.

D. compressa (Pers. ex Fr.) Tu!.; Sacc. Syll. Fung. VIII : 790. On pieces of dead wood, Kagan Valley : Sharhan.

## Helotium Fr.

H. citrinum (Hedw. ex Fr.) Fr.; Sacc. Syll. Fung. YIU : 224 ; Seaver, )nopercula te cup-fungi, p. 131. On fallen pieces of wood , dead branches and stumps of decid uous trees, Changla Gali ; Na thia Gali ; Kagan Valley : Shogran.

H. scutula (Pers. ex Fr.) Karst.; Sacc. Syll. Fung. VIII : 266 ; Seaver, Inoperculate cup-fungi, p. 119. On dead branches, Kagan Valley : Shogran.

H. virgultorum (Yahl ex Fr.) Fr.; Seaver, Inoperculate cup-fungi, p. 126 ; Sacc. Syll. Fung. VIII : 266 as *P hialea virgul torum.* On dead branches of *Sk immia laureol a,* Changla Gali.

## Scleroderris (Fr.) de Not.

S. salleana Sacc. & Cav.; Sacc. Sy!!. Fung. XVI : 765. On fallen bra nches of *Abies pindrow*, Kagan Valley : Shogran.

## Trichoscyphella Nannf.

T. calycina (Fr.) Nannf. in Nova Acta Reg. Soc. Sci. Upsal. Ser. iv, 8 : 270, 1932. On dead branches of *Abies pind row,* Kagan Valley : Shogran ; Swat : Bahrain.

## Velutaria Fuck.

V. rufo-olivacea (Alb. & Schw. ex Fr.) Fuck.; Sacc. Syll. Fung. VIII : 398 as *Lachnell a rufo-olivacea;* Korf, Mycologia 45 : 476 as *Velutarina rufo-olivacea.* On dead branches of *Rosa* sp., Kagan Valley : Shogran.

### Family : HYALOSCYPHACEAE

## Cistella Quel.

C. geelmuyderii Nannf. in Nova Acta Reg. Soc. Sci. Upsal. Ser. iv, 8 : 270, 1932 ; Dennis, Mycol. Pap. C. M. I., no. 32, p. 58, 1949. On decayed wood, Patriata, Murree Hills.

## Dasyscypha Fuck.

D. barbata (Kze.) Mass.; Sacc. Syll. Fung. VIII : 392 ; Dennis, Mycol. Pap. C. M. I., no. 32, p. 53, 1949. On dead branches of *Lonicera* sp., Kagan Valley : Sharhan.

D. bicolor Fuck.; Sacc. Syll. Fung. VIII : 393 ; Dennis, 1. c. p. 35 ; Seaver, lnoperculate cup-fungi, p. 250 as *Lachnella bicolor.* On dead branches of *Rosa* sp., Murree ; Charehan.

D. corticalis (Pers. ex Fr.) Mass.; Sacc. Syll. Fung. VIII : 393 ; Dennis, l. c. p. 39 ; Seaver, lnoperculate cup-fungi, p. 249 as *Lachnella corticalis.* On fallen branches of *Viburnum gra;-idifiorum ,* Murree.

D. indica (Cash) comb. nov. -Syn. *Dasyscyphella indica* Cash in Mycologia 40 : 724, 1948. On the bark of *Quercus d ilatata,* Murree ; Patriata.

### Family : GEOGLOSSACEAE

## Geoglossum Pers. ex Fr.

G. glabrum Pers. ex Fr.; Seaver, lnoperculate cup-fungi, p. 24 ; Sacc. Syll. Fung. VIII :43 under G. *ophioglossoides.* On the ground, Murree.

## Leotia Pers. ex Fr.

L. lubrica Pers. ex Fr.; Sacc. Syll. Fung. VIII : 609 ; Seaver, lnoperculate cup-fungi, p. 37. On the ground, Murree.

## Trichoglossum Boud.

T. velutipes (Peck) Durand ; Seaver, lnoperculate cup-fungi, p. 29 ; Sacc. Syll. Fung. VIII : 46 as *Geoglossum velutipes.* On th ground, Murree ; Ladhar, Sheikhupura Dist.

Order : LECANORALES

Family : PATELLARIACEAE

### Haematomyxa  Sacc.

H. pakistani Mueller & Ahmad in Sydowia 9 : 238, 1955. On dead branch -
es of *Berberis* sp., Murree ; of *Acacia modesta,* Salt Range :  Choa
8aidan Shah ; of *Olea cuspidata,* Choa Saidan Shah.

### Lecanidion Rebenh.

L. atratum (Hedw. ex Fr.) End!.; Sacc. Sy!!. Fung. VIII : 795. On the
bark of trees, Lahore ı Ladhar, Sheikhupura Dist.; Gujranwala; Choa
Saidan Shah.  Swat : Mingora ; Kagan Valley : Balakot, Shogran.

L. clavi:;porum (Berk. & Br.) Sacc.; Sacc. Syll. Fung. XVIII : 184. On the
bark of *Cordia myxa,* Ladhar, Sheikhupura Dist.

L. tetrasporum (Mass. & Morg.) Seaver ; Sacc. Sy!!. Fung. XVIII : 184.
On dead wood, Murree ; on fallen branches of *Berberis* sp., Swat :
Bahrain.

# Class : **BASIDIOMYCETES**

Subclass : HETEROBASIDIOMYCETES

Order : AURICULARIALES

Family : AURICULARIACEAE

### Auricularia  Merat

A. mesentrica Dicks. ex Fr.; Sacc. Sy!!. Fung. VI : 762 ; Bourd. & Galz.
Hym. Fr. p. 23. On the bark  of *Quercus dilatata* and *Q. incana,*
Murree ; Changla Gali.

A. pdtata Lloyd in Myc. Writ. 7 : 1117, 1922 ; Ahmad in Lloydia 6 :
242, 1943.  On the bark of *Cordia myxa,* and *Zizyphus jujuba,* Labor<!;
Gujranwala ; Sheikhupura ; Sangla Hill ; Sargodha.

### H.irneola Fr.

H. auricula (L. ex Merat) H. Karst.- Syn. *Auricularia auricula* (L. . ex
Merat) Underw. apud Barrett in Mycologia 2 : 12, 1911.- *A. auriculae-
judae* Schroet.; Bourd. & Galz. Hym. Fr. p. *15.-H irneola  auriculae-
judae* (Linn.) Berk.; Sacc. Syll. Fung. VI : 766. On  the trunks of
dead  trees, Changla Gali.

H. nigricans (Sw. ex Fr.) Donk in Reinwardtia 1 : 498.- Syn. *H . polytricha*
Mont.; Sacc. Syll. Fung. VI : 766.  On dead wood, Salt Range :
Choa Saidan Shah ; Lahore.

### Phleogena  Link

P. decorticata (Fr.) Martin in Univ. Iowa Stud. Nat. Hist. 18 : 69,  1944.-

Syn. *P.Jaginea* (Fr.) Link, Handb. Gewaechse 3 : 396, 1833. On logs, Changa Manga, Lahore.

## Family : TREMELLACEAE

### Ditangium Karst.

D. ccrasi (Tul.) Cost. & Duf.- Syn. *Craterocolla cerasi* Schum.; Sacc. Syll. Fung. VI : 778.- *Ditangium rubellum* ( Pers.) Pat. Ess. tax., p. 12. On dead branches of *Abies pindrow*, Changla Gali ; Lun Bagla (Azad Kashmir).

### Exidia Fr.

E. glandulosa Fr ; Sacc. Syll. Fung. VI : 773. On dead branches of deciduous trees, Murree ; Changla Gali ; Nathia Gali ; Kagan Valley : Shogran, Sharhan ; Swat : Kalam.

E. recisa Fr.; Sacc. Syll. Fung. VI : 772. On dead branches, Changia Gali.

E. saccharina Fr.; Sacc. Syll. Fung. VI : 777 as *Ulocolla saccharina* (Fr.) Bref. On coniferous wood, Murree ; Nathia Gali.

### Heterochaete Pat.

H. delicata (Kl. ex Berk.) Bres. in Hedwigia 53 : 77, 1912 ; Bodman, Lloydia 15 : 213, 1952. On dead branches, Sialkot ; Lahore.

### Phlogiotis Quel.

P. helvelloides (Fr.) Martin in Amer. Jour. Bot. 23 : 628, 1936.- Syn. *Gyrocephalus rufus* (Jacq.) Bref.; Sacc. Syll. Fung. VI : 995. On the ground, Murree ; Kagan Valley : Sharhan.

### Tremella Fr.

T. mcsentrica Fr.; Sacc. Syll. Fung. VI : 783. On dead wood, Swat : Kalam; Cbangla Gali. According to Prof. G. W. Martin the present collections are near this species but the basidia and basidiospores are distinct.

## Family : DACRYMYCETACEAE

### Calocera Fr.

C. cornea Fr.; Sacc. Syll. Fung. VI : 73 . On decayed wood, Kagan Valley : Sharhan.

C. vis::osa (Pers. ex Fr.) Fr. ; Sacc. Syll. Fung. VI : 73,2. On decayed logs, Murree ; Changla Gali ; Kagan Valley : Shogran.

### Dacrymyces Fr.

D. dcliqucscens (Merat) Duby ; Sacc. Syll. Fung. VI : 798. On comferous wood, Murree ; Changla Gali ; K;igan Valley ; Swat : Kalam.

## Dacryopinax Mart in

D. spathularia (Schw.) Mart in in Lloydia 11 : 116, 1948.- Syn. *Guepinia spathul aria* (Schw.) Fr.; Sacc. Syll. Fung. VI : 807. On dead wood , Changa Manga ; Gakkhar ; Ladhar, Sheikhupura Dist.

### Order : UREDINALES

#### Family : MEI,AMPSORACEAE

## Cerotelium Arth.

C. fici (Cast.) Arth. -Syn. *Kuehneola fici* (Cast.) Butl.; Syd. Monogr. Ured. 3 : 323 ; Sacc. Syll. Fung. XXIII : 790 ; Ahmad , Biologia 2 : 29, 1956. On leaves of *Ficus pal mata* , Lahore ; Changa Manga ; Sangla Hill.

## Chrysomyxa Unger

C. deformans (Diet.) Jacz.- Syn. *Barclayel la deformans* Diet.; Syd. Monogr. Ured. 3 : 522 ; Sacc. Syll. Fung. IX : 316 ; Butler & Bisby, p. 56 ; Ahmad, Biologia 2 : 29. On leaves of *Picea morinda,* Kurram Valley (Collett).

## Coleosporium Lev.

C. campanulre (Pers.) Lev.; Syd. Monogr. Ured. 3 : 628 ; Sacc. Syll. Fung. VII : 753 ; Arth. & Cummins, p. 399 ; Ahmad, Biologia 2 : 30. On leaves of *Campanul a colorata,* Kagan Valley : Batakundi, Shogran; Swat : Kalam ; of C. *canescens,* Kagan Valley : Naran ; of C. *evol vulacea,* Swat : Kalam.

C. clematidis Bard.; Syd. Monogr. Ured. 3 : 653 ; Sacc. Syll. Fung. IX : 317 ; Arth. & Cummins, p. 399 ; Ahmad, Biologia 2 : 30. On leaves of *Clematis grata,* Upper Topa, Murree Hills ; of C. *montana,* Lawrence College, Ghora Gali (R. R. Stewart) ; Gharial (R. R. Stewart).

## Cronartium Fr.

C. ribicola ischer ; Syd. Monogr. Ured. 3 : 567 ; Sacc. Syll. Fung. VII : 598 ; Malik & Khan, p. 523 ; Ahmad, Biologia 2 : 31. On leaves of *Ribes rubrum,* Kagan Valley : Shogran ; Hazara (S. A. Malik).

## Hyalopsora Magnus

H. polypodji (Pers.) P. Magn.; Syd . Monogr. Ured. 3 : 496 ; Ahmad, Biologia 2 : •33. On leaves of *Cystopteris fra gilis* (Linn.) Bernh.; Kagan Valley : Batakundi, Naran ; Swat : Kalam.

## Melampsora Cast.

M. epitea (Kze. & Schm.) Th uem.; Ahmad, Biologia 2 : 35. On leaves of *Salix* sp., Kagan Valley : Shogran.

M. euphorbiae (Schum.) Cast.- Syn. *M . hel ioscopiae* Winter ; Syd. Monogr. Ured. 3 : 377 ; Sacc. Syll. Fung. VII : 586 ; Malik & Khan, p. 523 ; Joerstad, p. 73 ; Butler & Bisby, p. *bO* ; Ahmad , Biologia 2 : 33. On leaves of *Euphorbia helioscopia*, Lahore ; Lyallpu r ; Rawalpindi ; Peshawar ; Wazirabad ; of *E. dracunculoid es*, Chillianwala ; Lahore; Lya llpur ; *E. cornigera*, Swat : Kala m; Kagan Valley : Shogran; Nathia Gali ; of *E. hypericifol ia*, Murree ; of *E. thomsoniana* , Barum Valley :Za potili ; of *E. k anaorica*, Quett a.

M. euphorbiae-gerardianae W. Muell.; Syd. Monogr. U red. 3 : 376 ; Sacc. Syll. Fung. XXIII : 382 ; Ahmad , Biologia 2 : 34. On leaves of *Eu phorbia falcata* , Swat : Khaza Khela ; of *Euphorbia* sp., Haza ra (S. A. Malik).

M. larici-caprearum Kleb.; Bu tler & Bisby, p. 60 ; A hmad, Biolo ia 2 : 35. On leaves of *S alix tetrasperma* , Kohat (Fletcher).

M. lini (Pers.) Lev.; Syd. Monogr. Ured. 3 : 381 ; Sacc. Syll. Fung. VII : 587 ; Ahmad , Biologia 2 : 34. On leaves and stems of *Linum usitatissimum*, Kalashah Kak u ; Sangla Hill.

M. populnea ( Pers.) Ka rst.- Syn. M. *tremul ae* Tul.; M. *recid ioid es* (DC.) Schroet.; Cummins, p. ·449 ; Ahmad , Biologia *2 :* 35. On lea ves of *Po pulus al ba*, Parachinar ; Abbottabad.

M. salicis-albae Kleb.; Ahmad, Biologia 2 : 35. On leaves of *Salix acmophyll a*, Swat : Khaza Khela.

### Phakopsora Diet.

·P. zizyphi-vulgaris (Henn.) Diet.; Syd. Monogr. Ured. 3 : 413 ; Sacc. Syll. Fung. XXI : 608 ; Sydow & Ahmad , p. 441 ; Malik & Khan, p. 524 ; A hmad , Biologia 2 : 36. On lea ves of *Z izy phus ju juba* , La hore ; Changa Manga ; of *Z . nummularia* , Chillian:wala ; Bhalike ; of *Z . sativa* ( *=Z . vul garis)*, Hazara (S. A. Malik).

### Pucciniastrum Otth

P. areolatum (Fr.) Otth- Syn. *Thekopsora areol ata* (Fr.) Magn.; *T.pad i* Groves ; Ahmad , B10logia 2 : 79. . On cone scales of *Picea morind a*, Kagan Vall_ey : Shogran ; Murree Hills :·Changla Gali.

P. agrimoniae (Diet.) Tranzsch.; Syd. Monogr. Ured. *3 :* 446 ; Malik & Khan, p. 524 ; Ahmad, Biologia 2 : 79. On *A grimonia eupatorium* , Hazara.

### Family : PUCCINIACEAE

### Diorchidi um Kalebbr.

D. digitariae Ahmad in Biologia 2 : 31, 1956. On lea ves of *Digitaria bicornis*, La hore (Abd ur Rehman).

## Endophyllum  Lev.

E. tuberculatum (Ell. & Keller m.) Arth. & Fromme ; Sacc. Syll. Fung.
XXIII : 849 ; Cummins, p. 448 .; Ahmad, Biologia 2 : 32. On leaves of
*Lavatera kashmiriana,* Kishenganga Valley (R. R. Stewart).

## Gymnosporangium  Hedw. f.

G. clavariaeforme (Jacq.) DC., Syd. Monogr. Ured. 3 : 59 ; Ahmad,
Biologia 2 : 33. On leaves of *Cotoneaster integrrima,* C. *'nummularia*
& *Crataegus oxyacantha,* Kishenganga Valley ; Swat : Kalam.

G. confusum Plowr.; Syd. Monogr. Ured. 3 : 56 ; Ahmad, Biologia 2 :
32. On leaves of *Crataegus oxyacantha,* Kishenganga Valley (R. R.
Stewart) ; of *Cotoneaster vulgaris,* Baluchistan : Ziarat.

G. distortum Arth. & Cummins ; Cummins, Mycologia 35 : 449 ; Ahmad,
Biologia 2 : 32. On leaves of *Cotoneaster bacillaris,* Kagan Valley :
Shogran ; Kishenganga Valley (R. R. Stewart).

## Phrag_midium  Link

P. barclayi Diet.; Syd Monogr. Ured. 3 : 150 ; Sacc. Syll. Fung. IX :
31S ; Ahmad, Biologia 2 : 40. On leaves of *Rubus lasiocarpus,* Changla
Gali, Murree Hills.

P. butleri Syd.; Syd. Monogr. Ured. 3 : 124 ; Sacc. Syll. Fung. XXI :
725 ; Malik & Khan, p. 524 ; Arth. & Cummins, p. 401 ; Ahmad,
Biologia 2 : 36. On leaves of *Rosa macrophylla,* Hazara (S. A. Malik);
of *Rosa* sp., Changla Gali (R. R. Stewart) ; Patriata, Murree Hills.

P. kamtschatke (Anders.) Arth. & Cummins in Mycologia 25 : 401.- Syn.
*Puccinia rosae* Bard.; *Gymnoconia rosae* (Bard.) Liro;- *Telconia rosae*
(Bard.) Syd., -*Trolliomyces rosae* (Bard.) Uelbr.; Joerstad, p. 74 ;
Ahmad, Biologia 2 : 37. On leaves of *Rosa webbiana,* Barum Valley,
Chitral (I. l. Chaudhri).

P. mucronatum (Pers.) Schlecht. -Syn. P. *discifiorum* (Tode) James ;
Syd. Monogr. Ured. 3 : 115 ; Ahmad, Biologia 2 : 37. On leaves of
*Rosa* sp., Rawalpindi (R. R. Stewart).

P. mysorense (Thirum. & Mundk.) Petr. -Syn. *Phragmotelium mysorense*
Thirum. & Mundk.; Ahmad, Biologia 2 : 41. On leaves of *Rubus
niveus,* Nathia Gali ; Changla Gali ; Murree.

P. nepalensi Bard.; Syd. Monogr. Ured, 3 : 100 ; Sacc. Syll. Fung. XI :
207 ; Malik & Khan, p. 524 ; Ahmad, Biologia 2 : 39. On leaves of
*Potentilla nepalensis,* Hazara (S. A. Malik.).

P. papillatum Diet. ; Syd. Monogr. Ured. 3 : 99 ; Sacc. Syll. Fung.

IX : 315 ; Ahmad, Biologia 2 : 39. On leaves of *Potentilla nepalensis,* Swat : above Kalam.

**P.** potentiHae (Pers.) Karst.; Syd. Monogr. Ured. 3 : 97 ; Sacc. Syll. Fung. VII : 743 ; Arth & Cummins, p. 401 ; Malik & Khan, p. 524 ; Ahmad, Biologia 2 : 40. On leaves of *Potentilla k leiniana,* Poonch (R. R. Stewart) ; of *P. argentata,* Baltistan : Astor Valley (R. R. Stewart) ; of *P. nepalensis,* Hazara (S. A. Malik).

**P.** rosae-rnoschatae Diet. ; Syd. Monogr. Ured. 3 : 125 ; Sacc. Syll. Fung. XXI : 725 ; Malik & Khan, p. 524 ; Ahmad, Biologia 2 : 38. On leaves of *Rosa moschata,* Murree ; of R. *webbiana,* Patriata, Changla Gali.

**P.** shogranense Petr. in Sydowia 8 : 162 ; Ahmad, Biologia 2 : 40. On leaves of *Rubus* sp., Kagan Valley : Shograll ; Swat : Miana.

**P.** tuberculatum J. Muell. -Syn. *P. egenulum* Syd. ; Syd. Monogr. Ured, 3 : 151 ; Sacc. Syll. Fung. XXIII : 823 ; Ahmad, Biologia 2 : 39. On leaves of *Rosa webbiana,* Kagan Valley : Batakundi ; Barum Valley : Shokor Shal (Wendelbo).

### Puccinia Pers.

**P.** absinthii DC. ; Syd. Monogr. Ured. 1 : 11 ; Sacc. Syll. Fung. VII : 837 ; Ahmad, Biologia 2 : 41. On leaves and stems of *Artemisia persica,* Barum Valley, Chitral (I. I. Chaudhd) ; of *A. parvifiora,* Changla Gali.

**P.** acetosae (Schum.) Koern ; Syd. Monogr. Ured. 1 : 581 ; Sacc. Syll. Fung. VII : 638 ; Ahmad, Biologia 2 : 42. On leaves and stems of *Rumex orientalis,* Kagan Valley : Naran.

**P.** allii (DC.) Rud. -Syn. *P. porri* (Sow.) Wint. ; Syd. Monogr. Ured. 1 : 614 ; Sacc. Syll. Fung. VII : 655 ; Ahmad, Biologia 2 : 42. On leaves of *Allium cepa,* Lyallpur ; Lahore.

**P.** ambigua (Alb. & Schw.) Lagerh.; Syd. Monogr. Ured. 1 : 216 ; Ahmad, Bio!ogia 2 : 42. On leaves of *Galium aparine,* Ghora Gali (Asghar Ali).

**P.** angelicae Schum.; Syd. Monogr. Ured. 1 : 356 ; Sacc. Syll. Fung. VII : 703 ; Ahmad, Biologia 2 : 43. On leaves of *Angelica glauca,* Swat : Kalam ; Poonch (R. R. Stewart).

**P.** argentata (Schultz.) Winter ; Syd. Monogr. Ured. 1 : 450 ; Sacc. Syll. Fung. VII : 639 ; Ahmad, Biologia 2 : 43. On leaves of *Impatiens brachycentra,* Kagan Valley : Sharhan, Batakuhdi ; Changla Gali.

**P.** aristidae Tracy ; Syd. Monogr. Ured. 1 : 727 ; Sacc. ·Syll. Fung. XI :

202 ; Ahmad , Biologia 2 :43.    On leaves of *Aristid a  ad scensionis* ,
Rawalpindi.

P. ba r beyi (Roum.) P. Magn.; Syd. Monogr. Ured. 1: 619 ; Sacc. SyJI.
Fung. X VI : 305 ; Ar th. & Cummins, p. 402 ; Butler & Bisby, p. 6 t ;
Ahmad , Biologia 2 : 44. On lea ves of *Asphod el us tenuifol ius,* very
common throughout the area.

P. barclayii nom. nov.- Syn. P. *joerstadii* Ahmad in Biologia 2 : 57, 1956
non P. *joerstad ii* Rytz., Veroeff. Geobot. Inst. Ruebel in Zu rich, 4 p.
86, 1927.- *P. nitid a* Bard.; Syd. Monogr. Ured . 1 : 574 ; Sacc. Syll.
Fung. IX : 307 ; Malik & K han, p. 425.    On lea ves of *Pol ygonum
d mplexicaul e* var. *s peciosum,* Swat : Kalam ; Hazara (S. A. Malik).

P. bithynica P. Magn.; Syd. Monogr. Ured. 8 : 394 ; Sacc. Syll. Fu ng.
XVII : 325 ; Ahmad, Biologia, 2 :45. On lea ves of *S al via hyd rangea,*
Bal uchistan : Hind u bagh (l. l. Chaud hri).

P. bullata (Pers.) Winter ; Syd. Monogr. Ured. 1 :403 ; Sacc. Syll. Fung.
VII :624.   On leaves and stems of *Peuced anum aucheri,* Quetta.

P. bu tleri Syd.; Sacc. Syll. Fung. XXI : 651 ; Ahmad , Biologia 2 : 46. On
leaves of *Launaea nudicaulis,* Lahore ; of L. *aspl enifolia ,* Lahore ;
Sangla Hill ; Sargod ha ; Gujrat.

P. calcitrapae DC. -Syn. P. *centaureae* DC.; Syd. Monogr. Ured. 1 :
39 ; Sacc. Syll. Fung. XVII : 286 ; Malik & Khan, p. 524 ; Butler &
Bisby, p. 65 ; Ahmad , Biologia 2 : S6. On leaves of *Centaurea calcitrapa* , Rawalpindi _; Swat : Barikot ; Peshawar ; of C. *phyl locephala ,*
Dargai.

P. carduoru m Jacky ; Syd. Monogr. Ured. 1 : 33 ; Sacc. Syll. Fung. XVI :
297 ; Ahmad , Biologia 2 : 46. On lea ves of *Card uus nutans* , Kagan
Valley :.Bataku ndi ; Shogran ; Swat : Kalam.

P, caricis (Schum.) Rebent.; Syd. Monogr. Ured. 1 : 648 ; Sacc. Syll.
Fung. VII : 626 ; A hmad, Biologia 2 : 47. On leaves of *Urtica  dioica,*
Pa triata, Murree Hills.

P. calthae Link ; Syd. Monogr. Ured. 1 : 540 ; Sacc. Syll. Fung. VII :
624 ; A hmad , Biologia 2 :_47. On leaves of *Caltha palustris ,* Kagan
Valley : Na ran.

P. carthami (Hutzelm.) Cord a ; Syd. Monogr. Ured . 1 : 35 ; Sacc. Syll.
Fun.g. VII : 846 ; Ahmad, Biologia 2 : 47. On leaves of *C arthamus
oxyacant ha ,* Sangla Hill ; Dargai ; Swat : Mingora, ; of C. *tinctorius,*
Chlllianwala ; Lahore.

cl?-i tralensis Joerstad , Nytt Mag. f, Bot. 1 : 45, 1952 ; Ahmad, Biologia

2 : 48. On leaves of *Pleurospermum stylosum*, Chitral State : Barum Valley (Wendelbo).

P. circaeae Pers.; Syd. Monogr. Ured. 1 : 422 ; Sacc. Syll. Fung. VII ; 686 ; Malik & Khan, p. 524 ; Ahmad , Biologia 2 : 48. On leaves of *Circaea alpina*, Changla Gali ; Kagan Valley : Naran.

P. cirsii Lasch ; Syd. Monogr. Ured. 1 : 55 ; Sacc. Syll. Fung. XVII : 292 ; Ahmad, Biologia 2 : 48. On leaves of *Cnicus argyracanthus*, .Swat : Madian ; of *C. wallichii*, Swat : Kalam ; Changla Gali ; of *Cnicus* sp., Kagan Valley : Shogran.

P. citrulli Syd. & Butl.; Sacc. Syll. Fung. XXIII : 719 ; Ahmad, Biologia

2 : 49.  On leaves of *Citrullus colocynthis* & *C. vulgaris*, Karachi.

P. clavata Syd.; Syd. Monogr. Ured. 1 : 845 ; Sacc. Syll. Fung. XVII : 356 ; Ahmad, Biologia 2 : 49. On leaves of *Clematis* sp., Baluchistan : Urak. (I. I. Chaudhuri).

P. collettiana Bard.; Syd. Monogr. Ured. 1 : 226 ; Sacc. Syll. Fung. IX : 306 ; Ahmad, Biologia 2 : 50. On leaves of *Rubia cordifolia*, Murree, Upper Topa.

P. coronata Corda ; Syd. Monogr. Ured. 1 : 699 ; Sacc. Syll. Fung. VII : 623 ; Arth. & Cummins, p. 402 ; Malik & Khan, p. 524 ; Ahmad, Biologia 2 : 50.    On leaves of *Agrostis pilosula*, Swat : Kalam ;  of *Rhamnus virgatus*, Kagan Valley : Shogran ; of *R. dahuricus*, Peshawar Valley.

P. cynodontis Lacroix ; Syd. Monogr. Ured. 1 : 748 ; Sacc. Syll. Fung. VII : 661 ; Sydow & Ahmad; p. 341 ; Ahmad, Biologia 2 : 50. On leaves of *Cynodon dactylon*, very common throughout the. area ; of *Plantago lanceolata*, Quetta (Asghar Ali).

P. cousiniae Syd. Monogr. Ured. 1 : 62 ; Sacc. Syll. Fung. XVII : 292. On laves of *Cousinia* sp., Quetta (M. Iqbal Qazi).

P. duthiae Ellis & Tracy ; Syd. Monogr. Ured. 1 : 726 ; Sacc. Syll. Fung. XIV : 352 ; Arth. & Cummins, p. 402 ; Ahmad, Biologia 2 : 51. On leaves of *Bothriochloa inermedia*, Rawalpindi ; Sangla Hill ; of *Dican- thium annulatum*, near Mogli Bungalow, Jhelum Di?t. (R. R. Stewart).

P. echinopsis DC.; Syd. Monogr. Ured. 1 ; 75 ; Sacc. Syll. Fung. XVII : 292 ; Ahmad, Biologia 2 : 51.. Oa leaves of *Echinops cornigera*, Swat : Kalam.

P. eremuri Korn.; Syd. Monogr. Ured. 1 : 622 ; Sacc. Syll. Fung. XVI : 305 ; Ahmad, Biologia 2 : 52. On leaves of *Eremurus himalaicus*, Kagan Valley: Batakundi ; of *E. persicus*, Baluchistan : Quetta, Ziarat.

**P.** extensicola Plowr.; Syd . Monogr. Ured. 1 : 667 ; Sacc. Syll. Fung. IX : 311 ; Cummins, p. 452 ; Ahmad, Biologia 2 : 52. On leaves of *Solidago virga-aurea*, Kagan Valley : Shogran ; Karen (R.R. Stewart).

**P.** flavipes Syd.·; Sacc. Syll. Fung. XXI : 684 ; Sydow & Ahmad, p. 440 ; Ahmad, Biologia 2 : 52. On leaves of *Fimbristylis dichotoma*, Chuharkana ; Sangla Hill ; of F. *schenoides*, Kalashah Kaku.

**P.** frankeniae Link ; Syd. Monogr. Ured. 1 : 446 ; Sacc. Syll. Fung. VII : 694 as *P. pulvinata*. On leaves of *Frankenia pulverulenta*, Lahore (Zainul Abidin).

**P.** gentianae (Str.) Roehl.; Syd. Monogr. Ured. 1 : 340 ; Sacc. Syll. Fung. VII : 604 ; Ahmad, Biologia 2 : 53. On leaves of *Gentiana kurroo*, Abbottabad (I. I. Chaudhri).

**P.** graminis Pers.; Syd. Monogr. Ured. 1 : 692 : Sacc. Syll. Fung. VII : 622 ; Ahma,d , Biologia 2 : 53. On leaves *of Triticum aestivum*, very common throughout the area ; of *Bromus japonicus*, Swat : Miana ; of *Agropyron semicostatum*, Miana : of *Agrostis munroana*, Kagan Valley : Batakundi ; of *Hordeum vulgare*, Sangla Hill ; Sind ; Lyallpur ; of *Cynodon dactylon*, Quetta (Asghar Ali).

**P.** helianthi Schw.; Syd. Monogr. Ured. 1 : 92 ; Sacc. Syll. Fung. VII : 605 ; Ahmad , Biologia 2 : 54. On leaves of *Helian,thus annuus*, Rawalpindi (Shaukat Ali).

**P.** heracleicola Cummins in Mycologia 35 : 452 ; Joerstad, p. 76 ; Ahmad, Biologia 2 : 55. On leaves of *Heracleum thomsoni* var. *glabior*, Chitral : Barum Valley (Wendelbo).

**P.** hieracii (Schum.) Mart.; Syd. Monogr. Ured. 1 : 95 ; Sacc. Syll. Fung. VII : 633 p.p.; Ahmad, Biologia 2 : *55*. On leaves of *Hieracium vulgatum*, Kagan Valley ; Shogran.

**P.** holboelli (Hornem.) Rostr.; Sacc. Syll. Fung. VII : 734 & IX : 292 ; Ahmad , Biologia 2 : 55. On leaves of *Erysimum hieraciifolium* , Naltar Valley, Gilgit (R. R. Stewart).

**P.** hysterium (Str.) Roehl.; Ahmad , Biologia 2 : 56. -Syn. *P. tragopogi* (Pers.) Winter ; Syd. Monogr. 1 : 167 ; Sacc. Syll. Fung. VII : 669. On leaves of *Tragopogon* sp., Kagan Valley : Besal (I. I. Chaudhri).

**P.** invenusta Syd.; Sacc. Syll. Fung. XXI : 686 ; Ahmad , Biologia 2 : 56. On leaves of *Phragmites karka*, Lahore.

**P.** iridis (DC.) Rabenh.; Syd. Monogr. Ured. 1 : 598 ; Sacc. Syll. Fung. VII 657 ; Ahmad , Biologia 2 : 56. On leaves of *Iris germanica*. Lahore.

**P.** isiacae (Thttem.) Wint.; Monogr..Ured. 1 : 792 ; Sacc. Syll. Fung. VII : 851 ; Ahmad, Biologia 2 : 16. On leaves of *Phragmites karka,* Quetta ; of *Lepidium d raba,* Quetta.

**P.** junci (Strauss) Wint.; Syd. Monogr. Ured. 1 : 642 ; Sacc. Syll. Fung. VII : 658 ; Ahmad, Biologia 2 : 57. On leaves of *Juncus* sp., Baluch- istan : Hanna Valley (Asghar Ali).

**P.** komarovii Tranzsch.; Syd. Monogr. Ured. 1 : 451 ; Sacc. Syll. Fung. XVII : 350 ; Arth. & Cummins, p. 403 ; Ahmad, Biologia 2 : 58. On leaves and stems of *Impatiens* sp., Poonch ; Changla Gali (R. R. Stewart).

**P.** kuehnii (Krueg.) Butl.; Sacc. Syll. Fung. XXIII : 744 ; Ahmad, Biologia 2 : 58. On leaves of *Saccharum spontaneum,* Lahore ; Lyallpur (A. Khan) ; of *S. munja,* Lahore (B. Dass).

**P.** leveillii Mont. ex G. Gay ; Sacc. Syll. Fung. XI : 185. -Syn. *P. geranii- syl vaticae* Karst. ; Syd. Monogr. Ured. 1 : 465 ; Sacc. Syll. Fung. VII : 682. On leaves of *Geranium pratense,* Kagan Valley : Shogran ; of G. *dol linum,* Satpura Nallah, Baltistan (R. R. Stewart) ; of
G. *rectum* Ti:-autv., Swat : Kalam ; of G. *collinum* var. *egl adulosum,* Barum Valley, Chitral (Wendelbo).

**P.** liberta Kern ; Sacc. Syll. Fung. XXII : 720 ; Ahmad, Biologia 2 : 59. On leaves of *Bilbostyl is barbata,* Sialkot.

**P.** longirostris Korn.; Syd. "Monogr. Ured. 1 : 205 ; Sacc. Syll. Fung. XVI: 303 ; Cummins, p. 554 ; Joerstad, p. 78 ; Ahmad, Biologia 2 : 59. On leaves of *Lonicera asperifolia,* Barum Valley : Shokor Shal (Wendelbo) ; Satpura Nalah above Skardu, Baltistan (R. R. Stewart).

**P.** major (Diet.) Diet.; Ahmad, Biologia 2 : 60. -Syn. *P. praecox* Bubak ; Syd. Monogr. Ured. 1 : 67 ; Sacc. Syll. Fung. XIV : 309. On leaves of *Dubyaea oligocephal a,* Kagan Valley : Shogran.

P. maydis Bereng.; Syd. Monogr. Ured. 1 : 830 ; Ah mad, Biologia 2 : 60 ; Sacc. Syll. Fung. VII : 659 as *P. sorghi* Schw. On leaves of *Zea mays,* Kagan ; Swat : Kulali ; Lahore.

**P.** melasmioides Tranz.; Syd. Monogr. Ured. 1 : 538 ; Sacc. Syll. Fung. XVII : 357 ; Joerstad, p. 78 ; Ahmad, Biologia 2 : 61. On leaves of
*Aquilegia pubifiora,* Swat : Mt. Ilam ; Murree ; of *A. fra grans,* Naltar Valley, Gilgit (R. R. Stewart).

**P.** menthae Pers.; Syd. Monogr. Ured. 1 : 282 ; Sacc. Syll. Fung. VII : 617 ; Arth. & Cummins, p. 403 ; Malik & Khan, p·. 524 ; Sydow & Ah mad, p. 440 ; Ahmad, Biologia 2 : 61. On leaves and stems of

*M entha syl vestris*, Chillianwala ; Quetta : Hanna Valley ; Swat : Mingora ; Poonch (R. R. Stewart) ; Kagan Valley : Naran ; Hasan-abdal·; Murree Hills Gharial (R. R. Stewart) ; Peshawar (Shaw) ; of *Origanum vul gare*, Kagan Valley :·Naran, Sharhan ; Changla Gali ; of *Calamintha umbrosa,* Kaga n Valley : Batak undi ; Changla Gali ; of *C. clinopodium*, Swat : Kalam ; Kagan Valley : Naran ; of *N epet a* sp., Kagan Valley : Saiful Maluk Sar (Shaukat Ali).

**P.** nepalensis Bard. & Diet.; Syd. Monogr. Ured. 1 : 578 ; Sacc. Syll. Fung. IX : 309 ; Malik & Khan, p. 524 ; A hmad , Biologia 2 : 62. On leaves and stems of *Rumex nepalensis,* Kagan Valley : Shogran ; Swat : Kalam ; Changla Gali ; Hazara (S. A. Malik).

P. oenanthes Diet.; Ahmad, Biologia 2· : 62. On leaves of *Oenanthe stolonifera,* Swat : Mingora.

P. philippinensis Syd .; Monogr. U red. 4 : 599 ; Sacc. Syll. Fung. XXIII : 720 ; Sydow & Ahmad , p. 441 ; Ahmad , Biologia 2 : 62. On leaves of *Cy perus rot und us,* La hore ; Sangla Hiil ; Lyallpur ; Pakpat-tan ; Multan.

**P.** phlomidis Thuem.; Syd. Monogr. Ured. 1 : 285 ; Joerst ad , p. 79. Ahmad, Biologia 2 : 63. On leaves of *Lamium rhomboid eum,* Ba ru m Valley : above Shokor Sha! (F. Jorstad).

**P.** phyllocladiae Cke.; Syd. Monogr. Ured. 1 : 617 ; Sacc. Syll. Fung. VII : 633 ; Ahmad , Biologia 2 : 63 ; Thind, Ind. Bot. Soc. Jour. 21 : 195. On stems and phylloclades of *As paragus gracilis,* Lahore ; Changa Manga.

**P.** pimpinellae (Str.) Ma rt.; Syd. Monogr. U red. I : 408 ; Sacc. Sy!!. Fung. VII : 616 p. p.; Art h. & Cu mmins, p. 403 ; Ahmad, Biologia 2 : 64. On leaves of *Pimpinella d iversifolia ,* Swat : Kalam ; Changla Gali (R. R. Stewart).

P. poarum Niels. in Bot. Tidssk. III, 2 : 34, 1877. -Syn. *P . poae-al pinaJ* Eriks. in Ark. f. Bot. 18 : 1, 1923 ; Biologia 2 : 64, 1956. On leaves of *Poa annua,* La hore. Dr Ivar Joerstad writes to inform tha t it is doubtful if *P. poarum* Niels. on *Poa a nnua* really is t his rust species. Records of *P. poarum* from Asia except Asia Minor and the western pa rt of the Soviet Union eastward to central Siberia are proba bly all dubious. *P. poarum* appears to be obligatorily alterna t-ing with *Tussilago farfara ,* and *Paa annua* to be rather resistan t.

**P.** poae-nemoralis Ot th; Ahmad , Biologia 2 : 64. On leaves of *Agrostis munroana,* Kaga n Valley : Batak u ndi.

P. pollinire Bard.; Syd. Monogr. Ured. 1 : 798 ; Sacc. Syll. Fung. IX : 313 ; Arth. & Cummins, p. 403 ; Ahmad, Biologia 2 : 65. On leaves of *Strobilanthes dalhousianus,* Murree Hills : Gharial ; Ghora Gali ; Murree.

P. polygoni-amphibii Pers.; Syd. Monogr. Ured. 1 : 569 ; Sacc. Syll. Fung. XVII : 394 ; Ahmad, Biologia 2 : 66. On leaves and stems of *Polygonum pterocarpum,* Swat : Kulali-Kalam.

P. prenanthes Kze. var. himalensis Barcl.; Syd. Monogr. Ured. 1 : 136 ; Sacc. Syll. Fung. XI : 189 ; Ahmad, Biologia 2 : 66. On leaves of *Lactuca brunoniana,* Kagan Valley : Shogran ; Changla Gali ; Poonch (R. R. Stewart).

P. propinqua Syd. & Butl.; Sacc. Syll. Fung. XXI : 692 ; Arth. & Cummins, p. 404 ; Ahmad, Biologia 2 : 66. On leaves of *Dicanthium annulatum,* Rawalpindi : Topi Park (R. R. Stewart).

P. prostii Moug.; Syd. Monogr. Ured. 1 : 638 ; Sacc. Syll. Fung, VII: 732; Cummins, p. 455 ; Malik & Khan, p. 524 ; Ahmad, Biolog-ia 2 : 66. On leaves of *Tulipa stellata,* Abbottabad (A. H. Khan) ; Margalla, Rawalpindi (R. R. Stewart).

P. pruni-spinosre Pers.; Syd. · Monogr. Ured. 1 : 484 ; Sacc. Syl\. Fung. VII : 648 ; Malik & Khan, p. 524 ; Ahmad, Biologia 2 : 67. On leaves of *Prunus persica,* Changa Manga ; Peshawar (S. A. Malik).

P. pulsatillae Kalchbr.; Syd. Monogr. Ured. 1 : 536 ; Ahmad, Biologia 2 : 68. On leaves of *Anemone obtusiloba,* Changla Gali ; Nathia Gali.

P. pulvinta Rabb.; Syd. Monogr. Ured. 1 : 76 ; Sacc. Syll. Fung. VII : 711 ; Ahmad, Biologia 2 : 68. On leaves of *Echinops echinatus,* Sangla Hill ; Lahore (B. Dass).

P. punctiformis (Str.) Roehl.; Ahmad, Biologia 2 : 68. -Syn. P. *suaveolens* (Pers.) Rostr.; Syd. Monogr. Ured. 1 : 55 ; Sacc. SyU. Fung. VII : 633 ; Sydow & Ahmad, p. 440 as P. *cirsii.* On leaves of *Cnicus arvensis,* Changa Manga ; Lahore.

P. purpurea Cke., Syd. Monogr. Ured. 1 : 803 ; Sacc. Sy!!. Fung. VII : 657 ; Ahmad, Biologia 2 : 69. On leaves of *Sorghum vulgare,* Lahore (Cheema).

P. pygmaea Erik.; Syd. Monogr. Ured. 1 : 741 ; Sacc. Syll.- Fung. XIV : 356 ; Ahmad, Biologia 2 : 69. On leaves of *Agrostis munroana,* Kagan Valley : Batakundi.

P. ranunculi-falcati Ahmad in Sydowia 8 : 163, 1954 ; Biologia 2 : 69. On leaves of *Ranmlculus Jalcatus,* Baluchistan : Ziarat.

**P.** ribis DC.; Syd. Monogr. Ured. 1 : 496 ; Sacc. Syll. Fung. VII : 679 ;
Malik & Khan, p. 524 ; Ahmad, Biologia 2 : 69.   On leaves of *Ribis
rubrum,* Swat : Kalam ; Hazara (S. A. Malik).

**P.** romagnoliana Maire & Sacc.; Syd. Monogr. Ured. 1 : 682 ; Sacc. Syll.
Fung. XVII : 374 ; Ahmad, Biologia 2 : 70.   On leaves of *Cyperus
di.fformis,* Chuh;irkana, Sheikhupura Dist.

**P.** rubigo-vera (DC.) Wint.; Ahmad, Biologia 2 : 70.   On leaves of
*Lol ium perenne ,* Murree ; of *Aquil egia pubiflora.* Kagan Valley :
Sharhan, Saiful Maluk Sar.

**P.** rufipes Diet.; Syd. Monogr. Ured. 1 : 757 ; Sacc. Syll. Fung. XVII :
177 ; Ahmad, Biologia 2 : 70. On leaves of *Imperata cylindrica,*
Chillianwala ; Chuharkana ; Changa Manga ; Lahore ; Sargodha.

**P.** saxifragae-ciliatae Bare!.; Syd. Monogr. Ured. 1 : 506 ; Sacc. Syll.
Fung. IX : 299 ; Arthur & Cum mins, p. 404 ; Cummins, p. 456 ;
Malik & Khan; p. 524 ; Ahmad, Biologia 2 : 71. On leaves of
*S axifraga cil iata* & *S. stracheyi ,* Kagan Valley : Shogran ; Changla
Gali ; Murree Hills ; Baltistan : Thalla La (R. R. Stewart).

**P.** schirajewskii Tranz.; Sacc. Syll. Fung. XXIII : 698 ; Ahmad, Biologia
2 : 72. On leaves of *Serratul a pallid a,* Murree : Lower Topa.

**P.** scirpi DC.; Syd. Monogr. Ured. 1 : 688 ; Sacc. Syll. Fung. VII : 659 ;
Ahmad, Biologia 2 : 72. On leaves of *S cirpus littoral is,* Sangla Hill ;
Chiniot ; Lahore (B. Dass).

**P.** silvatica Schroet.; Syd. Monogr. Ured. 1: 656 ; Sacc. Syll. Fung. Vil :
627 ; Ahmad, Biologia 2 : 73. On leaves of *Taraxacum officinal e,*
Quetta (Asghar Ali).

**P.** solmsii P. Henn.; Sacc. Syll. Fung. XIV : 357 ; Syd. Monogr. Ured.
1 : 568 ; Malik & Khan, p. 524 ; Ahmad, Biologia 2 : 73.   On leaves
of *Polygunum* sp., Hazara (S. A. Malik).

**P.** sonchi Rob.; Syd. Monogr. Ured. 1 : 154 ; Sacc. Syll. Fung. VII : 638 ;
Malik & Khan , p. 524 ; Ahmad , Biologia 2 : 73. On leaves of
*Sonchus arvensis,* Quetta (Asghar Ali) ; Upper Topa, Murree
(A . H. Khan) ; Hazara (S. A. Malik).

**P.** striiformis West ; Ahmad, Biologia 2 : 73.- Syn. P. *glumarum* (Schum.)
Eriks. & Henn.; Syd. Monogr. Ured. 1 : 706 ; Sacc. Syll. Fung. XVII :
380.   On leaves of *Triticum aestivum,* very common throughout the
area.

**P.** swertiae (Opiz.) Wint., Syd. Monogr. Ured. 1 : 342 ; Sacc. Syll. Fung.
VII : 613 ; Ahmad , Biologia 2 : 74. On leaves of *S wertia petiolata;*
Swat : Kalam; of *S. speciosa,* Kagan Valley : Shogran.

**P.** tanaceti DC.; Syd. Monogr. Ured. **1** : l61 ; Sacc. Syll. Fung. VII : 637; Ahmad , Biologia, 2 : 74. On leaves and stems of *Chrysanthemum griffit hii,* Barum Valley : Shokor Shal (Wendelbo).

**P.** tara xaci (Rebent. **I** Plowr.; Syd. Monogr. Ured. **1** : 164 ; Sacc. Syll. Fung. IX : 305 ; Ahmad, Biologia 2 : 74. On leaves of *Taraxacum officinale,* Swat : Kalam ; Kagan V_alley : Batakundi.

**P.** tricholepidis Syd.; Ahmad , :Siologia 2 : 75. On leaves of *Tricholepis stewartii,* Murree Hills : Dunga Gali, Changla Gali.

**P.** triticina Eri ks. ; Syd. Monogr. Ured. **1** : 716 ; Sacc. Syll. Fung. XVII ; 376 ; Ahmad, Biologia 2': 76. On leaves *of Triticum aestivum,* common throughout the area.

**P._** turgida P. & H. Syd. Monogr. Ured. 1 : 226 ; Sacc. Syll. Fung. XVII : 323 ; Ahmad , Biologia 2 : 76. On leaves of *Lycium europeum,* Lahore.

**P.** tuyutensis Speg.; Ahmad , Biologia 2 : 77.; Sacc. Syll. Fung. VII : 616. Syn . *P . cressae* (DC.) Lagerh .; Syd. Monogr. Ured. 1 : 320 ; Sacc. Sy!!. Fung. IX : 307. On leaves of *Cressa cretica,* Karachi (Jaffrey).

**P.** typha c Kalch br.; Sacc. Syll. Fung. XI : 198. On leaves of *Typha angustata ,* Thatta Dist., Sind.

**P.** u mbil ici Guep.; Syd. Monogr. Ured. 1 : 492 ; Sacc. Syll. Fu ng. VII : 700 ; Joerstad , p. 81 ; Ah mad , Biologia 2 : 77. On leaves of *S ed um het erodontum ,* Barum Valley : Shokor Shal (Wendelbo).

**P.** urticae Bard.; Syd. Monogr. Ured. **1** : 520 : Sacc. Syll Fung. IX : 299 ; Ahmad , Biologia 2 : 77. On leaves of *Urtica d ioica* Ka gan Valley.

**P.** versicolor Diet. & Holw.; Syd. Monogr. Ured. **1** : 724 ; Sacc. Syll. Fu ng. XIV : 352 ; Ahmad , Biologia 2 : 78. On leaves of *H eteropogon contort us,* Choa Saidan Shah.

**P.** violae (Sch um.) DC.; Syd. Monogr. Ured. 1 : 439 ; Sacc. Syll. Fung. VII : fi09 ; Malik & Khan, p. 524 ; Ahmad, Biologia 2 : 78. On leaves of *Vinl a ca nescens,* Swat : Kalam ; of *V. serpens,* Hazara (S. A. Malik); of *V. caespitosa,* Kagan Valley : Shogran.

**P.** wattia na Bard.; Syd . Monogr. Ured. 1 : 544 ; Sacc. Syll. Fu ng. IX : 298 ; Ahmad , Biologia 2 : 79. On leaves of *Clematis grata,* Swat : Miana ; Murree.

## Pucciniostele Tranzsch. & Korn.

**P.** clarkiana (Bard.) Diet.; Arth. & Cummins, p. 406 ; Cummins, p. 401i ; Ah mad , Biologia 2 : 80. On leaves of *Astil be rivul aris,* Kagan Va lley : Shar han ; Mu rree Hills : Changla Gali (R. R. Stewart).

## Ravenelia Berk.

R. mimosae-himalayae Ahmad in Biologia 2 : 80, 1956.    On leaves of
*Mimosa himalayana*, Lahore, Changa Manga.

R. sessilis Berk.; Syd. Monogr. Ured. 3 : 248 ; Sacc. Syll. .Pung. VII :
772 ; Ahmad, Biologia 2 : 81. On leaves and pods of *Albizzia lebbek*,
Sialkot ; Changa Manga.

R. taslimii Mundk.; Sydow & Ahmad, p. 441 ; Ahmad, Biologia 2 : 81.
On leaves of *Acacia modesta*, Changa Manga ; Taxilla ; Rawalpindi ;
Choa Saidan Shah.

## Trachyspora Fuck.

T. alchemillae tPers.) Fuck.· Ahmad , Biologia 2 : 82.-Syn. *Uromyces
alchemillae* (Pers.) Lev.; Syd. Monogr. Ured. 2 : 196 ; Sacc. Syll.
Fung. VII : 553. On leaves of *Alchemilla vulgaris*, Skardu, Baltistan
(R. R. Stewart).

## Uromyces Link

U. apludae Syd. & But!.; Syd. Monogr. Ured. 2 : 321 ; Sacc. Sy!!. Fung.
XXI : 591 ; Ahmad, Biologia 2 : 82. On leaves of *Apluda mutica*,
Lahore.

U. appendiculatus (Pers.) Link ; Syd . Monogr. Ured. 2 : 120 ; Sacc.
Syll. Fung. VII : 535 ; Ahmad, Biologia 2 :82.    On leaves of *Dolichos
lablab*, Swat : Kulali ; Hazara (S. A. Malik).

U. andropogonis-annulati Syd. & Butl.; Monogr. Ured. 2 : 320 ; Sacc.
Syll. Fung. XXI : 592 ; Sydow & Ahmad, p. 440 ; Arthur & Cummins,
p. 406 ; Ahmad, Biologia 2 : 82. On leaves of *Dicanthium annulatum*,
Chillianwala ; Sangla Hill ; Rawalpindi; Swat : Kulali-Kalam; Khangah
Dogran, Gujranwala Dist. (R. R. Stewart).

U. anthyllidis (Grev.) Schroet.; Syd. Monogr. Ured. 2 : 64 ; Sacc. Syll.
Fung. VII : 551; Ahmad , Biologia 2 : 83. On leaves of *Trigonella
gracilis*, Upper Topa, Murree ; of *T. incisa*, Sangla Hill ; Gakkhar ;
Chilli anwala.

U. capitatus Syd.; Monogr. Ured. 2 : 93 ; Sacc. Syll. Fung. XVIII : 250 ;
Ahmad, Biologia *2* : 83. On leaves of *Desmodium tiliaefolium*, Kagan
Valley : Sharhan ; Swat : Madian.

U. chenopodii Schroet. ; Syd. Monogr. Ured. 2 : 233 ; Sacc. Syll. Fung.
VII : 548 ;.Ahmad , Biologia 2 .: 83. On leaves and branches of *Suaeda
Jruticosa*, Sangla Hill ; Lahore.

U. ciceris-arietini (Grog.) Jacky ; Syd. Monogr. Ured. 2 : 84 ; Sacc.  Syll.

Fung. XI : 175. On leaves of *Cicer arietinum*, Sangla Hill ; Chillian-wala.

U. decoratus Syd.; Syd. Monogr. Ured. 2 : 88 ; Sacc. Sy!!. Fung. XXl : 549 ; Ahmad, Biologia 2 : 84. On leaves of *Crotolaria juncea*, Sialkot.

U. eragrostidis Tracy ; Syd. Monogr. Ured. 2 : 326 ; Sacc. Syll. Fung. XI : 182 ; Ahmad, Biologia 2 : 84. On leaves of *Desmostach ya bipinnata*, Lahore ; Sialkot ; Chenab Bank (Cheema).

U. fabae (Pers.) de Bary ; Syd. Monogr. Ured. 2 : 103 ; Sacc. Syll. Fung. VII : 531 p.p.; Sydow & Ahmad, p. 439 ; Ahmad, Biologia 2 : 84. On leaves of *Pisum sativum* and *Vicia sativa*, Chillianwala ; Peshawar ; of *Lat hyrus odoratus*, Peshawar (S. A. Malik); of *Vicia faba*, Ly allpur (Mitter).

U. fritillariae (Sehl.) Thuem.; Ahmad, Biologia 2 : 85. On leaves of *Fritil laria roylei*, Saiful Maluk (Kagan Valley).

U. geranii (DC.) Lev.; Syd. Monogr. Ured. 2 : 190 ; Ahmad, Biologia 2 : 85. On leaves of *Geranium aconitifol ius*, Kagan Valley : Shogran ; Swat ; :{(alam.

U. heteromallus Syd.; Sydow & Ahmad; p. 439 ; Ahmad, Biologia 2 : 85. On stems of *Haloxylun recuruum*, Lyallpur.

U. ignobilis (Syd.}, Arth.; Ahmad, Biologia 2 : 85. On lea ves of *Sporo-bolus pal lidus*, Lahore (Ak hlaq Ahmad).

U. kondoi R. Miura ; Cummins, p. 457 ; Ahmad, Biologia 2 : 86. On leaves of *Guldenstaedtia* sp., Rawalpind i (R. R. Stewart).

U. lespedezae-sericeae Ahmad in Biologia 2 : 86, 1956. On leaves of *Lesped eza sericea*, Abbottabad ; Upper Topa, Murree (A. H. Khan) ; Ghora Gali (Asghar Ali).

U. lineolatus (Desm.) Schroet.; Ahmad, Biologia 2 : 87.- Syn. *U. scirpi* (Cast.) Burr.; Syd. Monogr. Ured. 2 : 302 ; Sacc. Syll. Fung. VII : 558. On leaves of *Scirpus marit imus*, Lahore ; Sheikhu pura.

U. lycoctoni (Kalchbr.) Trotter ; Ahmad, Biologia 2 : 87. On leaves of *Aconitum laeve*, Kagan Valley : Saiful Maluk Sar.

U. minor Schroet.; Syd. Monogr. Ured. 2 : 134 ; Sacc. Syll. Fung. VII : 560 ; Sydow & Ahmad, p. 439 ; Ahmad, Biologia 2 : 87. On leaves of *Trifolium resupinatum*, Chillianwala ; Ladhar, Sheikhupura Dist.

U. nerviphilus (Grog.) Hotson ; Ahmad, Biologia 2 : 8· .- Syn. *U. fiectens* Lagerh.; Syd. Monogr. Ured. 2 : 360 ; Sacc. Syll. Fung. XXI : 541.. On leaves of *Trifolium repens*, Kagan Valley : Shogran.

U. orientale Syd.; Syd. Monogr. Ured. 2 : 102 ; Sacc. Syll. Fung. XXI : 547 ; Ahmad, Biologia 2 : 88. On leaves of *Indigo/era linifolia,* Ladhar, Sheikhupura Dist.

U. phacae-frigidae (Wahlenb.) Hariot; Ahmad, Biologia 2 : 18 ; Joerstad, p. 82. On leaves of *Astragalus coluteocarpus,* Chitral : Barum Valley, Zapotili (Wendelbo).

U. polygoni-aviculare (Pers.) Karst.; Ahmad, Biologia 2 : 88.- Syn. *U. polygoni* (Pers.) Fuck.; Syd. Monogr. Ured. 2 : 236 ; Sacc. Syll. Fung. VII : 533 ; Malik & Khan, p. 524. On leaves of *Polygonum aviculare,* Kagan Valley : Sharhan ; Quetta Valley ; of *P. viviparum,* Hazara (S. A. Malik) ; Swat : Madian.

U. proeminens (DC.) Lev.; Syd. Monogr. Ured. 2 : 158 ; Sacc. Syll. Fung. VII : 553 p.p.; Ahmad, Biologia 2 : 89. On leaves of *Euphorbia hypericijolia,* Gilgit (R. R. Stewart) ; Muzaffarabad.

U. punctatus Schroet.; Ahmad, Biologia 2 : 89. -Syn. *U. astragali* (Opiz) Schroet.; Syd. Monogr. Ured. 2 : 07 ; Sacc. Syll. Fung. VII : 550 p.p. On leaves of *Oxytropis* sp., Kagan Valley : Batakundi.

U. rumicis (Schum.) Wint:; Syd. Monogr. Ured. 2 : 238 ; Sacc. Syll. Fung. VII : 344 ; Sydow & Ahmad, p. 439 ; Ahmad, Biologia 2 : 89. On leaves of *Rumex dentatus,* Lahore ; Changa Manga ; Chillianwala.

U. setariae-italicae (Diet.) Yoshino ; Syd. Monogr. Ured. 2 : 339 ; Sacc. Syll. Fung. XVII : 457 ; Sydow & Ahmad. p. 440 ; Ahmad, Biologia 2 : 89. On leaves of *Setaria lutescens,* Lahore, Sheikhupura Dist:

U. striatus Schroet.; Syd. Monogr. Ured. 2 : 115 ; Sacc. Syll. Fung. VII : 542 ; Ahmad, Biologia 2 : 90. On leaves of *Medicago sativa,* Sargodha ; Ladhar, Sheikhupura Dist.; Chillianwala ; of M. *lupulina,* Poonch (R. R. Stewart) ; of M. *denticulata,* Chillianwala ; of *Lens esculenta,* Sialkot.

U. striolatus Tranz.; Syd. Monogr. Ured. 2 : 17S ; Sacc. Syll. Fung. XXI : 562 ; Joerstad, p. 83 ; Ahmad, Biologia 2 : 90. On leave of *Euphorbia* off. *esula,* Barum Valley, Chitra!.

U. superfluus H. & P. Svd. Monogr. Ured. 2 : 337 ; Sacc. Syll. Fung. XXI : 593 ; Ahmad, Biologia 2 : 90. On leaves of *Panicum antidotale,* Changa Manga ; Karachi.

U. thallungii. Maire ; Sacc. Syll. Fung. XXIII : 537 ; Ahmad, Biologia 2 : 90. On leaves of *Rumex vesicarius,* Karachi.

U. trifolii (Hedw. f.) Lev.; Syd. Monogr. Ured. 2 : 132 ; Sacc. Syll. Fung. VII : 534 p.p.; Arthur & Cummins, p. 406 ; Malik & Khan,

p. 524 ; Ahmad , Biologia 2 : 91. On leaves of *Trifolium resupinatum* , Islamia College, Peshawar (R.R. Stewart) ; Sangla Hill- ; Chillianwala ; Peshawar (Shaw).

U. trifolii-repentis (Cast.) Liro ; Syd. Monogr. Ured. 2 : 131 ; Sacc. Syll. Fung. XXI : 542 ; Ahmad , Biologia 2 : 91. On leaves of *Trifolium repens*, Kagan Valley ; Gilgit (R.R. Stewart).

U. tuberculatus Fuck.; Syd. Monogr. Ured. 2 : 163 ; Ahmad, Biologia 2 : 91 ; Sacc. Syll. Fung. VII : 553 as *U. proeminens* p.p. On leaves of *Euphorbia* sp., Quetta (Asghar Ali).

U. vaierianae-wallichii (Diet.) Arth. & Cumm. in Mycologia 25 : 406, 1933 ; Ahmad , Biologia 2 : 92. On leaves of *Valeriana wallichii* , Changla Gali ; Kagan Valley : Shogran.

## FORM GENERA

## Aecidium Pers.

*t\.* calianthum Syd.; Ahmad, Biologia 2 : 94 ; Malik & Khan, p. 523. On leaves of *Desmodium tiliaefolium*, Hazara (R. R. Stewart).

A. clematidis DC.; Ahmad, Biologia 2 : 94. On leaves of *Clematis* sp., Kagan Valley : Sharhan.

A. colchici Ahmad in Biologia 2 : 94. 1956. On leaves of *Colchicum luteum*, Upper Topa, Murree (I. I. Chaudhri) ; Abbottabad (A.H. Khan).

A. crypticum Kalchbr. & Cke.; Syd. Monogr. Ured. 4 : 41 : Sacc. Syll ; Fung. VII : 900 ; Arthur & Cummins, p. 398 ; Malik & Khan, p. 523. Ahmad , Biologia 2 : 95. On leaves of *Gerbera lanuginosa* , Kagan Valley : Shogran ; Ghora Gali ; Swat.

A. euphorbiae Gmel.; Ahmad , Biologia 2 : 95. On leaves and stems of *Euphorbia* aff. *esula*, Barum Valley : Chitral ; of *Euphorbia* sp., Kagan Valley : Naran (I. I. Chaudhri) .

A. hederae Wakefield ; Ahmad, Biologia 2 : 95. -Syn. *A. hederae* Arth. & Cummins, in Mycologia 25 : 398 ; Cummins, p. 442. On leaves of *Hedera nepalensis*, Murree.

A. merenderae Syd.; Syd. Monogr. Ured . 4 : 286 ; Sacc. Syll. Fung. XXI : 784 ; Ahmad, Biologia 2 : 95. On leaves of *Merender'a persica*, Salt Range (Drummond).

A. montanum But!.; Syd. Monogr. Ured . 4 : 248 ; Sacc. Syll. Fung. XXI : 753 ; Arthur & Cummins, p. 399 ; Cummins, p. 447. On *Berberis ceratophylla,* Murree ; of *B. petiolaris*, Murree ; Nathia Gali ;

Changla Gali ; Kagan Valley : Shogran ; of *Berberis vulgaris,* Ziarat, Baluchistan ; of *Berberis* sp., Barum Valley : Chitral (I. I. Chaudhri).

A. orbiculare Bard.; Syd. Monogr. Ured. 4 ; 256 ; Sacc. Syll. Fung. XI : 213 ; Ahmad, Biologia 2 : 96. On leaves of *Clematis* sp., Gilgit (I. I. Chaudhri).

A. ranunculacearum DC.; Ahmad, Biologia 2 : 96. On leaves of *Ranunculus hirtellus* Deosai Plains (R. R. Stewart).

A. stcwartianum Cumm. in Mycologia 35 : 450, 1943. On leaves of *Heracleum candicans,* Kishenganga Valley (R. R. Stewart) ; Kagan Valley : Nadi-Kund.

### Monosporidium Bard.

M-r andrachnis Barcl.; Syd. Monogr. Ured. 4 : 364 ; Sacc. Syll. Fung. IX : 297 ; Malik & Khan, p. 523 ; Ahmad, Biologia 2 : 93. On leaves of *Andrachne cordifolia,* Changla Gali ; Murree Hills.

### Peridermium Link

P. indicum Colley & Taylor ; Ahmad, Biologia 2 : 93 ; Malik & Khan, p. 523. On leaves of *Pinus excelsa,* Hazara (S. A. Malik).

P. thomsoni Berk.; Syd. Monogr. Ured. 4 : 4 ; Sacc. Syll. Fung. VII : 837 ; Ahmad, Biologia 2 : 93. On leaves of *Picea morinda,* Kagan Valley : Sharhan.

### Uredo Pers.

U. dalbergiae P. Henn.; Syd. -Monogr. Ured. 4 : 476 ; Sacc. Syll. Fung. XVII : 445 ; Ahmad, Biologia 2 : 92. On leaves of *Dalbergia sissoo,* Changa Manga.

U. otostegiae Ahmad in Biologia 2 : 92, 1956. On leaves of *Otostegia limbata,* Balakot ; Poonch (R. R. Stewart).

U. ravennae Maire ; Syd. Monogr. Ured. 4 : 538 ; Ahmad, Biologia 2 : 93. On leaves of *Erianthus ravennae,* Chuharkana ; Lahore.

.U. rottboelliae Diet.; Syd. Monogr. Ured. 4 : 546 ; Sacc. Syll. Fung. XVII : 457 ; Ahmad, Biologia 2 : 93. On leaves of *Hemarthria compressa,* Lahore ; Changa Manga ; Sangla Hill.

U. vicatiae Syd.; Syd. Monogr. Ured. IV : 441 ; Sacc. Syll. Fung. XXI : 789 ; Ahmad, Biologia 2 : 93. On leaves of *Vicatia coniifolia,* Poonch (R. R. Stewart). ·

### Order : USTILAGINALES

### Family : USTILAGINACEAE

### Cintractia Cornu

C. axicola (Berk.) Cornu ; Sacc. Syll. Fung. VII     480 ; Mundk. &

Thirumal., p. 41 ; Zundel, p. 20.    On *Fimbristylis tenera*, Pakpattan ; Kalashah Kaku.

C. caricis (Pers.) Magn.; Zundel, p. 22 ; Mundk. & Thirumal, p. 41 ; Joerstad, p. 85. On *Carex wendelboi* and *Kobresia laxa*, Barum Valley: Chitral ; on *Eriophorum comosum*, Murree.

C. limitata Clint.; Sacc. Syll. Fung. XVII : 480 ; Zundel, p. 32.    On *Cyperus rotundus*, Ladhar, Sheikhupura Dist.

## Melanopsichium    Beck

M. austro-americanum (Speg.) Beck ; Sacc. Syll. Fung. XVII : 484 ; Zundel, p. 45 ; Mundk. & Thirumal., p. 46 as M. *pennsylvanicum* Hirschhorn.    On *Polygonum glabrum*, Lahore.

## Pericladium    Pass.

P. grewiae Pass., Sacc. Syll. Fung. VII :838 ; Mundk. & Thirumal., 47 ; Zundel, p. 49. On *Grewia villosa*, Kalachitta Hills, Attock Dist. (R.R. Stewart).

## Sorosporium    Rud.

S. ladharense Sydow in Sydow & Ahmad, p. 443 ; Mundk.    - Thirumal., p. 53 ; Zundel, p. 65.    On *Cymbopogon jwarancusa*, Ladhar, Sheikhupura Dist.

S. penniseti'Mundkur  ; Mundk. & Thirumal., p. 54 ; Zundel, p. 69.    On *Cenchrus ciliaris*, Lahore.

S. saponariae Rud.; Zundel, p. 72 ; Joerstad , p. 85. On *Silene moorcroftiana*, Barum Valley : Chitral.

S. tumefaciens McAlpine ;    Sacc. Syll. Fung. XXI : 514 ; Mundk. & Thirumal.; p. 54 ; Zundel, p. 77. On *Chrysopogon mantanus*, Murree.

## Sphacelotheca    de Bary

S. andropogonis (Opiz) Bubak ; Mundk. & Thirumal., p. 9 ; Sydow & Ahmad, p. 442 ; Fischer, p. 130 : Zundel, p. 95 as *S. ischaemi*. On *Bothriochloa ischaemum*, Ladhar, Sheikhupura Dist.

S. andropogonis-annulati (Bref.) Zundel ; Sacc. Syll. Fung. XIV : 419 ; Mundk. & Thirumal., p. 10 ; Zundel, p. 80. On *Dicanthium annulatum*, Swat : Kulali ; Lahore ; Lahar, Sheikhupura Dist.

S. apludae (Syd.) Zundel in Ustil. of the world, p. 81 ; Mundk. & Thirumal., p. 10. . On *Apluda aristata*, Murree.

S. cruenta (Kuehn) Potter ; Sacc. Syll. Fung. VII : 455 as *Ustilago cruenta* ; Mundk & Thirumal., p. 13 ; Sydow & Ahmad. p. 442 ; Zundel, p. 86. · On *Sorghum halepense*, Lahore ; Sheikhupura ; Gujranwala ; Sialkot.

S. cypericola Mundk. & Pavgi in Indian Phytopath. 1 : 111 ; Mundk. & Thirumal., p. .13. On *Gyperus difformis,* Ladhar, Sheikhupura Dist.

S. erianthi (Syd.) Mundkur ; Sacc. Syll. Fung. XXIII : 610 as *Ustilago erianthae ;* Mund k. & Thirumal.,, p. 15 ; Zundel, p. 90. On *Erianthus ravennae,* Lahore.

S. hydropiperis (Schum) de Bary ; Sacc. Syll. Fung. XXI : 508 ; Mundk. & Thirumal., p. 15. On *Polygonum* sp., Swat :Kalam ;. Murtee.

S. lanigeri (Magn.) Maire ; Zundel, p. 96 ; -Syn. *S. consueta* Syd.; Sydow & Ahmad, p. 442 ; Mundk. & Thir,umal., p. 12.- *S. schoenanthi,* (Syd. & Butl.) Zundel in Mycologia 12 : 136. On *Cymbopogon jwaranctisil ,* Shahkot Hills ; Karachi ; on, C. *schoenant hus,* Hasana bdal ; Margalla (Rawalpindi) ; Swat : Mingora.

S. monilifera (Ell. & Ev.) Clinton ; Mundk. & Thirumal., p. 17 ; Zundel, p. 100 ; Sacc. Syll. Fung. XVII : 417 as *Ustilago warneckeana.* On *Hetropogon contortus,* Swa.t : Madian ; Abbottabad.

S. montaniensis (Ell. & Hollw.) Clint.; Zundel, p. 100 ; -Syn. *S. strangulan3* (lssats.) Clint. On *Eragrostis poa-eoides,* Murree ; Swat : Kalam.

S. pappophori (Pat.) Zundel in Ustil. of the world, p. 104. Sacc. Syll. Fung. XXI : 504 as *Ustil ago pa ppo phori.* On *Ennea pogon* sp., Baluchistan : Spinikarez (I. I. Chaudhri).

S. ophiuri (P. Henn.) Ling in Sydowia 7 : 237. -Syn. *S. cornuta ;* Mundk. & Thirumal., p. 12. On *Rottboellia exaltata,* Murree.

S. punjabensis Syd.; Sydow & Ahmad , p. 442 ; Mundk. & Thirumal., p. 18 ; Zundel, p. 106. *On Cenchrus setigerus* (= C. *bifiorus* Hk. f.), Sargodha ; Lahore ; Ladhar, Sheikhupura Dist.

S. reiliana (Kuehn) Clint.; Zundel, p. 106 ; Mundk. & Thirumal., p. 18 ; Sacc. Syll. Fung. VII : 471 as *Ustil ago reiliana.* On *Z ea mays,* Lahore ; Swat State .: Kulali ; on *Sorghum vul gare* and *Sorghum hal epense,* Jhelum ; Murree ; Rawalpindi..

S. rottboelliae (Syd. & Butl.) Mundk.; Zundel, p. 108 ; Mund k. & Thirumal., p. 19 ; Sacc. Syll. Fung. XXI :418 as *Ustil ago rottboel liae.* On *Hemarthria compressa,* Kagan Valley : Batak undi ; Swat : Barikot; Ladhar, Sheikhupura Dist.

S. sacchari (Rabenh.) Cifferi ; Zundel, p. 108 ; Mundk. & Thirumal., p. 19 ; Sacc. Syll. Fung. VII : 456 as *Ustil ago sacchari-ciliaris.* On *Saccharum munja,* Lahore ; Muzaffargarh.

S. schweinfurthiana (Thuem.) Sacc.; Sacc. Syll. Fung. XXI :509 ; Sydow & Ahmad, p. 412 ; Mu ndk. & Thirumal., p. 21 ; Zundel, p. 109. On

*Imperata cylindrica,* Lahore ; Sargodha ; Peshawar ; Ladhar, Sheikhupura Dist.

S. sorghi (Link) Clint.; Sacc. Syll. Fung. XVII : 487 ;  Mundk. & Thirumal., p. 21 ; Sydow & Ahmad , p. 442 ; Zundel, p. 110; G. W. Fischer,
p. 149.  On *Sorghum vulgare,* throughout the area.

S. stewartii Mundk.; Zundel, p. 111 ; .Mundk. & Thirumal., p. 21.     On
*Pennisetum Jlacidum₁* Baltistan  (R. R. Stewart).

S. tenuis (Sym.) Zundel ; Mundk. & Thirumal., p. 22 ; Zundel, p.  112;
Sacc. Syll. Fung. XXI : 506 as *Ustilago tenuis.*    On *Bothriochloa
pertusa,* Murree ; Muzaffafabad.

S. tricholaenae (P. Henn.) Mundk .; Mundk. & Thirumal. p. 23 ; Zundel,
p. 113.  On *Tricholaena teneriffae,* Sind.

S. vryburgii Zundel in Mycologia  23 : 298, 1931 ; Zundel, p.  114.     On
*Themeda ana.ther.a,* Murree ; Muzaffarabad.

### Thecaphora Fingerhuth

T. atterima Tul. ; Sacc. Syll. Fung. VII : 508 ; Zundel, p.  117 ;
Ahmad,Biologia , 1 : 140.  On *Carex* sp., Quetta .

### Tolyposporium Woron.

T. ehrenbergii (Kuehn) Pat.; Sacc. Syll.  Fung. XXI : 516 ; Mundk. &:
Thirumal., p. 56 ; Zundel, p. 128.- Syn. *T. filiferum* W. Busse ; *Sorosporium ehrenbergii* Kuehn.     On *Sorghum vulgare,* Jhelum ; Multan.

T. evernium Sydow ; Mundk. & Thirumal., p. 57 ; Sydow & Ahmad, p.
443 ; Zundel, p. 129. On *Paspalum distichum,* Lahore ; Akalgarh ;
Chuharkana.

T. penicillariae Bref.; Sacc. Syll. Fung. XIV : 426; Mundk. & Thirumal.,
p. 57 ; Zundel, p. 132.  On *Pennisetum typhoides,* Lahore ;  Sialkot.

### Ustilago (Pers.) Roussel

U. avenae (Pers.) Rostr.; Sacc. Syll. Fung. IX : 283 ; Mundk. & Thirumal.;
p. 25 ; G. W. Fischer, p. 242 ; Zundel, p. 141.     On *Avena sativa,*
Lahore ; Sialkot ; Gujranwala ; Sheikhupura ; Multan.

U. commellinae (Komarov) Zundel in Ustil. of the world,  p.  151, 1953.
On *Commellina benghalensis,* Murree ; Rawalpindi.

U. cordai Liro ; Sydow & Ahmad, p. 441 ; Mundk. & Thirumal., p. 26 ;
Zundel, p. 215 as a synonym of *U. utriculosa.* On *Polygonum barbatum,*
Ladhar, Sheikhupura Dist.; Kalashah Kaku.

U. crameri Koernicck; Sacc. Syll. Fung. VII : 455 ; Mundk. & Thirumal.\

p. 27 ; G. W. Fischer, P. 254 ; Zundel, p. 153.    On *Setaria italica*, Murree ; Muzaffarabad.

U. cynodontis P. Henn.; Sacc. Syll. Fung. XIV :416; Mundk. & Thirumal, p. 28 ; G. W. Fischer, p. 255 ; Zundel, p. 154.    On *Cynodon dactylon*, very common throughout the area.

U. egenula Syd. & Butf.; Sacc. Syll. Fung. XXIII : 609 ; Sydow &. Ahmad , p. 441; Mundk. & Thirumal., p. 28 ; Zundel, p. 158.    On *Eragrostis japonica*, Ladhar, Sheikhupura Dist.

U. euphorbiae Mundkur ; Zundel, p. 160 ;  Mundk. & Thirumal., p. 29. On *Euphorbia dracunculoides*, Kalashah Kaku.

U. hordei (Pers.) Lagerh.; Sacc. Syll. Fung. IX: 263: Mundk. & Thirumal., p. 28 ; Zundel, p. 166.   On *Hordeum vulgare*, common throughout.

U. idonea Syd.; Sydow & Ahmad , p. 422 ; Mundk. & Thirumal., p. 30 ; Zundel, p. 170. On *Dactyloctenium scindicum*, Sheikhupura ; Sangla Hill.

U. indica Syd. & But!.; Sacc. Syll. Fung. XXIII : 610 ; Mundk. & Thirumal., p. 30 ; Zundel, p. *110:* On *Eulaliopsis binata*, Swat : Mingora ; Murree ; Jhelum.

U. kolleri Wille ; Zundel. p. 174 ; Mundk. & Thirumal., p. 30.    On *Avena sativa*, Sind.

U. maydis (DC.) Corda ; Zundel, p. 179 ; G. W. Fischer, p. 281; Mundk. & Thirumal., p. 31 ; Sacc. Syll. Fung. VII : 472 as *U. zeae* Unger.  On *Zea mays*, Swat ; Kagan Valley ; Murree.

U. morinae Padwick & Azmatullah ; Zundel, p. 181; Mundk. & Thirumal., p. 32.   On *Marina* sp., Poonch (R. R. Stewart).

U. neglecta Niess!; Sacc. Syll. Fung. VII : 472 ; Zundel, p. 183 ; Fischer, p. 286; Mundk. & Thirumal p. 32.    On *Setaria lutescens*, Murree.

U. nepalensis Liro ;  Mundk. & Thirumal., p. 32 ; Zundel, p. 46 as *Melanopsichium nepalensis.* On *Polygonum alatum*, Kagan Valley : Batakundi.

U. nuda (Jensen) Rostrup ; Zundel, p. 184 ; Fischer,  p. 287 ; Mundk. & Thirumal., p. 33.   On *Hordeum vulgare*, Skardu, Baltistan.

U. panici-frumentacei Bef. ; Sacc. Syll. Fung. XIV : 414 ; Zundel, p. 187 ; Mundk. & Thirumal., p. 34 ; Sydow & Ahmad, p. 442. On *Echinochloa frumentacea*, Ladhar, Sheikhupura Dist.

U. paradoxa Syd. & Butl.; Sacc. Syll. Fung. XXIII : 611 ; Zundel, p. 189 ; Mundk. & Thirumal., p. 34.   On *Echinochloa frumentacea*, Sind.

U. rabenhorstiana Kuehn ; Sacc. Syll. Fung. VII : 471 ; Zundel, p. 194 ; Mundk. & Thirumal., p. 35. On *Digitaria cruciata*, Kagan Valley : Naran.

U. royleana Syd. & But!.; Sacc. Syll. Fung. XXI : 499 ; Zundel, p. 196 ; Mundk. & Thirumal., p. 36. On *Digitaria royleana*, Murree.

U. schismi Bubak ; Zundel, p. 197. On *Schismus arabicus*, Dargai.

U. scitaminea Syd. var. sacchari-barberi Mundkur in Kew Bull. 1939 : 529, 1940 ; Mundk. & Thirumal., p. 36 ; Zundel, p. 199. On *Saccharum officinarum*, very common throughout the area.

U. sparsa Underw,; Sacc. Syll. Fung. XIV : 416 ; Sydow & Ahmad, p. 441 ; Zundel, p. 202 ; Fischer, p. 296 ; Mundk. & Thirumal., p. 37. On *Dactyloctenium aegyptium*, Lahore ; Sialkot ; Sangla Hill; Lyallpur; Multan ; Rawalpindi.

U. spermophora Berk. & Curt.; Sacc. Syll. Fung. VII : 466 ; Sydow & Ahmad, p. 441; Zundel, p. 203; Fischer, p. 301; Mundk. & Thirumal., p. 37. On *Eragrostis poCEoides*, Pakpattan ; Gujranwala ; Rawalpindi ; Multan.

U. trichophora (Link) Kze.; Sacc. Syll. Fung. VII : 462 ; Zundel, p. 211 ; Mund k. & Thiru mal., p. 38. On *Echinochloa colonum*, Murree ; Rawalpindi.

U. tritici (Pers.) Rostru p ; Sacc. Syll. Fung. IX : 282 ; Zundel, p. 212 ; Mundk. & Thirumal., p. 39 ; G. W. Fischer, p. 287 as a synonym of *U. nuda*. On *Triticum vulgare*, very common everywhere.

U. utriculosa (Nees) Unger ; Sacc. Syll. Fung. VII : 476 ; Zundel, p. 215 ; Mundk. & Thirumal., p. 39. On *Polygonum barbatum* and *P. glabrum*, Lahore.

U. violacea (Pers.) Fckl.; Sacc. Syll. Fung. VII : 474 ; Zundel, p. 218 ; Joerstad , p. 85. On *Dianthus angulatus*, Barum Valley : Chitral. On *Stel laria media* Swat : Bahrain ; on *Lychnis apetal a*, Kagan Valley : Saiful Maluk Sar (Shaukat Ali).

### Family : TILLETIACEAE

### Doassansia Cornu

D. sagittarire (West) Fischer ; Sacc. Syll. Fung. VII : 503 ; Zundel, p. 231. On *Sagittaria guayanensis*, Gakkhar.

### Entyloma de Bary

E. fuscum Schroet.; Sacc. Syll. Fung. VII : 488 ; Zundel, p. 251 ; G. W. Fischer, p. 94 ; Mund k. & Thirumal., p. 68. On *Papaver rhoeas*, Lahore.

E. ranunculi (Bonord.) Schroet.; Sacc. Syll. Fung. VII : 488 ; Zundel, p. 263 ; Mundk. & Thirumal., p. 70 ; G. W. Fischer, p. 91 as a synonym of *F. ficarim.*  On *Ranuncul us* sp., Changla Gali

### Neovossia Koern.

N. barclayana Bref.; Sacc. Syll. Fung. XVI: 375 ; Zundel, p. 272; Mundk. & Thirumal., p. 60.  On *Pennisetum flaccid um,* Murree.

N. horrida (Takahashi) Padwick & Azmatullah ; Zundel. p. 278 ; Mundk. & Thirumal., p. 61.  On *Oryza sativa,* Hafizabad ; Kalashah Kaku.

N. indica (Mitra) Mundkur ; Zundel, p. 278 ; Mundk. & Thirumal., p. 62.  On *Triticum vulgare,* Gujranwala.

### Tilletia Tul.

T. caries (DC.) Tulasne ; Zundel, p. 284 ; Mundk. & Thirumal., p. 63 ; Sacc. Syll. Fung. VII : 481 as *T. tritici.*  On *Triticum vulgare,* Gilgit.

T. eleusines Sydow ; Zundel, p. 287 ; Mundk. & Thiru mal., p. 64.  On *Dactyloctenium aegyptium,* Lahore ; Sialkot ; on *Acrachne racemosa,* Murree.

T. foetida (Wallr.) Liro ; Zundel, p. 289 ; Mundk. & Thirumal., p. 64.  On *Triticum vulgare,* Gilgit.

T. tumefaciens Sydow ; Sacc. Syll. Fung. XXIII : 621 ; Zundel, p. 301 ; Mundk. & Thirumal., p. 66.  On *Panicum antidotale,* Lyallpu r ; Lahore ; Changa Manga ; Lad har, Sheik hupura Dist. •

### Urocystis Rabenh.

U. anemones (Pers.) Schroet.; Sacc. Syll. Fung. XVII : 491 ; Zundel, p. 308 ; Mundk., & ThirumaJ., p. 71.  On *Anemone obtusiloba,* Changia Gali.

U. colchici (Schlecht.) R abenh.; Zundel, p. 313 ; Mundk. & Thirumal., p. 72.- Syn. *U. colchici-lutei* Zundel.  On *Colchicum luteum,* Abbottabad.

U. magica Pass.; Sacc. Syll. Fung. VII : 517 ; Zundel, p. 326 ; Mundk. & Thirumal., p. 72. On *Allium rubellum,* Rawalpindi ; Quetta.

### Family : GRAPHIOLACEAE

### Graphiola Poit.

G. phoenicis Poiteau ; Sacc. Syll. Fung. XVII : 493.  On *Phoenix dactylifera,* common throughout the area.

Subclass : HOMOBASIDIOMYCETES

## Series A.   HYMENOMYCETES

Family : THELEPHORACEAE

### Coniophora  DC. ex Pers.

C. fusispora (Cke. & Ell.) Cke. in Sacc. Syll. Fung. VI : 650, 1888 ; Burt, Mo. Bot. Gard. Ann. 4 : 243, 1917. On the ground and on decayed wood, Murree ; Patriata ; Kagan Valley : Shogran.

### Corticium Pers. ex Fr.

C. polygonoides Ka rst. in Symb. Myc. Fenn. 8 : 12, 1881 ; Bou rdot & Galzin, Hym. Fr.  p. 227, 1928 ; Sacc. Syll. Fung. VI : 638.- Syn. *Lyomyces pol ygonoides* Ka rst. Finl. Basidsv. p. 419.- *Aleurodiscus pol ygonoides* (Karst.) Pil at in Ann. Myc. 24 : 219, 1926. On dead branches, Charehan, Murree Hills.

C. porosu m Berk. & Curt.; Sacc. Syll. Fung. VI : 609.- Syn. *Gloeocystidium porosum* (B. & C.) Wakef. ex Bou rd. & Galz. Hym. Fr. p. 253, 1928.- *Gloeocystidiellum porosum* (B. & C.) Donk, Nederl. Mycol. Ver. Med. 18-20 : 156, 1931.   On dead wood, Mu rree,

C. portentosum Berk. & Curt. in Grevillea 2 : 3, 1873 : Sacc. Syll. Fung. VI : 636 ; Bourd. & Galz. Hym. Fr. p. 225, 1928. On dead wood, Murree ; on a log of *Salvad ora ol eoides,* Changa Manga.

C. punctulatum Cooke in Grevillea 6 : β2, 1878 ; Sacc. Syll. Fu ng. VI : 614 ; Bu r t, Mo. Bot. Gard. Ann. 13 : 179, 1926.- Syn. *H ypochnus cremicolor* Bres.; *Penio phora sordid a* (Schroet.) Hoeh n. & Litsch.; *Gloeocystid ium eichleri* (Bres.) Hoehn. & Litsch.; G. *al bo-stramineum* Hoehn. & Litsch.   On dead wood , Murree.

### Epithele Pat.

E. typhae ( Pers. ex Fr.) Pat. in Soc. Myc. Fr. 1899, p. 202 ; Bourd. & Galz. Hy m. Fr. p. 246 ; Rea, Brit. Bas. p. 671. On leaves of *Saccli- arum mimja,* Ladhar, Sheik h upura.

### Duportella Pat.

D. velutina Pat. in Philippine Jour. of Sci. 10 : 87, 1915 ; Sacc. Syll. Fung. XVIII : 531. On dead branches of *Vernonia elaeagnifolia,* Lahore ; on bark of *Cordia myxa ,* Ladhar, Sheikhupu ra Dist. According to Talbot (Bothalia 6 : 46, 1951) it is a synonym of D. *tristicula* (B. & Br.) Reinking.

### Hymenochaete Lev.

H. cinnamomea (Pers.) Bres. ; Sacc. Syll. Fung. XXIII : 530 (name only) ; Bourd. & Galz. Hym. Fr. p. 389 ; Burt , Mo. Bot. Gard. Ann. 5. 345, 1918. On dead branches of *Quercus dil atata,* Murree.

**H.** leonina Berk. & Curt.; Sacc. Syll. Fung. VI : 597; Massee, Linn. Soc. Bot. Jour. 27 : 107, 1890 ; Burt, Mo. Bot. Gard. Ann. 5 : 353, 1918. On stumps of *Pinus excelsa,* Murree.

**H.** mougeotii (Fr.) Cke.; Sacc. Syll. Fung. VI : 593 ; Bourd. & Galz. Hym. Fr. p. 388 ; Massee, Linn. Soc. Bot. Jour. 27 : 111, 1890. On the bark of trees, Changla Gali ; Murree, Patriata ; Kagan Valley.

**H.** nigricans (Lev.) Bres.; Sacc. Syll. Fung. XXIII : 510 & 530 (name only).   On fallen branches, Murree.

**H.** rheicolor (Mont.) Lev.; Sacc. Syll. Fung.  VI : 589 ; Massee,  Linn. Soc. Bot. Jour. 27 : 98, 1890.   On dead branches, Murree ; Patriata.

**H.** rubiginosa Dicks. ex Lev.; Sacc. Syll. Fung. VI : 589 ; Bourd. & Galz. Hym. Fr. p. 390 ; Burt, Mo. Bot. Gard. Ann.  5 : 332, 1918.  On dead wood, Murree.

**H.** semistupposa Petch.  On a prostrate log, Nathia Gali.

**H.** tabacina (Sow.) Lev.; Sacc. Syll. Fung. VI : 590 ; Bourd. & Galz. p. 388 ; Burt, Mo. Bot: Gard. Ann. 5 : 325, 1918. On fallen  branches, Murree ; Nathia Gali,

## Pellicularia Cke.

**P.** filamentosa (Pat.) Rogers in Farlowia 1 : 113, 1943.- Syn. *Corticium sol ani* (Prill. & Dell.) Bourd. & Galz. Soc. Myc. Fr. Bull. 27 : 248, 1911.- C. *vagum* subsp. *solani* (Prill. & Del.) Bourd. & Galz. Hym. Fr. p. 242, 1928.- *Botryobasid ium sol ani* (Prill. & Del.) Donk, Nederl. Myc. Ver. Med. 18-20 : 117, 1931. On living leaves or stems of *Solanum tuberosum, Lyco persicum escul entum, Trifolium al exand erinum, S esamum ind icum.* The sclerotial stage has been described under the name *Rhizoctonia solani* Kuehn.

## Peniophora Cke.

**P.** cinerea (Pers.) Cke. in ₁Grevillea 8 : 20,  1880 ; Sacc. Syll. Fung. VI : 643 ; Burt, Mo. Bot. Gard. Ann. 12 : 348, 1925.- Syn. *P . l ilacina* (Schw.) Massee, Linn. Soc. Bot. Jour. 25 : 147, 1889. On dead branches of *Skimmia l aureola, Rosa* sp., and *Quercus dil at ata,* Mu r ree ; Patriata ; Shogran ; Kalam.

P. filamentosa (Berk. & Curt.) Burt ; Mo. Bot. Gard. Ann. 12: 320, 1925; Bourd. & Galz. Hym. Fr. p. 311, 1928.  On dead branches, Murree.

**P.** gigantea (Fr.) Massee, Linn. Soc. Bot. Jour. *25* : 142, 1889 ; Burt, Mo. Bot. Gard. Ann. 12 : 216, 1925 ; On dead wood of *Pinus excelsa* and *Abies pindrow ,* Murree ; Patriata ; Shogran.

**P.** roumeguerii (Bres.) Hoehn. & Litsch.; Burt, Mo. Bot. Gard. Ann. 12 : 270, 1925.- Syn. *P. molleriana* (Bres.) Sacc.; Sacc. Syll. Fung. XI : 128 ; Bourd. & Galz. Hym. Fr. p. 316. On dead wood, Murree.

**P.** pubera (Fr.) Sacc.; Sacc. Syll. Fung. VI : 646 ; Bourd. & Glaz. Hym. Fr. p. 316 ; Burt, Mo. Bot. Gard. Ann. 12 : 313, 1925. On dead wood, Murree ; Patriata.

**P.** sedimenticola Ahmad in Biologia 1 : 265, 1955. On the ground, Ladhar, Sheikhupura Dist.; Lahore.

**P.** versiforme (Berk. & Curt.) Bourd. & Galz. in Hym. Fr. p. 327. 1928.- Syn. *P. carbonicola* (Pat.) Massee, Linn. Soc. Bot. Jour. 25 : 144, 1889.- *Stereum versiforme* Berk. & Curt. in Grevillea 1 : 164, 1873. On dead branches, Murree.

## Sparassis Fr.

S. crispa Wulf. ex Fr.; Sacc. Syll. Fung. VI : 690 ; Bourd. & Galz. Hym. Fr. p. 84, 1928. On the ground, Swat : Kalam.

## Stereum Hill ex S. F. Gray

S. chailletii (Pers. ex Fr.) Fr.; Sacc. Syll. Fung. VI : .566 ; Bourd. & Galz. Hym. Fr. p. 378 ; Lentz, Agr. Monogr. 24, U. S. Dept. of Agric. p. 33, 1955.- Syn. *Lloydella chailletii* (Pers. ex Fr.) Bres. in Lloyd, Mycol. Writ. 1, Mycol. Notes 6 : 51, 1901. On a stump of *Pinus excelsa*, Murree.

S. elegans Meyer ex Fr.; Sacc. Syll. Fung. VI : 553 ; Lloyd, Mycol. Writ. 4, Stip. St. p. 24, 1913. On the ground attached to buried wood, Lahore ; Sangla Hill.

S. fuscum Schrad. ex Quel.; Sacc. Syll. Fung. XIV : 217. On dead wood, Murree ; Nathia Gali.

S. guasapatum Fr.; Sacc. Syll. Fung. VI : 560 ; Lentz, Agr. Monogr. 24, U. S. Dept. of Agric. p. 51, 1955 ; Rea, Brit. Bas. p. 663 as *S. spadiceum.* On dead wood, Murree.

S. hirsutum (Willd. ex Fr.) S. F. Gray ; Sacc. Syll. Fung. VI : 563. On dead wood, Murree ; Nathia Gali ; Changla Gali ; Kagan Valley ; Swat. Very Common.

**S. nitidulum** Berk.; Sacc. Syll. Fung. VI : 552 ; Lloyd, Mycol. W_rit. 4, Stip. St. p. 23, 1913. On the ground attached to buried wood, Sangla Hill ; Changa Manga.

S. ostrea (Blume & Nees ex Fr.) Fr.; Sacc. Syll. Fung. VI : 571 ; Lentz, Agr. Monogr. 24, U. S. Dept. of Agric. p. 27, 1955.- Syn. *S.fasciatum*

(Schw.) Fr.; Sacc. Syll. Fung. VI : 560.- *S. lobatum* Fr.; Sacc. Syll. Fung. VI : 568. On dead wood, Murree.

S. papyrinum Mont.; Sacc. Syll. Fung. VI : 576 as *Stereum membranaceum.* On dead wood, Murree ; Patriata.

S. petalodes Berk.; Sacc. Syll. Fung. VI : 557 ; Lloyd, Mycol. Writ. 4, Stip. St. p. 32, 1913. On the ground attached to buried wood, Lahore.

S. purpureum (Pers. ex Fr.) Fr.; Sacc. Syll. Fung. VI : 563 ; Lentz, Agr. Monogr. 24, U. S. Dept. of Agric. p. 41, 1955. On mossy bark of *Quercus dilatata,* Murree ; Patriata ; of *Pinus excelsa,* Charehan.

S. sanguinolentum (Schw.) Fr.; Sacc. Syll. Fung. VI : 564 ; Bourd. & Galz. Hym. Fr. p. *373 ;* Lentz, Agr. Monogr. 24, U. S. Dept. of Agric. p. 48, 1955. On dead wood, Nathia Gali.

S. pusillum Berk.,; Sacc. Syll. Fung. VI : 559 ; Lloyd, Mycol. Writ. 4, Stip. St. p. 26, 1913 ; Massee, Linn. Soc. Bot. Jour. 27 : 174, 1890. On dead rhizomes of *Desmostachya bipinnata,* Ladhar, Sheikhupura Dist.; Lahore.

S. schomburgkii Berk.; Sacc. Syll. Fung. VI : 568 ; Lloyd, Mycol. Writ. 6 : 960.- Syn. *Hymenochaete schomburgkii* (Berk.) Mass. in Linn. Soc. Bot. Jour. 27 : 115, 1890. On dead branches of *Marus alba,* Changa Manga ; on a prostrate log, Kagan Valley : Kagan.

S. subpileatum Berk. & Curt.; Massee, Linn. Soc. Bot. Jour. 27 : 192, 1890 ; Lentz, Agr. Monogr. 24, U. S. Dept. of Agric. p. 36, 1955.- Syn. *Lloydella subpileata* (B. & C.) Hoehn. & Litsch.;- *Stereum insigne* Bres.;- *Stereum sepium* Burt. On trunk of dead trees, Murree ; Nathia Gali ; Patriata ; Changla Gali ; Kagan Valley ; Swat.

### Thelephora Ehrh. ex Fr.

T. anthocephala Bull. ex Fr. var. clavularis Quel.; Sacc. Syll. Fung. VI : 528 as *T. clavularis* Fr.; Rea, Brit. Bas. p. 652 as *Phylacteria clavularis.* On the ground, Murree.

T. caryophyllea Schaeff. ex Fr.; Sacc. Syll. Fung. VI : 528 ; Burt, Mo. Bot. Gard. Ann. 1 : 209, 1914 ; Rea, Brit. Bas. p. 652 as *Phylacteria caryophyllea.* On the ground, Swat : Kalam.

T. fimbriata Schw. ex Fr.; Sacc. Syll. Fung. VI : 542 ; Burt, Mo. Bot. Gard. Ann. 1 : 222, 1914. On the ground, Murree.

T. palmata Scop. ex Fr.; Sacc. Syll. Fung. VI : 529 ; Burt, Mo. Bot. Gard. Ann. 1 : 201, 1914 ; Rea, Brit. Bas. p. 652 as *Phylacteria palmata.* On the ground, Murree ; Patriata.

T. penicillata Fr.; Sacc. Syll. Fung. VI : 539 under *T. spiculosa* Fr. On the ground, Patriata.

T. terrestris Eh r h. ex Fr.; Sacc. Syll. Fu ng. VI : 536 ; Burt, Mo. Bot. Gard. Ann. 1 : 219, 1914 ; Rea, Brit. Bas. p. 653 as *Phylacteria terrestris.* On the ground, Nat hia Gali ; Changla Gali.

### Family : HYDNACEAE

### Auriscalpium S. F. Gray

A. vulgare S. F. Gray ; Miller & Boyle, Iowa St. N.H. 18 : 54, 1943.- Syn. *H yd num auriscal pium* Linn. ex Fr. ; Sacc. Syll. Fung. VI : 445.- *Pleurod on auriscal pium* ( Linn. ex Fr.) Pat. ; Bourd. & Galz. Hym. Fr. p. 439, 1927. On decayed cones of conifers, Patriata, Murree Hill.

### Grandinia Fr.

G. mutabilis (Pers.) Bourd. & Galz.; Miller & Boyle, Iowa St. N.H. 18 : 14, 1943 ; Cejp, Monogr. Hydn. p. 37, 1928.- Syn. *Odontia mutabilis* ( Pers.) Bres. in Annal. Mycol. 9 : 426, 1911. On leaves of *Saccharum munja,* Lahore ; Ladhar, Sheikh upura Dist.

### Hericium Pers. ex S. F. Gray

H. caput-ursi (Fr.) Corner.- Syn. *H yd num caput-ursi* Fr.; Sacc. Syll. Fung. VI : 448.- *H ericium coralloid es* sensu Banker, Coker and Miller. On decayed wood , Murree ; Swat : Kalam ; on logs of *Cedrus deod ara,* Kalam, Bahrain.

**H.** erinaceum Pers.; Sacc. Syll. Fung. VI : 449 as *H yd num erinaceum;* Cejp, Monogr. Hydn., p. 99, 1928 as *Dr yod on erinaceus.* On a decayed oak log, Changla Gali.

**H.** coralloides Pers. ex S. F. Gray ; Sacc. Syll. Fung. VI : 446 as *H ydnum coralloid es.*- Syn. *H ericium laciniatum* sensu Banker, Coker <i nd Miller. On a trunk of *Quercus d ilatata,* 11;urree ; Swat : Bahrain, Kalam.

### . Hydnum Linn. emend. S. F. Gray

**H.** caeruleum Hornem. ex Fr. ; Sacc. Syll. Fung. VI : 438.- Syn. *Calod on caeruleus* (Horn. ex Fr.) Quel.; Ka rst. Finl. Basidsv. p. 358.- *Hyd nellum caerul eum* (Horn. ex Fr.) Karst.; Donk, Medd. B. Mus. Ut recht 9 : 52, 1936. On the gro und, Swat : Ba hrain.

**H.** imbricatum Linn. ex Fr.; Sacc. Syll. Fung. VI : 430 .- Syn. *S arcod on imbricatum* (Linn. ex Fr.) Quel.; Bou rd. & Galz. Hym. Fr. p. 448, 1928. One the ground, Swat : Kalam.

**H.** nigrum Fr.; Sacc. Syll. Fung. VI : 442.- Syn. *Cal odon nigrum* (Fr.) Quel. Fl. Myc. p. 444.- *P hell odon r1iger* (Fr.) Karst. in Rev. Myc, 31 : 19, 1881. On the ground, Swat : Bahrain.

H. repandum Linn. ex Fr.; Sacc. Sy!!. Fung. VI : 435 ; Bou rd. & Galz. Hym. Fr. 445, 1928.- Syn. *Tyrod on repand us* (Linn. ex Fr.) Karst. in Rev. Myc. *3 :* l9, 1881.- *Dentinum repand um* (Linn.) S. F. Gray ; Miller & Boyle in Iowa St. N.H. 18 *:* 58, 1943.- *S arcod on repand um* (Linn. ex Fr.) Quel. Fl. Myc. p. 446. On the grou nd , K agan Valley ; Mu rree.

## Mycoacia Donk

M. fragillissima (Berk. & Curt.) Miller & Boyle in Iowa St. N.H. 18 : 42, 1943.- Syn. *H yd num fragil lissimum* Berk. & Cu rt. in Grevillea 1 : l00, 1873 ; Sacc. Syll. Fung. VI : 475.- *Oxyd ontia Jra gil lissima* (Berk. & Curt.) Miller in Mycologia 25 : 364, 1933. On sandy soil and on the bark of trees, Lahore ; Ladhar, Sheikhupu ra Dist.

## Odontia Pers. amend. Fr.

O. arguta (Fr.) Quel.; Sacc. Syll. Fu ng. XXIII : 484 ; Rea, Brit. Bas. p. 648, 1922 ; Miller & Boyle, Iowa St. N.H. 18 : 32, 1943. On dead wood , Lad har, Sheikhupu ra Dist.; on a stump of *Pinus excel sa ,* Mu rree.

O. corrugata Fr.; Sacc. Syll. Fung. VI : 501. On dead branches of *Dalber gia sissoo,* Lahore.

O. hydnoides (Cke. & Mass.) v. Hoehn.; Miller & Boyle in Iowa St. N.H. 18 : 23, 1943; Sacc. Sy!l. Fung. VI : 646 as *Peniophora hyd noid es* Cke. & Mass. On wood of *Dal bergia sissoo,* Lahore.

O. queletii Bourd. & Galz.; Sacc. Syll. Fung. XXIII : 484 ; Cejp, Monogr. Hydn. p. 50, 1928. On the grou nd and on dead wood, Ladha r, Sheikhupura Dist.

### Family : CLAVARIACEAE

### Clavaria Fr. s. str.

C. rosea Fr. Syst. Myc. 1 : 48, 18 21 ; emend. Coker, Clav. U.S. & Ca nada, p. 40, 1923 ; Corner, Ann. Bot. Monogr. 1 : 248, 1950. On the ground, Lahore.

C. ver micularis Fr. Syst. Myc. I : 484, 1821 ; Corner, Ann. Bot. Monogr. l· : 251, 1950. On the ground , Mu rree ; Patriata ; Kagan Valley : S l0gran ; Swat : Kalam.

—**var.** sphaerospora Bourd. & Galz. in Hym. Fr. p. 110, 1928 ; Corner, Ann. Bot. Monogr. 1 : 254. 1950. On the ground, Pa triata.

### Clavariadelphus Donk

C. truncata (Quel.) Donk in Rev. Nieder!. Homobas. Aphyll. 2 : 73,

1933 ; Corner, Ann. Bot. Monogr. 1 : 282, 1950.- Syn. *Clavaria truncata* Quel. Fl. Myc. Fr. p. 460 ; Bonrd. & Galz., p. 119. On the ground, Murree ; Kagan Valley : Shogran.

## Clavulina Schroet.

C. cinerea (Fr.) Schroet. in Krypt. Fl. Schles. Pilze, p. 442, 1888 ; Corner, Ann. Bot. Monogr. 1:308, 1950.- Syn. *Clavaria cinerea* Fr., Syst. Myc. 1 : 466, 1821 ; Sacc. Syll. Fung. VI : 695. On the ground, Changla Gali.

—-var. gracilis Rea in Trans. Brit. Mycol. Soc. 6 : 62. On the ground, Changla Gali:

C. cristata (Fr.) Schroet. in Krypt. Fl. Schles. Pilze, p. 442, 1888 ; Corner, Ann. Bot. Monogr. 1 : 312, 1950.- Syn. *Clavaria cristat a* Fr., Syst. Myc. 1 : 473; 1821 ; Sacc. Syll. Fung. VI : 695. On the ground, Murree.

C. rugosa (Fr.) Schroet. in Krypt. Fl. Schles. Pilze, p. 442, 1888 ; Corner, Ann. Bot. Monogr. 1 : 336, 1950.- Syn. *Clavaria rugosa* Fr., Syst. Myc. 1 : 473, 1821. On the ground, Changla Gali.

—-var. alcyonaria Corner in Ann. Bot. Monogr. 1 : 337, 1950. On the ground, Swat : Kalam.

## Clavulinopsis v. Ov.

C. corniculata (Fr.) Corner in Ann. Bot. Monogr. 1: 362, 1950.- Syn. *Clavaria cornicul ata* Fr., Syst. Myc. 1 : 471, 1821. On the ground, Murree ; Kagan Valley.

## Lachnocladium Lev.

L. fulvum Corner in Ann. Bot. Monogr. 1 : 424, 1950. On the ground, Changa Manga.

## Ramaria S. F. Gray

R. apiculata (Fr.) Donk in Rev. Niederl. Homobas. Aphyll. 2 : 105, 1938; Corner in Ann. Bot. Monogr. 1 : 555, 1950.- Syn. *Clavaria apiculata* Fr., Syst. Myc. 1 : 470, 1821 ; Sacc. Syll. Fung. VI : 705. On the ground, Swat : Bahrain.

R. flaccida (Fr.) Ricken in Vadem., p. 254, 1918 ; Corner in Ann. Bot. Monogr. 1 : 576, 1950.- Syn. *Clavaria fiaccid a* Fr., Syst. Myc. 1 : 471, 1821 ; Sacc. Syll. Fung. VI : 702. On the ground , Charehan iMurree ; Swat : Kalam.

R. flava (Fr.) Quel. in Fl. Myc. p. 466, 1888 ; Corner in Ann. Bot. Monogr. 1 : 577, 1950.- Syn. *Cl avaria flava* Fr., Syst. Myc. 1 : 467.

1821 ; Sac-..Syll. Fung. VI : 692. On the groumJ,,,Patriata ; Murree: Swat : Kala.m,t Bahrain.

R. fragillima (Sacc. & Syd.) Corner in Ann. Bot. Monogr: 1 : 588, 1950.- Syn. *Clavaria fra gil lima* Sacc. & Syd. in Syll. Fung. XVI : 206, 1902.

On the ground , Swat : Bahrain.

R. maif pnk in Niederl. Homobas. Aphyll. 2 : 106, 1933 ; Corner, n .n n ·Bot. Monogr. 1 : 60+, 1950.- Syn. *Clavaria pal lida* Bres. non ...;Betk': & Curt. On the ground, Murree ; Changla Gali.

R. moelleriana (Bres. & Rou m.) Corner in Ann. Bot. Monogr. 1 : 606, l950.- Syn. R. *pol y pus* Corner in Ann. Bot. Monogr. 1 : 614, 1950.- *Lachnocl ad ium moellerianum* Bres. & Roum. On decayed wood, Patriata.

R. stricta (Fr.) Quel. in Fl. Myc. p. 464, 1888 ; Corner in Ann. Bot. Monogr. 1 : 623, 1950.- Syn. *Cl avaria stricta* Fr., Syst. Myc. 1 : 468, 1821. On the ground, Patriata ; Murree.

Family : MERULIACEAE

## Merulius Hall. ex Fr.

M. aureus Fr.; Sacc. Syll. Fung. VI : 415 ; Burt , Mo. Bot. Gard. Ann. 4 : 342, 1917 ; Bourd. & Galz. Hym. Fr. p. 351. On a log of *Pinus excelsa,* Kagan Valley : Shogran.

M. corium Fr.; Sacc. Syll. Fung. VI : 413 ; Burt, Mo. Bot. Gard. Ann. 4 : 322, 1917. On dead branches of *Viburnum grandifiorum,* Patriat a.

M. lacrymans Wulf. ex Fr.; Sacc. Syll. Fung. VI : 419 ; Burt, Mo. Bot. Gard. Ann. 4 : 340, 1917 ; Bourd. & Galz. p. 352 s *Gyro phana l acry-mans.* On a log of *Cedrus deod ara,* Swat : Kalam.

, , M..-,0:.1olluscus Fr.; Sacc. Syll. Fung. VI : 416 ; Burt, Mo. Bot. Gard. Ann. 4 : 352 under *M .fugax ;* Rea, Brit. Bas. p. 624 ; Bourd. & Galz. Hym. Fr. p. 351. On dead wood , Patriata.

"l'1· piwtri (Fr.) Burt in Mo. Bot. Gard. Ann. 4 : 356, 1917 ; Sacc. Syll. Funi. · VI : 464 as *H yd num pinastri ;* Bburd. & Galz. Hym. Fr. p. 355 *:Gy;ophana pinastri.* On dead wood , Nat hia Gali.

M. rufus Pers. ex Fr.; Sacc. Syll. Fung. VI : 417 ; Burt, Mo. Bot. Gard. Ann, 4 ; 338, 1917. On dead wood , Chare han ; Murree Hills.

M. terrettri1 kPeck) Burt , Mo. Bot. Gard. Ann. 4 : 346, 1917 ; Rea, Brit. Bas. p. 653. On the ground, Changla Gali ; Nathia Gali.

M. tremellosus Schrad. ex Fr.; Sacc. Syll. Fu ng. VI : 411 ; Bu rt , Mo. Bot. Gar&;. Ann. 4 : 312, 1917. On coniferous logs, Charehan ; Nathia Gali.

Family : BOLETACEAS

Boletus Dill. ex Fr.

B. luridus Schaeff.; ex Fr. Sacc. Sy!!. Fung. VI : 34. On .the,,, l'.ound,

Strobilomyce.s Berk.

Changla Gali.

S. floccopus (Yahl ex Fr.) Karst.; Sacc. Sy!!. Fung. VI : SO. 6n the ground, Ghora Gali ; Patriata.

Xerocomus Que!.

X. indicus Singer in Pap. Mich. Acad. Sci. 52 : 104, 1946. On the ground, Ladhar, Sheikhupura Dist.

Family : POLYPORACEAE

Daedalea Pers. ex Fr.

D. flavida Lev. Sacc. Sy!!. Fung. VI: 381. On stumps of *Dalbergia sissoo*, Lahore ; Sialkot (Nawaz).

D. gollanii Massee in Kew Bull. 1908, 217, 1908 ; Sacc. Syll. Fung. XXIII : 450. On stump◇ of *Quercus* sp., Murree ; Changla Gali ; Patriata.

Fistulina Bull. ex Fr.

F. hepatica Huds: ex. Fr. ; Sacc. Syll. Fung. VI : 54. On living trees of *Quercus dilatata*, Changla Gali ; Swat: Kalam.

Fornes Fr.

F. ajazii Husain in Mycologia 44 : 823, 1952. On living trees of *Lonicera quinquelocul aris*, Charehan ; Patriata.

F. badius Berk.; Sacc. Syll. Fung. VI : 175. On living trees of *Acaeia modesta* and *A. arabica*, Lahore ; Sangla Hill ; Sialkot ; Sind.

F. borneonensis (Lloyd) n. comb.- Syn. *Trametes borneonensis* Lloyd in Mycol. Writ. 7 : 1113, 1928. On coniferous logs, Kagan Valley ; Sharhan ; Swat : Kalam, Bahrain.

F. conchatus (Pers. ex Fr.) Gill.; Sacc. Syll. Fung. VI : 174. On a living tree of *Cedrel a serrata*, Charehan, Murree Hills.

F. demidoffii Lev.; Sacc. in Sy!!. Fung. VI : 189, 1888.- Syn. *P .juni perinus* (von Schrenk) Sacc. & Syd. in Syll. Fung. XVI : 151. On a living tree of *Juniperus macropod a*, Ziarat (A. H. Khan).

F. fastuosus Lev.; Sacc. Sy!!. Fung. VI : 172. On *Quercus incana*, Murree.

F. fomentarius Linn. ex Fr. Sacc. Sy!!. Fung. VI : 179. On living trees of *Juglans regia*, Murree ; Kagan Valley : Shogran ; Nathia Gali ; Swat. Very common.

F. igniarius (Linn. ex Fr.) Gill.; Sacc. Syll. Fung. VI : 180. On a living tree of *Salix* sp., Chitral (I.I. Chaudhri).

F. lividus Kalchbr.; Sacc. Syll. Fung. VI : 206. On a living tree of *Morus alba,* Lahore ; Changa Manga.

F. pini (Thore ex Fr.) Karst.; Sacc. Syll. Fung. VI : 345 as *Trametes pini.* On living trees of *Pinus excelsa* and *Abies pindrow,* Murree; Charehan; Gulerah Gali ; Swat : Kalam ; Kagan Valley : Shogran, Sharhan.

——var. abieties f. micropora Pilat ; Atlas Champign. Eur. III : 521 as *Phellinus.* On a stump of *Pinus excelsa,* Patriata.

F. pinicola Swartz ex Fr.; Sacc. Syll. Fung. VI: 167. On living trees of *Pinus excelsa* and *Abies pindrow ,* Nathia Gali ; Kagan Valley : Sharhan.

F. populinus (Fr.); Sacc. Syll. Fung. VI : 197.- Syn. *Fornes connatus* (Fr.) Gill. On the trunk of a dead tree, Changla Gali.

F. ribis (Schum. ex Fr.) Gill.; Sacc. Syll. Fung. VI : 184. On a decayed stump, Murree ; Patriata.

——f. rosae (Jacq.) Pilat ; Atlas Champign. Eur. III : 529 as *Phellinus.* On a living plant of *Rosa* sp., Swat : Madian.

F. robustus Karst.; Sacc. Syll. Fung. IX : 179. On a coniferous   log, Kagan Valley : Nadi-Sharhan.

F. scruposus (Fr.) G.H. Cunningham in Plant Disease Bull. No. 79, p. 11, 1948 ; Sacc Syll. Fung. VI : 121 as *Polporus scruposus* ; Corner, Brit. Myc. Soc. Trans. 17 : 79 as *Polyporus gilvus* var. *scruposus.* On living trees of *Cornus macrophylla, Viburnum grandifiorum* and *Juglans regia,* Murree ; Kagan Valley : Shogran ; Swat : Kalam.

F. torulosus Pers. ex Lloyd in Mycol. Writ. 3, Polp. Issue No. 3, p. 48, 1910 ; Pilat , Atlas Champign, Eur. III : 501 as *Phellinus torulosus* (Pers.) B. & G. On living trees of *Quercus dilatata,* Swat : Kulali.

### Fuscoporia Murr.

F. laevigata (Fr.) G.H. Cunningham in Plant Disease Bull. No. 73, p. 9, 1948 ; Sacc. Syll. Fung. VI : 326 as *Poria laevigata* Fr. On trunks of *Pyrus pashia ,* Patriata ; of *Citrus aurantium,* Lahore ; on a prostrate log, Sialkot (Nawaz).

F. punctata (Fr.) G.H. Cunningham in Plant Disease  Bull. No.  73,  p. 11, 1948 ; Sacc. Syll. Fung. VI : 309 as *Poria punctata*  Fr. On trunk of *Olea cuspidata,* Swat : Mingora.

### Ganoderma Karst.

G. applanata {Pers. ex Wahlr.) Pat.; Sacc. Syll.  Fung. VI : 176 as *Fornes appl andius.*- Syn. G. *zeucophaeum* (Mont.) Pat. On living trees of *Zizyphus Jujuba, Marus alba, Acacia modesta,* Changa Manga ; Sialkot; Sangla Hill ; Rawalpindi.

G. australe (Fr.) Pat.; Sacc. Syll. Fung. VI : 176 as *Fornes australis.*- Syn. *Fome vegetus* Fr.; Sacc. Syll. Fung. VI : 179. On stumps, Murree ; Patriata.   -

G. colossus (Fr.)   res.; Sacc. Syll. Fung. VI : 138 as .*Po/yporus colossus* Fr.   On a dead stump of *Bambusa* sp., Lahore ; Changa Manga.

G. lucidum (Leyss; ex Fr.) Karst.; Sacc. Syll. Fung. VI : 157 as *Fornes*
•   *lucidu;* (Leyss. ex Fr.) Fr.   At the base of *Dalbergia sissoo, Marus alba* and *Zizyphus jujuba ,* Lahore ;  Sialkot ;  Gujranwala ;  Changa Manga ; Sangla Hill.

### Hexagona  Pat.

H. discopoda Pat. & Har.; Sacc. Syll. Fung. XI : 98.   On dead branches of *Mangifera indI"ca,* Sh-ahdara.

### Irpex  Klotz.

I. flavus Klotz."; Sace. Syll. Fung. VI : 486.   On logs of *Dalbergia sissoo* and *Marus alba,* Changa Manga.

### Lenzites  Fr.

L. adusta Massee in Kew Bulletin 1910, p. 250, 1910.   On logs of *Morus qlba ,* Changa Manga.   Very common.

L. betulina Linn. ex Fr.; Sacc. Syll. Fung. V :?38.  On   logs· of deciduous trees, Murree; Charehan; on stumps of *Prunus cornuta,* Kagan Valley : Shogran.

L. striata Swartz ex Fr.; Sacc. Syll. Fung. V :643.   On coniferous logs, ' -· Kagan v'alley "! Paras ; Sialkot ; Murree ; Patriata ; Sangla Hill.

L. subferruginea Berk.; Sacc. Syll. Fung. V :643.  On coniferous logs,

Nt:urree ; Nathia Gali ;. Shogran ; Kalam.  Very common.

### Polyporus Mich. ex Fr.

:P: adstqs Willd .·ex Fr.; Sacc.. Syll. Fung. VI : 125.  On decayed stumps, Murree ; Nathia Gali ; Patriata ; Swat ; Kagan Valley ; on a stump of *Marus alba,* Changa Manga.

f. arcularius Batsch ex Fr.; Sacc. Syll. Fung. VI : 67.. On fallen branches, Kagan Valley : Shogran ; Swat : Kalam.

P. biennis ( Bull. ex FrJ Fi:.; Sacc. Syll. Fung. VI : 77. On the ground near trunks of deciduous trees, Sangla Hill ; Sialkot (Nawaz).

P. candidulus,Lev.; Sa"cc. Syll. Fung. VI : 126. On  a  decayed  stump, Murree ; Charehan.

- P.:ca(cllttcnsis..Bose in Annal. Mycol. 23 : 179, 1925. On living trees of
*Iaarix articulata* and *Salvadora oleoides,* Lahore ; Sangla Hill.

**P.** cuticularis Bull. ex Fr.; Sacc. Syll. Fung. VI : 128. On living trees of
*Quercus dilatata,* Murree ; Patriata ; Swat : Kalarn.

**P.** dickinsii Berk.; Sacc. Syll. Fung. VI : 94. On dead wood, Murree
(Asghar Ali) ; Changla Gali.

**P.** dryaedeus Pers. ex Fr.; Sacc. Syll. Fung. VI : 136. On a stump of
*Pinus excelsa,* Murree.

**P.** elatinus Berk.; Sacc. Syll. Fung. VI : 141. On a coniferous log, Swat :
Kalarn.

**P.** friabilis Bose in Ind. Bot. Soc. Jour. 11 : 300, 1921 ; Lloyd, Mycol.
Writ. 7 : 1148, 1928. On the ground and among dead leaf bases of
*Saccharum munja,* Lahore ; Sangla Hill ; Sargodha ; Chiniot.

**P.** gilvus (Schw.) Fr.; Sacc. Syll. Fung. VI : 121. On logs, Sialkot
(Nawaz) ; Changa Manga.

**P.** grammocephalus Berk.; Sacc. Syll. Fung. VI : 92. On a living tree
of *Cordia obliqua,* Sialkot.

**P.** hispidus Bull. ex Fr.; Sacc. Syll. Fung. \TI : 129. On living trees of
*Zizyphus jujuba,* Lahore ; of *Tamarix articulata,* Panjnad ; of *Morus
alba,* Balakot ; of *Quercts incana,* Murree.

**P.** hookeri Lloyd, in Mycol. Writ. 4, Ap. p. 348 ; Sacc. Syll. Fung.
XXIII : 366. On logs, Kagan Valley : Shogran.

**P.** leucomelas Pers. ex Fr.; Sacc. Syll. Fung. VI : 58. On the ground,
in a coniferous forest, Swat : Bahrain.

**P.** nummularius Bull. ex Fr.; Sacc. Syll. Fung. VI : 85. On fallen
branches, Kagan Valley : Shogran.

P. ostreiformis Berk.; Sacc. Syll. Fung. VI: 110. On living trees of *Acacia
arabica, Melia azedarach, Prunus persica,* Lahore ; Gujranwala ;
Sangla Hill.

**P.** schwcinitzii Fr.; Sacc. Syll. Fung. VI : 76. On decayed stumps and
attached to buried pieces of wood, Murree ; Patriata ; Kagan
Valley : Shogran.

**P.** squamosus Huds. ex Fr.; Sacc. Syll. Fung. VI : 79. On living trees
of *Juglans regia,* Kagan Valley : Shogran ; Swat : Kalam.

**P.** stipticus Pers. ex Fr.; Sacc. Syll. Fung. VI : 113. On a log of *Picea
morinda,* Swat : Kalam.

**P.** sulphureus Bull. ex Fr.; Sacc. Syll. Fung. VI : 104. At the base of
*Quercus dilatata,* Changla Gali.

**P.** tephroleucus Berk.; Sacc. Syll. Fung. VI: *275* as *Polystil'R*  ;;.-
On logs of *Picea morinda,* Swat : Kalam ; Changla Gali.

**P.** tinctorius Quel., in Bull. Soc. Bot. Fr., p. 216, 1881.- Syn. *Xanthochrous tinctorius* (Quel.) Pat. in Bull. Soc. Myc. Fr. 13 : 201, 1897. On a living tree of *Pistacea khinjuk,* Baluchistan : Shingar (A. H. Khan).

**P.** umbellatus Pers. ex Fr.; Sacc. Syll. Fung. VI : 95. On the ground, Changla Gali.

**P.** varius Pers. ex Fr.; Sacc. Syll. Fung. VI : 84. On decaying coniferous logs, Kagan Valley : Nadi-Sharhan ; Changla Gali.

### Polystictus Fr.

P. abietinus Dicks. ex Fr.; Sacc. Syll. Fung. VI :265. On dead branches of coniferous trees, Swat : Kalam, Bahrain ; Murree ; Patriata ; Nathia Gali.

**P.** cinnabarinus Jacq. ex Fr.; Sacc. Syll. Fung. VI : 245.- Syn. *Polystictus sanguineus* Linn. ex Fr.; f?acc. Syll. Fung. VI : 229. On dead branches of *Betula utilis,* Swat : Kalam.

**P.** cinnamomeus Jacq. ex Gray ; Sacc. Syll. Fung. VI : 210. On the ground, Murree ; Charehan ; Kalam ; Kagan Valley : Shogran ; Nathia Gali.

P. hirsutus Wulf. ex Fr.; Sacc. Syll. Fung. VI : 257. On logs of *Acacia arabica,* Sialkot ; of Morns *alba,* Changa Mana.

**P.** leoninus Klotzsch in Linnaea 8 : 486, 1833 ; Sacc. Syll. Fung. VI :235. On *Mangifera indica,* Lahore ; Sialkot (Nawaz).

**P.** occidentalis Klotzsch; Sacc. Syll. Fung. VI :274. On dead wood, Murree.

P. perennis Linn. ex Fr.; Sacc. Syll. Fung. VI : 210. On the ground, Swat : Kalam ; Changla Gali.

**P.** proteus Berk.; Sacc. Syll. Fung. VI: 250. On logs of *Dalbergia sissoo* and Morns *alba,* Lahore ; Changa Manga ; Sangla Hill- ; Sialkot (Nawaz).

**P.** pubescens Schum. ex Fr.; Sacc. Syll. Fung. VI : 135 as *Poly porns pubescens.* - Syn. *Polystictus velutinus* Fr.; Sacc. Syll. Fung. VI : 258. On logs of *Dalbergia sissoo,* Sialkot (Nawaz).

**P.** tomentosus Fr.; Sacc. Syll. Fung. VI : 208. Attached to buried pieces of coniferous wood, Swat : Kalam ; Patriata ; Shogran.

**P.** versicolor Linn. ex Fr.; Sacc. Syll. Fung. VI : 253. On stumps and decayed logs, Murree ; Patriata; Changla Gali ; Nathia Gali ; Shogran; Kalam. Very common.

P xanthopus fr:; $ace Syll. Fung, VI : 21 S: ,On deaa wood, Murree.

P. zonatus Fr.-; Sacc. Stll. Fung. VI : 260,    On dead wood, Rawblpindi ; Sialkot. ·

" ·Poria· (Pers.) S. F. Gray

P. ravenalae Berk. & Br.; Sacc. Syll. Fung. VI: 307.    On petioles of palm ieaves ;sp. *'Ijhoenix actylifera*, Lahore.

Trametes Fr.

T. incert (Currey) Qke.; Sac. Sy!!. Fung. VI : 352;, 0),1 logs, Murre.

T. lactinia Berk.; Sacc. Sy!!. Fung. VI : 343.    On logs_ of *Marus alba,* Changa Manga. Common.

T· sua":eolens (Linn•-ex Fr.) Fr.; Sacc. Syll. Fung_. YI : 338.  On ded t   wo<ρ     rree· ; G,hora Gali (Asghar Ali).

Family : AGARICACEA.E          i. O

Agaric'l,.ls L. ex fr.

A. augustus Fr.: Sacc. Syll. Fung.. V : 993.  ·on the grou!1d , bahore;

Amanifa Pers. ex S. F. Gray

A. nana  Singer.   On the ground, Lahore ; Sangla   Hill ; Gujranwala.
· C:cirnmon.

A. vaginata (13ull. ex Fr.) Que!.; Sacc. Syll. Fung. V :21 as *Amanitopsis.*
· On the ground, Murree ; Nathia Gali ; 'Swat -: Bahrai .

Asterop hora  Ditm. 'ex S. F."Gray

A. parasitica (Bull. ex Fr.) Singer ; Sacc. SylJ..Fung. V :501  as *Nyctalis parasitica* Bull. ex Fr, Parasitic on *Russula* sp., Swat : K;alam ; Chare'han:

Bolbitius Fr.

B. t'ener Berk.; Sacc; syn:- Fung. V·: 1076'; Giriai, Ind Bot. Soc. Jour. 15 : 279.  On dung, Lahore.

B. viellinus Pers. ex Fr.; Sacc. SyU. Fung. V :°i074 : Mahju, p. 161.  On· du_pg, Lahore.

Clitopilus (Fr.) Quel.

e. ·pleurotelioides    uhner) Josserand: On tfre ground antl""on dead wooel eadhar, Sh(!ikbupura Dist.

C. scyphoidcs (Fr.) Singer ; Sacc. Syll. Fung. V : 310 iJ.S *Omphalia scyplwi-d s.*   On sandy soil,- Labore ; Ladhar, Sheikhupub Dist.

Coprinus (Pers.,ex Fr.) S. F. Gray_

C. ciner,eμs. (Schaeff.),Cke.; Sacc. Sy!!. Fung. V : 1088 ; Ginai, p. 277. On dung, Lahore.

C. comatus (Muell. ex Fr.) S. F. Gray ; Sacc. Syll. Fung. V : 1079. On the ground, Lahore ; Gujranwala ; Murree.

C. ephemerus Bull. ex Fr.; Sacc. Syll. Fung. V : 1106 ; Mahju, p. 161. On dung, Lahore.

C. filiformis Berk. & Br.; Sacc. Syll. Fung. V : 1111 ; Ginai, p. 278. On dung, Lahore.

C. gibbsii Mass. & Crossl.; Sacc. Syll. Fung. XVII : 93 ; Ginai, p. 278. On dung, Lahore.

C. hendersonii (Pers.) Berk.; Sacc. Syll. Fung. V : 1097 ; Ginai, p. 278. On dung, Lahore.

C. niveus Pers. ex Fr.; Sacc. Syll. Fung. V : 1088 ; Mahju, p. 160. On dung, Lahore.

C. nycthemerus Fr.; Sacc. Syll. Fung. V : 1100 ; Ginai, p. 278. On dung, Lahore.

C. papillatus Batsch ex Fr.; Sacc. Syll. Fung. V : 1093 ; Mahju, p. 161. On dung, Lahore.

C. radiatus Bolt. ex Fr.; Sacc. Syll. Fung. V : 1101 ; Mahju, p. 161. On dung, Lahore.

C. stellaris Quel.; Sacc. Syll. Fung. V : 1101 ; Ginai, p. 278. On dung, Lahore.

### Gomphus S. F. Gray

G. clavatus S. F. Gray ; Sacc. Syll. Fung. VI : 519 as *Craterellus.* On the ground, Murree.

G. floccosus (Schw.) Singer ; Sacc. Syll. Fung. V : 491 as *Cantharellus floccosus.* On the ground, Nathia Gali.

——var. excavatus Sm. & Morse. On the ground, Murree ; Dunga Gali.

### !vlacrolepiota Singer

M. rachodes (Vitt.) Singer ; Sacc. Syll. Fung. V : 29 as *Lepiota rachodes* Vitt. On the ground, Lahore.

### Marasmius Fr.

M. graminum (Lib.) Berk.; Sacc. Syll. Fung. V : 542. On dead leaves of grasses, Lahore ; Gujranwala ; Rawalpindi.

### Montagnites Fr.

M. arenarius (DC.) Morse in Mycofogia 40 : 256, 1948 ; Ahmad, Gaster.

W. Pak., p. 78. In sandy soil, Lahore ; Chuharkana ; Ladhar, Sheikhupura Dist.; Multan ; Bahawalpur. Very common.

### Naematoloma Karst.

N. fasciculare (Huds. ex Fr.) Karst.; Sacc. Syll. Fung. V : 1029 as *Hypholoma Jascicul are* Huds. ex Fr. On the ground, 1v1urree ; Swat : Kalam.

### Panaeolus (Fr.) Que!.

P. sphinctrus (Fr.) Que!.; Sacc. Syll. Fung. V : 1121 as P. *campanul atus.* On richly manured soil, Lahore.

P. papilionaceous (Bull. ex Fr.) Que!.; Sacc. Syll. Fung. V : 1122. On manure heaps, Ladhar, Sheikhupura Dist.

P. fimicola (Fr.) Gillet ; Sacc. Syll. Fung. V : 1124. On dung, Ladhar, Sheikhupura Dist.

### Pholiota (Fr.) Que!.

P. squarrosa Muell. ex Fr.; Sacc. Syll. Fungt. V : 749. On the ground, Swat : Kalam ; Murree.

### Pleurotus (Fr.) Que!.

P. ostreatus (Jacq. ex Fr.) Que!.; Sacc. Syll. Fung. V : 355. On a dead tree *of Jtlglans regia,* Swat : Kaiam.

### Schizophyllum Fr.

S. commune Fr.; Sacc. Syll. Fung. V : 655. On various hosts. Common throughout the area.

### Stropharia (Fr.) Que!.

S. semiglobata (Batsch ex Fr.) Quel.; Sacc. Syll. Fung. V : 1022 ; Ginai, p. 277. On dung, Lahore.

### Termitomyces Heim

T. eurhizus (Berk.) Heim ; Sacc. Sy!!. Fung. VI : 85 as *Armil laria eurhiza* Berk. -Syn. *Raja pa eurhizus* (Berk.) Singer in Lloydia 8 : 142, 1945. On termite nests, Gakkhar ; Lahore ; Sangla Hill.

### Volvariella Speg.

V. pusilla (Pers. ex Fr.) Singer ; Sacc. Syll. Fung. V : 663 as *Volvaria parvul a.* On the ground, Ladhar, Sheikhupura Dist. ; Lahore.

V. taylori (Berk:) Singer ; Sacc. Syll. Fung. V : 658 as *Vol varia taylori* Berk. On the ground, Ladhar, Sheikhupura Dist.

V. volvacea (Bull. ex Fr.) Singer ; Sacc. Syll. Fung. V : 657 as *Volvaria volvacea* Bull. ex Fr. On the ground, Lahore ; Sangla Hill ; Dunga Gali.

## Series B. GASTEROMYCETES
### Order : HYMENOGASTR ALES
### Family : HYMENOGASTRACEAE

### Melanogaster Corda

M. ambiguus (Vitt.) Tul.; Sacc. Syll. Fung. VII : l65 ; Ahmad, Gaster. W. Pak., p. 3. On the ground, Murree.

M. durissimus Cke.; Sacc. Syll. Fung. VII: l67; Ahmad, Gaster. W. Pak., p. 3. On the ground, Chitral.

### Rhizopogon Fr.

R. flavus Petch in Ann. Roy. Bot. Gard. Peradeniya 6 : 207, l917 ; Ahmad, Gaster. W. Pak., p. 4. On the ground, Mu rree ; Changla Gali ; Kagan Valley : Shogran, Sharhan ; Swat : Bahrain, Kalam, Miana, Mt. Ilam.

### Family : PROTOPHALLACEAE
### Protubera A. Moeller

P. maracuja A. Moeller ; Sacc. Syll. Fung. XI : 156 ; Ahmad, Gaster. W. Pak., p. 5. On the ground, Lahore ; Sargodha ; Ladhar, Sheikhu-pura Dist.

### Family : SECOTIACEAE
### Secotium Kze.

S. acuminatum Mont.; Sacc. Syll. Fung. VII : 53. -Syn. S. *agaricoid es* (Czem.) Hollos. On the ground, Swat : Bahrain ; Kulali ; Kagan Valley : Shogran.

### Order : GASTROSPORIALES
### Family : GASTROSPORIACEAE

### Gastrosporium Mattirolo

G. simplex Mattirolo ; Sacc. Syll. Fung. XVII : 243 ; Pilat, Bull. Myc. Soc. Fr. 50 : 37-49 ; Ahmad, Sydowia 4 : 124 ; Gaster. W. Pak., p. 6. Hypogeal, encircling roots of *Cynod on dactylon*, Ladhar, Sheikhupura Dist.

### Order : SCLERODERMAT ALES
### Family : SCLERODERMATACEAE

### Scleroderma Pers.

S. bovista Fr.; Sacc. Syll. Fung. VII : 135. On the ground, Patriata.

S. flavidum Ell. & Ev.; Sacc. Syll. Fung. VII : 139. On the ground, Kagan Valley : Shogran.

S. verrucosum (Vaill.) Pers.; Sacc. Syll. Fung. VII : 136; Ahmad, Gaster. W. Pak., p. 9. On the ground, Murree ; Changla Gali ; Nathia Gali ; Kagan Valley ; Swat. Very common.

Order : LYCOPERDALES

·Family : LYCOPERDACEAE

Bovista Dill. ex Fr.

B. bovistoides (Cke. & Mass.) Ahmad in Publ. Dept. Bot. Panjab Univ. No. 11, p. 15, 1952. On mossy ground along road side, Changla Gali ; Patriata.

B. concinna Ahmad in Sydowia 3 : 335, 1949 ; Gaster. W. Pak.,  p. 17. On the ground, Murree, Upper Topa.

B. lycoperdioides (Cke.) Ahmad in Publ. Dept. Bot. Panjab Univ.  No. 11, p. 17, 1952. On the ground, Changla Gali ; Muzaffarabad Dist.

B. plumbea Pers.; Sacc. Syll. Fung. VII : 96 ; Ahmad , Gaster. W. Pak., p. 15. On the ground, Changla Gali, Kagan Valley : Batakundi ; Swat : Kalam.

Calvatia Fr.

C. craniiformis (Schw.) Fr.; Sacc. Syll. Fung. VII : 106. On the ground, Swat : Bahrain ; Kalam.

C. cyathiformis (Bose) Morgan ; Ahmad , Gaster. W. Pak., p. 27 ; Sacc. Syll. Fung. VII : 123 as *Lycoperdon cyathiforinis* Bose. On the ground, Chitral : .Barum Valley.

Disceseda Czern.

D. cervina (Berk.) Hollos ; Ahmad , Gaster. W. Pak.. p. 11. On the ground, Ladhar, Sheikhupura Dist.

Lanopila Fr.

L. wahlbergii Fr.; Sacc. Syll. Fung. VII : 95.  On the ground, Ladhar, Sheikhupura Dist.

Lycoperdon Tourn. ex Pers.

L. echinella (Pat.) Ahmad in Ind. Bot. Soc. Jour. 20 : 138 ; Gaster. W. Pak., p. 25. On a patch of *Funaria hygrometrica* , Ladha r, Sheikhupura Dist.

L. acuminatum Bose ; Coker, Gaster. U. S. & Canada, p. 78. On moss-covered logs, Patriata.

L. atropurpureum Vitt.; Sacc. Syll. Fung. VII: 123 & 477. On the ground, Swat : Kalam.

L. glaberescens Berk.; Sacc. Syll. Fung. VII : 122 & 480 ; Ahmad, Gaster. W. Pak., p. 24.  On the ground, Changla Gali.

L. oblongisporum Berk. & Curt.; Sacc. Syll. Fung. VII : 122 ; Ahmad, Gaster. W. Pak., p. 24. On the ground, Kagan Valley : Shogran.

L. perlatum Pers.; Sacc. Syll. Fung. VII : 106 ; Ahmad, Gaster. W. Pak., p. 21. -Syn. *L. gemmat um* Batsch ex Fr. On the ground , Murree ; Changla Gali ; Patriata ; Swat : Ba hrain ; Kagan Valley : Shogran ; Sharhan. Very common.

L. pratense Pers.; Ahmad, Gaster. W. Pak., p. 20 as *L. hiem.,al e* Bull. On the ground, Murree ; Patriata ; Swat : Kagan Valley.

L. pusillum ( Batsch) Pers.; Ahmad , Gaster. W. Pak., p. 23. On the ground, Lahore ; Gujranwala ; Rawalpindi ; Ladhar, Sheikh1pura Dist.

L, pyriforme Schaeff. ex Fr.; Sacc. Syll. Fung. VII : 117 ; Ahmad, Gaster. W. Pak., p. 22. On the ground, very common throughout the hills.

L. rimulatum Peck ; Coker, Gaster. U. S. & Canada, p. 75. On the ground, Swat : Bahrain ; Patriata ; Charehan.

L. trachysporum (Lloyd) Ahmad in Ind. Bot. Soc. Jour. 21 : 285, 1942 ; Gaster. W. Pa k., p. *25.* Amongst moss on exposed rocks, Mu rree ; Changla Gali.

L. umbrinum Pers.; Ahmad, Gaster. W. Pak., p. 19. On the grou nd , Murree ; Nathia Gali.

L. polymorphum Vitt.; Gast er. W. Pak., p. *22.* On the ground, Murree ; Kagan Valley.

## Mycenastrum Desv.

M. corium (Guers.) Desv.; Ahmad , Gaster. W. Pak., p. 13. On the ground, Changa Manga.

### Family : GEASTRACEAE

### Geastrum Pers.

G. clelandii Lloyd ; Ahmad , Gaster. W. Pak., p. 30. On the ground, Kagan Valley near Naran.

G. coronatus (Schceff.) Schroet., Sacc. Syll. Fung. IX : 271. On the ground Swat : Kalam.

G. drummondii Berk.; Sacc. Syll. Fu ng. VII : 79. On the ground, Swat : Kalam.

G. hygrometricum Pers.; Sacc. Syll. Fung. VII : 90 as *Astraeus hy gro-metricus* (Pers.) Morga n On the ground , Murree ; Patriata ; Swat : Kalam ; Kagan Valley.

G. panjabense Ahmad in Sydowia 127, 1950 ; Gaster. W. Pak., p. 33.
On the ground, Sargodha ; Shorkot ; Ladhar, Sheikhupura Dist.

G. mammosum Fr.; Sacc. Sy!!. Fung. VH : 85. On the ground, Swat :
Kaiam.

G. saccatus Fr.; Sacc. Syll. Fung. VII : 86 ; Ahmad, Gaster. W. Pak., p.
32. On the ground, Kagan Valley.

G. schmidelli Vitt.; Sacc. Syll. Fung. VII : 76 ; Ahmad, Gaster. W. Pak.,
p. 77. On the ground, Shogran ; Patriata ; Swat : Kalam.

G. triplex Jungh.; Sacc. Syll. Fung. VII : 74 ; Ahmad, Gaster. W. Pak.,
p. 31. On the ground, Swat : Kalam ; Kagan Valley : Shogran ;
Murree ; Patriata ; Nathia Gali.

Family : TULOSTOMATACEAE

Battarrea Pers.

B. stevenii (Lib.) Fr.; Sacc. Syll. Fung. VII : 66 ; Ahmad, Gaster. W.
Pak., p. 36. On the ground, Peshawar.

Phellorina Berk.

P. inquinans Derk.; Sacc. Syll. Fung. VII : 145; Ahmad, Gaster. W. Pak.,
p. 60. In sandy wastes, Sargodha ; Multan ; Bahawalpur; Sind; Gujranwala ; Jhang.

Podaxis Desv.

P. pistillaris (L. ex Pers.) Fr.; Sacc. Syll. Fung. VII : 59 ; Ahmad, Gaster.
W. Pak., p. 57. In sandy soil, very common. throughout the area.

Schizostoma Ehrenb.

S. laceratum Ehrenb.; Long, Mycologia 35: 23 ; Ahmad, Gaster. W. Pak.,
p. 54. In sandy soil, Sargodha ; Sangla Hill ; Jhang.

S. mundkuri (Ahmad) Long in Mycologia 35 : 27 ; Ahmad, Gaster. W.
Pak., p. 55. In sandy soil, Shorkot, Jhang.

Tulostoma Pers.

T. amnicola Long & Ahmad in Farlowia 3 : 243 ; Ahmad, Gaster. W.
Pak., p. 41. On the ground, Lahore.

T. balanoides Long & Ahmad in Farlowia 3 : 242 ; Ahmad, Gaster. W.
Pak., p. 50. In sandy soil, Ladhar, Sheikhupura Dist.

T. cineraceum Long in Lloydia 10 : 123, 1947. On the ground, Skardu
plain, Baltistan.

T. crassipes Long & Ahmad in Farlowia 3 : 256 ; Ahmad, Gaster. W.
Pak., p. 53. On the ground, Gakkhar ; Ladhar, Sheikhupura Dist.

T. evanescens Long & Ahmad in Farlowia 3 : 235 ; Ahmad, Gaster. W. Pak., p. 41. On the ground, Ladhar, Sheikhupura Dist.

T. exitum Long & Ahmad in Farlowia 3 : 254 ; Ahmad, Gaster. W. Pak., p. 45. On the ground, Ladhar, Sheikhupura Dist.

T. hygrophilum Long & Ahmad in Farlowia 3 : 238 ; Ahmad, Gaster. W. Pak., p. 42. On the ground amongst grass, Ladhar, Sheikhupura Dist.

T. inonotum Long & Ahmad in Farlowia 3 : 246 ; Ahmad, Gaster. W. Pak., p. 42. On the ground, Ladhar, Sheikhupura Dist.

T. mussooriense P. Henn.; Long & Ahmad, Farlowia 3 : 234. On the ground, Patriata ; Swat : Kalam.

T. operculatum Long & Ahmad in Farlowia 3 : 246 ; Ahmad, Gaster. W. Pak., p. 46. On the ground, Sargodha.

T. parvissimum Long & Ahmad in Mycologia 3 : 87 ; Farlowia 3 : 250 ; Ahmad, Gaster. W. Pak., p. 46. On the ground, Ladhar, Sheikhupura Dist.

T. perplexum Long & Ahmad in Farlowia 3 : 257 ; Ahmad, Gaster. W. Pak., p. 48. On the ground, Ladhar, Sheikhupura Dist.

T. pluriosteum Long & Ahmad in Farlowia 3 : 235 ; Ahmad, Gaster. W. Pak., p. 43. On the ground, Ladhar, Sheikhupura Dist.

T. puncticulosum Long & Ahmad in Farlowia 3 : 246 ; Ahmad, Gaster. W. Pak., p. 47. In sandy soil, Ladhar, Sheikhupura Dist.

T. volvulatum Borsz.; Sacc. Syll. Fung. VII : 61 ; Long & Ahmad, Farlowia 3 : 258 ; Ahmad, Gaster. W. Pak., p. 51. In sandy soil, Sargodha ; Jhang ; Bahawalpur ; Ladhar, Sheikhupura Dist.

T. vulgare Long & Ahmad in Farlowia 3 : 248 ; Ahmad, Gaster. W. Pak., p. 46. On the ground, Ladhar, Sheikhupura Dist.

T. xerophilum Long ; Long & Ahmad, Farlowia 3 : 240 ; Ahmad, Gaster. W. Pak., p. 49. On the ground, Kirana Hill near Sargodha.

### Order : PHALLALES

### Family : CLATHRACEAE

### Simblum Klotz.

S. sphaerocephalum Schlecht.; Sacc. Syll. Fung. VII : 16 ; Ahmad, Gaster. W. Pak., p. 70. On the ground among grass, Lahore ; Ladhar, Sheikhupura Dist.

## Family : PHALLACEAE

### Dictyophora    Desv.

D. indusiata (Vent. ex Pers.) Desv.; Ahm1d, Gaster. W. Pak., p. 69.
   On the ground, Lyallpur.

### ltajahya A. Moeller

I. rosea (Delile) Fischer ; Ahmad, Gaster. W. Pak., p. 64. On the ground,
   Lahore; Ladhar, Sheikhupura *Dist.;* Gujranwala; Bahawalpur: Pallah.

### Phallus  L. ex Pers.

P. celebicus P. Henn.; Ahmad, Gaster. W. Pak., p. 67. On the ground
   among grass, Ladhar, Sheikhupura *Dist.*

P. impudicus Linn. ex Pers.; Sacc. Syll. Fung. VII : 8 as *Ithyphallus* im-
   *pudicus* ; Ahmad, Gaster. W. Pak., p. 66. On the ground, Kagan
   Valley : Shogran ; Batakundi ; Murree ; Swat : Mingora.

P. rubicundus (Bose) Fr.; Sacc. Syll. Fung. VII : 11 as *Ithyphallus*
   *rubicundus* ; Ahmad, Gaster. W. Pak., p. 67. On the ground, Kagan
   Valley : Balakot, Mahandri.

## Order : NIDULARIALES

## Family : SPHAEROBOLACEAE

### Sphaerobolus  Tode ex Pers.

S. stellatus Tode ex Fr.; Sacc. Syll. Fung. VII : 46 ; Ahmad, Gaster.
   W. Pak., p. 73. On decayed wood and on dung, very common
   throughout the area.

## Family : NIDULARIACEAE

### Crucibulum Tul.

C. vulgare Tul.; Sacc. Syll. Fung. VII : 43 ; Ahmad, Gaster. W. Pak.,
   p. 75. On the ground, Kagan Valley : Shogran ; Patriata.

### Cyathus Brown ex Pers.

C. stercoreus _(Schw.) de Toni ; Sacc. Syll. Fung. VII : 40 ; Ahmad,
   Gaster. W. Pak., p. 76. On the ground, dung heaps and dead branches, common throughout the area.

## FUNGI   IMPERFECT!

## Order : SPHAEROPSIDALES

## Family : SPHAEROPSIDACEAE

### Ascochyta  Lib.

A. rabiei (Pass.) Labrousse ; Sacc. Syll. Fung. III : 397 as *A. pisi.*   On leaves, branches and pods of *Cicer arietinum*, Sargodha ; Campbellpur ; Mianwali ; Sangla Hill ; Taru ; near Peshawar.

## Botryodiplodia Sacc.

**B.** acacigena Penz. & Sacc. ; Sacc. Syll. Fung. XVIII : 331. On *Acacia f arnesiana*, Ladhar, Sheikhu pura Dist.

B. ambigua Petr. in Sydowia 8 : 173, 1954. On dead branches of *Cap paris aphyl la*, Ladhar, Sheikhu pura Dist.

B. anceps Sacc. & Syd. ; Sacc. Syll. Fung. XXV : 314. On dead branches of *Morus alba*, Changa Manga.

B. azedarachta nom. nov.- Syn. *B. meliae* Ahmad in ·sydowia 8 : 174, 1954 (non *B. meliae* Ell. & Ev.). On naked wood of *M el ia azed arach*, Ladhar, Sheikhu pura Dist.

B. deodarae Petr. in Sydowia 8 : 178, 1954. On dead branches of *Cedrus deod ara*, Kagan' Valley : Shogran.

**B.** gossypii Ell. & Barth. ; Sacc. Syll. Fung. XVIII: 332. On dead branches of *Gossypium* sp., Ladhar, Sheikhupura Dist.

**B.** lecanidion (Speg.) Petr. & Syd. Repert. Spec. Nov. Regni Veg. Fedde Beib. Bd. 42 (2) : 161, 1927 ; Sacc. Syll. Fung. XI : 517 as *N othopatel la lecanidion*. On dead branches of *Citrus aurantium*, Lahore.

**B.** mangiferae (Koord.) Petr. in Sydowia 8 : 174, 1954. On fallen leaves of *M angifera indica*, Ladhar, Sheikhu pura Dist.

**B.** nerii Sydow in Annal. Mycol. 14 : 203, 1916. On dead branches of *N erium odorum*, Lahore.

**B.** ricinicola Ahmad in Sydowia 8 : 155, 1954. On dead branches of *Ricil lus communis*, Lahore.

## Camarosporium Schulz.

C. berberidis Cke. ; Sacc. Syll. Fung. X : 341. On dead branches of *Berberis* sp., Murree.

C. capparidis Ahmad in Sydowia 5 : 393, 1951 ; Sydowia 8 : 175. On dead branches of *Cap pari s aph yll a* & *S al vadora ol eoid es*, Ladha r, Sheikhu pu ra Dist. ; Changa Manga, Lahore.

C. oleae Politis in Pragmat. Ak a d. Athen, No. 4, p. 32, 1935. On dead branches of *Olea cuspid ata*, Swat : Khaza Khela.

C. origa ni Milostzova in Trans. Inst. Bot. Charkov. 2 : *12*, 1937. On dead branches of *Origanum uul gare*, Swat : Mingora.

C. pegani Bubak ; Sacc. Syll. Fung. XXV : 402.    On dead branches of *Peganum harmla,* Swat : Mingora.

## Ceuthospora Grev. ex Fr.

C. oleae Kalchbr. & Cke. ; Sacc. Syll. Fung. III : 278.  On fallen leaves of *Olea cuspidata,* Swat : Mingora, Khaza Khela.

## Coleophoma Hoehn.

C. mangiferae Ahmad in Sydowia 8 : 176, 1954.   On fallen leaves of *Mangifera indica,* Ladhar, Sheikhupura Dist.

C. oleae (DC.) Petr. & Syd. ; Sacc. Syll. Fung. III : 112 as *Phoma oleae.* On fallen leaves of *Olea cuspidata,* Choa Saidan Shab ; Swat : Mingora, Khaza Khela.

## Coniothyrium   Corda

C. fuckelii Sacc. ; Sacc. Syll. Fung. III : 306.  On dead branches of *Rosa* sp., Ladhar, Sheikhupura Dist. ; of *Rubus fruticosus,* Swat : Mingora.

C. withaniae Ahmad in Sydowia 5 : 393, 1951.  On dead branches of *Withania somnifera,* Ladhar, Sheikhupura Dist.

## Cytospora Ehrenb. ex Fr.

C. ambiens Sacc. ; Sacc. Syll. Fung. III ; 268. On dead branches of *Rosa* sp., *Rubus fruticosus* and *Salix* sp., Murree : Mingora ; Ghora Gali.

C. rosarum Grev. ; Sacc. Syll. Fung. III : 253. On branches of *Rosa moschata,* Murree ; Ghora Gali.

C. salicis (Cda.) Rabb. ; Sacc. Syll. Fung. III : 261. On dead branches of *Salix* sp., Ghora Gali.

## Cytosporella Sacc.

C. corticola Ahmad in Sydowia 5 : 391, 1951.   On the bark of *Cordia obliqua,* Ladhar, Sheikhupura Dist.

C. lignicola Ahmad in Sydowia 5 : 391, 1951. On naked wood of *Acacia arabica,* Ladhar, Sheikhupura Dist.

C. verrucosa Petr. in Sydowia 8 : 176, 1954. On the bark of *Salvadora oleoides,* Changa Manga, Lahore.

## Darluca Cast.

D. filum (Biv.) Cast. ; Sacc. Syll. Fung. III : 410. On *Uredo rottboelliae,* on *Hemarthria compressa,* Ch;inga Manga ; on uredo- stage o'f *Puccinia kuehnii, P. cynodontis, Uromyces andropogonis-annulati,* Lahore.

## Dendrophoma Sacc.

**D.** punicina Sacc.; Sacc. Syll. Fung. XVIII : 225 as *Phoma.* On dead branches of *Punica granatum*, Lahore ; Multan ; Choa Saidan Shah.

## Dichomera Cooke

**D.** gymnosporia Ahmad in Biologia 1 : 197, 1955. On dead branches of *Gymnosporia royleana,* Swat : Barikot.

**D.** macrospora Ahmad in Biologia 1 : 197, 1955. On dead branches of *Berberis lycium,* Murree.

## Dilophospora Desm.

**D.** alopecuri (Fr.) Fr.; Sacc. Syll. Fung III : 600 ; Joerstad, p. 85. On leaves of *Calamagrostis pseudophragmites,* Barum Valley : Zapotili (Wendelbo).

## Diplodia Fr.

**D.** albozonata Dur. & Mont.; Sacc. Syll. Fung. III : 334 ; Ahmad, Sydowia 5 : 395. On dead branches of *Zizyphus jujuba,* Ladhar, Sheikhupura Dist.

**D.** asclepiadea Cke. & Ell.; Sacc. Syll. Fung. III : 365 ; Ahmad, Sydowia 5 : 394. On dead branches of *Calotropis procera,* Ladhar, Sheikhupura Dist.

**D.** aurantii Catt.; Sacc. Syll. Fung. IH : 330 ; Ahmad, Sydowia 5 : 394. On the bark of *Citrus aurantium,* Ladhar, Sheikhupura Dist.

**D.** bombacina Ahmad in Sydowia 5 : 394, 1951. On leaves of *Bombax malabaricum,* Lahore.

**D.** dalbergiae Died.; Sacc. Syll. Fung. XXV : 280 ; Ahmad, Sydowia 5 : 394. On dead branches of *Dalbergia sissoo,* Ladhar, Sheikhupura ; Dist. Changa Manga.

**D.** mori Westd.; Sacc. Syll. Fung. III : 351 ; Ahmad, Sydowia 5 : 394. On dead branches of *Marus alba,* Wazirabad ; Lahore ; Ladhar, Sheikhupura Dist.

**D.** rosarum Fr.; Sacc. Syll. Fung. III : 338 ; Ahmad, Sydowia 5 : 394. On dead branches of *Rosa* sp., Ladhar, Sheikhupura Dist.

**D.** salvadorina Ahmad in Sydowia 5 : 395, 1951. On dead branches of *Salvadora oleoides,* Ladhar, Sheikhupura Dist.

**D.** sicula Scalia ; Ahmad, Sydowia 5 : 394. On dead petioles of *Phoenix dactylifera,* Lahore.

**D.** viticola Desm.; Sacc. Syll. Fung. III : 332 ; Ahmad, Sydowia 5 : 394. On dead branches of *Vitis vinifera,* Ladhar, Sheikhupura Dist.

**D.** withaniae Ahmad in Sydowia 5 : 395, 1951.   On dead branches of *Withania somnifera*, Ladhar, Sheikhupura Dist.

**D.** zeae (Schw.) Lev.; Sacc. Syll. Fung. XXII : 1001. -Syn. D. *maydis* (Berk.) Sacc., Syll. Fung. III : 373.   On culms of *Zea mays*, Patriata.

### Diplodina   Westend.

**D.** capparidincola Ahmad in Sydowia 8 : 177, 1954.  On dead branches of *Capparis aphylla*, Ladhar, Sheikhupura Dist.

D. panici Ahmad in Sydowia 5 : 392, 1951. On dead culms of *Panicum antidotale*, Changa Manga ; Ladhar, Sheikhupura Dist.

### Diplodiella  (Karst.) Sacc.

**D.** milleri Ahmad in Sydowia 5 : 393, 1951. On stones of *Zizyphus jujuba*, Ladhar, Sheikhupura Dist.

### Dothiorella Sacc.

**D.** advena Sacc. ; Sacc. Syll. Fung. III : 240. On dead branches of *Viburnum grandifiorum*, Patriata. This is the imperfect stage of *Botryosphaeria quercum*.

**D.** berengeriana Sacc. ; Sacc. Syll. Fung. III : 238. On dead branches of Morus *alba*, Changa Manga. This is the imperfect stage uf *Botryosphaeria dothidea*.

**D.** chenopodii Ahmad in Sydowia 8 : 177, 1954. On dead branches of *Chenopodium album*, Ladhar, Sheikhupura Dist.

**D.** ficina Ahmad in Sydowia 5 : 392, 1951. On dead wood of *Ficus palmata*, Ladhar, Sheikhupura Dist.

**D.** graminicola Ahmad in Sydowia 5 : 391, 1951.   On dead runners of *Cynodon dactylon*, Ladhar, Sheikhupura Dist.

**D.** ladharensis Ahmad in Sydowia 8 : 178, 1954.   On dead leaves of *Mangifera indica*, Ladhar, Sheikhupura Dist.

D. lagerstroemiae Ahmad in Sydowia 5 : 392, 1951.   On the bark of *Lagerstroemia indica*, Lahore.

**D.** peucedani Ahmad in Sydowia 8 : 178, 1954.   On dead stems of *Peucedanum graveolens*, Ladhar , Sheikhupura Dist.

### Fusicocum Corda

F. asparagi Ahmad in Sydowia 5 : 390, 1951.   On dead branches of *Asparagus* sp., Lahore.

F. euphorbiae Ahmad in Sydowia 5 : 390, 1951.   On dead branches of *Poinsettia pulcherrima*, Lahore.

F. lahoreanurn Ahmad in Sydowia 5 : 390, 1951.  On dead branches of
*T hevetia neriifolia*, Lahore.

## · Haplosporella Speg.

H. bakeriana Sacc. ; Sacc. Syll. Fung. XXV : 261.  On dead branches
of *Acacia farne siana*, Changa Manga.

H. dalbergiae (Died.) Petr. & Syd. ; Sacc. Syll. Fung. XXV : 250 as
*Pleosphaero psis.* On dead branches of *Dalber gia sissoo*, Ladhar ;
Changa Manga.

H. gossypii tDied.) Pet r. & Syd. ; Sacc. Syll. Fung. XXV : 250 ; Petr. &
Ah mad, p. 179. On dead branches of *Gossypium* sp., Ladha r,
Sheikhupura Dist.

H. hesperidica Speg. ; Sacc. Syll. Fung. III :323.   On dead branches of
*Citrus* sp., Lahore.

H. rnoricola Berl. ; Sacc. Syll. Fung. X : 275.  On ·dead branches of
*M arus alba*, Changa Manga.

H. nerii Sacc. ; Sacc. Syll. Fung. III : 324. On dead branches of *N erium
odorum*, Lahore.

H. prosopidina Petr. in Sydowia 8 : 179, 1954.   On dead branches of
*Proso pis julif lora*, Changa Manga.

H. prosopidincol3; Ahma d in Sydowia 8 : 180, 1954.   On branches of
*Prosopis juli fiora* , Changa Manga.

H. salvadorae Petr. in Sydowia 8 : 180, 1954, On dead wood and
branches of *S alvadora oleoid es*, Changa Manga ; Ladhar, Sheikhupura
Dist.

## Hendersonia Sacc.

H. astericola Ahi:nad in Biologia 1 : 197, 1955.  On dead sterns of
*Aster bellid ioi des*, Swat : Mingora.

H. astragalina Karst.  On dead branches of *Astragalus* sp., Chitra l.

H. leptostrornatis Petr. in Sydowia 8 : 181, 1954. On *Leptostroma
ahmad ii* Petr. on *Pinus excel sa*, Kagan Valley : Shogran.

H. obtusa Cke. ; Sacc. Syll. Fung. III : 423.  On dead branches of
*J asminum* sp., Lad ha r, Sheikhupura Dist. ; Lahore.

H. rubi (West.) Sacc. ; Sacc. Syll. Fung. III : 424 & X : 821.   On dead
branches of *Rubus Jruticosus*, Swat : Mingora.

## Macrophorna (Sacc.) Berl. & Vog.

M. triticina Ahmad in Sydowia 2 : 79, 1948.  On dead culrns of *Triticum
vul gare*, Sheikhupura.

## /Iacrophornina  Petrak

**M. phaseoli** (Maubl).   Ashby in Brit. Myc. Soc. Trans. 12 : 111, 1927.
On various hosts, common.

## Microdiplodia   Allesch.

**M. agaves** (Niessl.) Tassi ; Sacc. Syll. Fung. XVIII : 323.- Syn. *Diplod ia
agaves* Niessl. ; Sacc. Syll. Fung. III : 371. On leaves of *Agave
americana*, Lahore ; Sialkot.

## Phorna  Sacc.

**P.** .cassiae Sacc. ; Sacc. Syll. Fu ng. III : 66 ; Ah mad & Lod hi, p. 269.
On dead branches of *Cassia occid entalis*, Lahore.

**P.** changana  Ahmad in Sydowia 8 : 112, 1954.   On dead branches of
*Atri pl ex l aciniata*, Changa Manga.

**P.** gossypii Sacc. ; Sacc. Syll. Fung. III : 121.   On dead branches of
*Gossypium* sp., Ladhar, Sheikhupura Dist.

**P.** grarninis West. ; Sacc. Syll. Fung. III : l67.  On runners of *El eusine
fia gel l ifera* , Ladhar,  Sheikhupura Dist.

**P.** herbarurn West. ; Sacc. Syll. Fung. III : l33.   On dead branches of
*C henopod ium al bum,* Lad har, Sheikhu pura Dist.

**P.** rnangiferae  Ahmad  in Sydowia 2 : 78, 1948.   On dead branches of
*M angifera ind ica*, Lad har, Sheikhupura Dist.

**P.** nyctaginea F. Tassi var. boerhaaviae Ahmad in Sydowia 2 : 78, 1948.
On dead branches of *Boer haavia d iffusa*, Ladhar, Sheikhu pu ra Dist.

**P.** psidii Ahmad in Sydowia 2 : 78, 1948. On dead branches of *Psid ium
guava*, Lahore.

**P.** zizyphina Ahmad in Sydowia 2 : 78, 1948.  On dead branches of
*Zizy phus jujuba* , Lad har, Sheikhupura Dist.

## Phornopsis  Sacc.

**P.** jasrnini (Cke.) Traverso ; Sacc. Syll. Fung. X : 146 as *Phoma jasmini.*
On dea d branches *of ]asminum sambac*, Lahore.

**P.** phytolaccae (Berk. & Curt.) n. comb. ; Sacc. Syll. Fun g. III : 139 as
*Phoma phytol accae* B. & C. On dead branches of *Phytolacca acinosa*,
Kagan Valley : Shogran.

**P.** rnangiferae Ahmad in Sydowia 8 : 183, 1954.   On fallen leaves of
*M angifera ind ica,* Ladhar, Sheikhupura Dist.

## Phyllosticta  Pers. ex Desm.

**P.** cycadina Ahmad in Sydowia 2 : 77, 1948. On leaves of *Cycas
revol uta*, Lahore.

**P.** ficina Ahmad in Sydowia 2 : 77, 1948. On leaves of *Ficus elastica*, Lahore.

**P.** phytolaccae Cke. ; Sacc. Syll. Fung. III : 57. On leaves of *Phytolacca acinosa*, Murree.

**P.** pirina Sacc. ; Sacc. Syll. Fung. III : 7. On leaves of *Pyrus communis*, Lyallpur ; Hazara.

**P.** typhina Sacc. & Maub. ; Sacc. Syll. Fung. III : 60. On leaves of *Typha angustata*, Choa Saidan Shah.

**P.** zizyphi Thuem. ; Sacc. Syll. Fung. III : l5. On leaves of *Zizyphus jujuba*, Sialkot.

### Phyllostictina Syd.

**P.** solierii (Mont.) Petr. & Syd.- Syn. *Macrophoma asphod eli* Ahmad in Sydowia 2 : 69, 1948. On peduncles of *Asplwdelus tenuifolius*, Ladhar, Sheikhupura Dist. ; Sialkot.

### Pleuroplaconema Petrak

**P.** punicae Chaudhuri & Singh in Bull. Soc. Myc. Fr. 50 : 155, 1934. On branches of *Punica granatum*, Lahore.

### Septoria Sacc.

S. ah madii Petr. in Sydowia 8 : 1l4, 1954. On *Abelia trifiora*, Kagan Valley : Shogran.

S. aitchisoni Syd. ; Sacc. Syll. Fung. XVIII : 386. On leaves of *Jasminum humile*, Kurram Valley.

S. alhagiae Ahmad in Biologia 1 : l98, 1955. On leaves of *Alhagi maurorum*, Bahawalpur : Pallah.

S. arcuata Cke. ; Sacc. Syll. Fung. III : 499. On leaves of *Ficus bengalensis*, Lahore ; Lyallpur.

S. gei Rob. & Desm. ; Sacc. Syll. Fung. III : 510. On leaves of *Geum urbanum*, Kagan Valley : Shogran.

S. lepidii Desm. ; Sacc. Syll. Fung. III : 519. On leaves of *Lepid ium draba*, Baluchistan : Kahan.

S. tritici Desm. ; Sacc. Syll. Fung. III : 561. On leaves of *Triticum vulgare*, Lyallpur ; Lahore ; Sbeikhupura ; Peshawar.

S. violae West. ; Sacc. Syll. Fung. III : 518. On leaves of *Viola canescens*, Swat : Kalam.

### Sirodiplospora Naumov.

S. tamaricis Syd. in Annal. Mycol. 37 : 444, 1939. On *Tamarix articulat a*, Lahore ; Pakpattan.

Family : LEPTOSTROMATACEAE.

## Discosia Lib.

D. artocrcas Tade ex Fr. ; Sacc. Sy!!. Fung. III : 365.   On fallen leaves of *Quercus dilatata*, Murree ; Charehan ; Patriata.

## Leptostroma Fr.

L. ahmadii Petr. in Sydowia 8 : 181, 1954.   On living and dead needles of *Piuns excelsa*, Kagan Valley : Shogran.

## Leptothrium Kunze ex Wallr.

L. gleditschiae Ahmad in Biologia 1 : 198, 1955. On spines of *Gleditschia triacanthos*, Lahore.

## Sirothyrium Syd.

S. taxi Sydow in Annal. Mycol. 14 : 218, 1916.   On leaves of *Taxus baccata*, Murree.

Family : EXCIPULACEAE

## Dinemasporium Lev.

D. graminum ( Berk.) Lev. ; Sacc. Syll. Fung. III : 683 & XI : 560. On dead runners of Cynodon *dactylon* & *Eleusine flagelifera* , Ladhar , Sheikhupura Dist.

D. herbarum (Cke.) Groves ; Sacc. Syll. Fung. III : 685 as D. *hispidulum* var. *herbarum* Cke. On dead branches of *Capparis aphylla*, Ladhar, Sheikhupura Dist.

Family : ZYTHIACEAE

## Plenozythia Syd.

P. euphorbiae Syd. ; Sacc. Syll. Fung. XXV     486.   On stems of *Euphorbia cornigera*, Changla Gali.

## Polystigmina Sacc.

P. pallescens Petr. m Sydowia 8 : 183, 1954.   On living leaves of *Prunus cornuta*, Kagan Valley.

## Zythia Fr.

Z. versoniana Sacc. ; Sacc. Syll. Fung. III : 614. On the stalks and immature fruits of *Punica granatum*, Quetta (S. A. Malik) ; Choa Saidan Shah. This is the imperfect stage of *Nectriella versoniana*, Sacc. & Penz. The conidial stage alone has been recorded in West Pakistan

Order : MELANCONIALES

Family : MELANCONIACEAE

### Ahmadia Petr.

A. pcntatropidis Petr. in Annal. Mycol. 37 : 445, 1939. On living leaves of *Pentatropis cynanchoides,* Lahore ; Domeli, Jhelum.

### Ahmadinula Petr.

A. excelsa Petr. in Sydowia 7 : 375, 1953. On dead branches of *Clematis* sp., Murree ; Changla Gali.

### Amphichaeta McAlp.

A. punicac Chaudhuri & Singh in Brit. Myc. Soc. Trans. 19 : 139, 1935. On dead branches of *Punica granatum,* Lahore.

### Colletogloeum Petr.

C. dalbergiae (Ahmad) Petr. in Sydowia 7 : 369, 1953.- Syn. *Septogloeum dalbergiae* Ahmad in Sydowia 7 : 269, 1953. On pods of *Dalbergia sissoo,* Ladhar, Sheikhupura Dist.

### Colletotrichum Corda

C. arthraxonis (Ahmad) n. comb.- Syn. *Vermicularia arthraxonis* Ahmad in Biologia 1 : 198, 1955. On leaves of *Arthraxon serrulatus,* Swat : Madian.

C. capsici (Syd.) Butl. in Sci. Monogr. Imp. Agr. Res. Counc. p. 152, 1933 ; Malik & Khan, p. 525. On *Capsicum annuum,* Hazara (S. A. Malik).

C. clerodendri Died.; Sacc. Syll. Fung. XXV : 578. On dead branches of *Clerodendron inerme,* Lahore.

C. cryngii (Cda.) n. comb.- Syn. *Vermicularia eryngii* (Cda.) Fckl. ; Sacc. Syll. Fung. III : 227. On dead branches of *Eryngium coeruleum,* Swat : Khaza Khela.

C. dematium (Pers. ex. Fr.) Groves ; Sacc. Syll'. Fung. III : *255* as *Vermicularia dematium.* On dead herbaceous stems, very common throughout the area.

C. gloeosporioides Penzig ; Sacc. Syll. Fung. III : 735 ; Malik & Khan. p. 525. On leaves and branches of *Citrus aurantium,* C. *medica* and *Mangifera indica.* Common throughout the area.

C. graminicolum (Ces.) Wilson.-Syn. C. *falcatum* Went. On leaves and culms of *Sorghum vulgare, Saccharum officinarum,* Lahore ; Lyallpur ; Gujranwala ; Gujrat. This is the imperfect stage of *Glomerella tucumanensis.*

C. hihisci Poll. ; Sacc. Syll. Fung. XIV : 1015. On *Hibiscus esculelltus,* Lahore.

C. lagenarium (Pass.) Ell. & Halst. ; Sacc. Syll. Fung. III : 719 as *Gloeosporium.* On *Lagenaria vulgaris,* Ladhar, Sheikhupura Dist.

C. lebbek (Syd.) Petr. ; Sacc. Syll. Fung. XXV : 547 as *Gloeosporium lebbek.* On fallen pods of *Albizzia lebbek,* Ladhar, Sheikhupura Dist.

C. mirabilis (Bres.) n. comb.- Sacc. Syll. Fung. XXV :552 as *Gloeosporium mirabilis* Bres. On dead branches of *Mirabilis jalapa,* Shahdara.

C. poinsettiae (Sacc.) Petr. ; Sacc. Syll. Fung. III : 793 as *Gloeosporium intermedium.* On dead branches of *Poinsettia pulcherrima.* Lahore.

C. musarum (Cke. & Mass.) Petr. ; Sacc. Syll. Fung. X : 461 as *Gloeosporium musarum.* On leaves of *Musa paradisiaca,* Lahore.

### Cryptostictis Fuckel

C. caudata (Preuss.) Sacc. in Syll. Fung. III : 444. On dead branches of *Rosa* sp., Lahore.

### Coryneum Nees ex Fr.

C. kunzei Corda ; Sacc. Syll. Fung. III : 778. On dead branches of *Quercus ilex,* Swat : Kulali.

C. umbonatum Nees ; Sacc. Syll. Fung. III : 777. On dead branches of *Quercus* sp., Swat : Kalam.

### Melanconium Link ex Fr.

M. juglandinum Kze. ; Sacc. Syll. Fung. III : 753. On branches of *Juglans regia,* Kagan Valley.

### Microstroma Niess!

M. juglandis (Bereng.) Sacc. in Syll. Fung. IV : 9. ; Ahmad & Lodhi, p. 269. On leaves of *Juglans regia,* Dadder, Abbottabad.

### Pestalotia de Not.

P. funerea Desm. ; Sacc. Syll. Fung. III :791 ; Ahmad & Ladhi. p. 269. On dead leaves of *Taxus baccata,* Murree.

P. phoenicis Vize Sacc. Syll. Fung. III : 796. On petioles of *Phoenix dactylifera,* Lahore.

### Septogloeum Sacc.

S. acaciae Syd. in Annal. Mycol. 12 : 489, 1914 ; Sacc. Syll. Fung. XXV : 591; Sydow & Ahmad, p. 446. On living leaves of *Acacia arabica,* Sargodha ; Sialkot.

### Thyrsidium Mont. ex Dur.

T. hcdericolum (de Not.) Dur. & Mont. ; Sacc. Syll. Fung. III : 761. On dead branches of *Hedera nepalensis,* Shogran.

### Order : MONILIALES
### Family : MONILIACEAE

### Acladium Link. ex Sacc.

A. niveum (Lev.) Sacc. in Syll. Fung. IV : 87 ; Ginai, p. 279 (1936). On dung, Lahore.

### Arthrobotrys Corda

A. superba Corda ; Sacc. Syll. Fung. IV : 181; Mahju, p. 162. On dung, Lahore.

### Aspergillus Mich. ex Fr.

A. calyptratus Oud. ; Thom & Raper, p. 185 as a synonym of *A. Jumigatus* ; Chaudhuri & Umar, p. 84. In garden and field soil, Punjab.

A. candidus Link ; Thom & Raper, p. 207 ; Chaudhuri & Umar, p. 86. Isolated from air, Lahore.

A. flavipes (Bain. & Sartoris) Thom & Church ; Thom & Raper, p. 179 ; Chaudhuri & Umar, p. 85. Isolated from alkaline soil.

A. flavus Link ; Thom & Raper, p. 263 ; Chaudhuri & Umar p. 90 ; Mahju, p. 157. Isolated from soil and air, Lahore.

A. fumigatus Pres. ; Thom & Raper, p. 148 ; Chaudhuri & Umar, p. 79. Isolated from soil and air. Lahore.

—-var. tumescens Blumentritt ; Chaudhuri & Umar, p. 80 ; Thom & Raper, p. 151 as a synonym of *A. Jumigatus.* Isolated from soil and air, Lahore.

A. humicola Chaudhuri & Sachar in Ann. Myc. 32 : 97. According to Thom & Raper, p. 193, Neill (Trans. & Proc. Roy. Soc. New Zealand 69 : 237-264) correctly places this species with *A. variecolor.* Isolated from humus soil, Lahore.

A. luchuensis Inui ; Thom & Raper, p. 229 ; Chaudhuri & Umar, p. 88. Isolated from air, Lahore.

A. nidulans (Eid.l Wint. ; Thom & Raper, p. 156 ; Chaudhuri & Umar, p. 81. Isolated from soil, air and citrus fruits. Lahore.

A. niger van Tiegh. ; Thom & Raper, p. 216 ; Chaudhuri & Umar, p. 86. Isolated from air, Lahore.

A. sachari Chaudhuri in Ann. Myc. 32 : 95 ; Chaudhuri & Umar, p. 88; Blochwitz leaves this species in *A. quercina* but Thom & Raper

p. 278, cast doubt on this because of the colourless, smooth conidiophores. Isolated from alkaline soil,' Lahore.

A. sydowi (Bain. & Sart.) Thom & Church ; Thom & Raper, p. 184 ; Chaudhuri & Umar, p. 83. Isolated from air and soil, Lahore.

A. tamarii Kita ; Thom & Raper, p. 254 ; Chaudhuri & Umar, p. 89. Isolated from soil and air, Lahore.

A. terreus Thom ; Thom & Raper, p. 195 ; Chaudhuri & Umar, p. 85. Isolated from soil and air, Lahore.

A. versicolor (Yuill.) Tiraboschi ; Thom & Raper, p. 190 ; Chaudhuri & Umar, p. 82. Isolated from soil and air, Lahore.

### Beauveria Yuill.

B. bassiana (Bals.) Yuill. ; Sacc. Syll. Fung. IV . 119 as *Botrytis* ; Mundkur & Ahmad, p. 9. On a beetle *( Hypera variabilis* Hbst.), Ladhar, Sheikhupura Dist.

### Botrytis Pers. ex Fr.

B. vulgaris Fr. ; Sacc. Syll. Fung. IV : 128 ; Ginai, p. 719 (1939). On grapes, Quetta Valley.

### Cephalosporium Corda

C. sacchari Butl. in Mem. Dept. Agr. Ind. Bot. Ser. 6 : 181, 1913 ; Malik & Khan, p. 525. On culms of *Saccharum officinarum,* Hazara (S. A. Malik).

### Dactylaria Sacc.

D. purpurella Sacc. ; Sacc. Syll. Fung. IV : 195 ; Ginai, p. 279 (1936). On dung, Lahore.

### Oedocephalum Preuss

O. glomerulosum (Bull.) Sacc. in Syll. Fung. IV : 4 ; Mahju, p. 162. On dung, Lahore.

### Penicillium Link. ex Fr.

P. atramentosum Thom ; Raper & Thom, p. 381 ; Chaudhuri p. 95. Isolated from air, Lahore.

P. casei Staub. ; Raper & Thom. p. 401 ; Chaudhuri, p. 97. Isolated from air, Lahore.

P. chloroleucon Biourge ; Chaudhuri, p. 95 ; Raper & Thom, p. 345, believe that it is synonymous with *P. corylophilum* Diercks. Isolated from air, Lahore.

P. citrinum Thom ; Raper & Thom, p. 345. On rotting citrus fruits, Lahore.

**P.** cyaneo-fulvum Biourge ; Raper & Thom, p. 371 ; Chaudhuri, p. 96. Isolated from air, Lahore.

**P.** expansum Link. emend. Thom ; Raper & Thom, p. 512. Causing soft rot in apples, Quetta.

**P.** fellutanum Biourge ; Raper & Thom, p. 212 ; Chaudhuri, p. 94. Isolated from air, Lahore.

**P.** pinophilum Hedgecock ; Chaudhuri, p. 98 ; Raper & Thom, p. 620, regard this as probably synonymous with *P. funiculosum* Thom. Isolated from humus soil, Lahore.

**P.** puberulum Bainier ; Raper & Thom, p. 497 ; Chaudhuri, p. 98. Isolated from air, Lahore.

**P.** steckei Zaleski ; Raper & Thom, p. 350 : Chaudhuri, p. 96. Isolated from soil and air, Lahore.

**P.** terrestre Jensen ; Raper & Thom, p. 450 ; Chaudhuri, p. 98. Isolated from garden soil, Lahore.

**P.** viridi-varians Cha,.u dhuri & Sachar in Annal. Mycol. 32 : 98, 1932 ; Chaudhuri, p. 93. According to Raper & Thom, p. 846, from the inadequate description given, the species appears to belong in the section Divaricata, possibly approximating *P. nalgiovensis* Laxa. Isolated from soil, Lahore.

### Piricularia Sacc.

**P.** oryzae Cavara ; Sacc. Syll. Fung. X : 563. On *Oryza sativa*. Common.

### Ramularia Sacc.

**R.** decipiens Ell. & Ev. ; Sacc. Syll. Fung. IV : 215 ; Sydow & Ahmad, p. 446. On leaves of *Rumex dentatus,* Lahore ; Sangla Hill ; Swat : Kalam ; Gujrat.

**R.** urticae Ces. ; Sacc. Syll. Fung. IV : 216. On leaves of *Urtica* sp., Murree.

### Sepedonium Link ex Fr.

S. chrysospermum Link ex Fr. ; Sacc. Syll. Fung. IV : 146. On *Boletus* sp., Murree ; Kagan Valley.

### Spicaria Auct.

S. silvatica Oudem. ; Sacc. Syll. Fung. XVIII : 538 ; Chaudhuri & Sachar, p. 98. Panjab garden soils.

### Stephanoma Wallr.

S. strigomm Wallr. ; Sacc. Syll. Fung. IV : 754. Parasitic on *Humaria hemisphaerica ,* Murree.

## Trichoderma Pers. ex Fr.

T. glaucum Abbott in Iowa State College Jour. Sci. 1 : 15 ; Hukam Chand, p. 325.  Isolated from Lahore soils.

T. koningi Oudem. ; Sacc. Syll. Fun g. XVIII : 512 ; Chaudhuri & Sachar, p. 92.  Isolated from soil, Lahore.

## Trichothecium Link ex Fr.

T. roseum Link ; Sacc. Syll. Fung. lV : l78 ; Kheswala , p. 296 ; Chaud huri & Sachar, p. 98 as *Cephal ot hecium roseum* Cda. On *Pyrus malus,* Quetta ; Panjab soils.

T. inaequale Mass. & Salm. ; Sacc. Syll. · Fu ng. XVIII : 539. On dead branches of *Gossypium* sp., and on dung, Ladhar, Sheikh upura Dist.

## Family : DEMATIACEAE •
## Alternaria Nees ex Wa!lr.

A. brassicae (Berk.) Sacc.; Sacc. Syll. Fung. IV : 546 & X : 679.   On *Brassica campestris ,* Sangla Hill.

——f. phaseoli Brun.; Sacc. Syll. Fung. XIV : 1098 ; Malik & Khan, p. 526.   On *Vicia faba ,* Sind ; Peshawar.        •

A. citri Pierce ; Sacc. Syll. Fung. XVIII : 623 ; Chaud huri, p. 96 (1936) ; Malik & Khan, p. 524. On leaves of *Citrus sinensis ,* Lahore ; of *Citrus* sp., _ffazara (S. A. Malik).

A. dianthi Stev. & Hall; Sacc. Syll. Fung. XXII: 1410. On *H ibiscus tiliaceous, Jasminum* sp. and *Calend ula officinal is,* Lahore (H. Chaudhuri).

A. humicola Oud.; Sacc. Syll. Fung. XVIII : 624. Isolated from Pu njab field soils.

A. malvae Roum. & Let.; Sacc. Syll. Fung. X : 679. Isolated from soil, Lahore.

A. macrospora Sacc.; Sacc. Syll. Fung. IV : 546 as a variety of *A. brassicae.* On *Gossypium* sp., Hazara (S. A. Malik).

A. solani (Ell. & Martin) Jones & Grout ; Sacc. Syll. Fung. IV : 530 as *M acrosporium* ; Malik & K han, p. 524. It causes early blight of potato.

A. tenuis Nees ; Sacc. Syll. Fung. IV : 545 ; Lod hi & Naeem, p. 242. Isolated from seeds, Lahore.

## Cercospora Pres.

C. abelmoschi Ell. & Ev.; Chu pp, p. 367; Sydow & Ahmad , p. 446 as C. *hibisci* Tracy & Earle. On leaves of *H ibiscus cannabinu s ,* Pasru r ; Lahore.

C. achyranthis Syd. in Ann. Myc. 7 : l71 ; Chupp, p. 29.   On leaves of *Achyrant hes aspera ,* Pasrur (Zain).

C. ahmadii Petrak in Sydowia 9 : 495, 1955. On leaves of *Marsdenia roylei,* Murree.

C. annulata Cke.; Sacc. Syll. Fung. IV : 475 ; Chupp, p. 392 ; Malik & Khari, p. 525. On leaves of *Ficus* sp., Hazara (S. A. Malik).

C. asparagi Sacc.-; Sacc. Syll. Fung. IV : 4'i7 ; Chupp, p. 343 ; Malik & Khan, p. 525. On phylloclades of *Asparagus* sp., Hazara (S. A. Malik).

C. beticola Sacc.; Sacc. Syll. Fung. IV : 456 ; Chupp, p. 111 ; Malik & Khan, p. 525 as C. *anthelmintica* Atkinson. On leaves of *Beta vulgaris,* Lahore ; on *Chenopodium ambrosioides,* Peshawar.

C. blumeae Thuem.; Sacc. Syll. Fung. IV : 445 ; Ahmad & Lodhi, p. 269 ; Chupp, p. 124. On leaves of *Blumea membranacea,* Lahore.

C. calotropidis Ell. & Ev.; Sacc. Syll. Fung. XVI : 1072 ; Sydow & Ahmad, p. 446 ; Chupp, p. 71. On leaves of *Calotropis procera,* Lahore ; Sangla Hill.

C. cannabina Wakef.; Sacc. Syll. Fung. XXV : 884 ; Ahmad & Lodhi, p. 269 ; Chupp, p. 393. On leaves of *Cannabis sativa,* Lahore ; Peshawar.

C. cruenta Sacc.; Sacc. Syll. Fung. IV : 435 ; Chupp, p. 298. On leaves of *Phaseolus mungo* var..*radiatus,* Gilgit.

C. davisii Ell. & Ev.; Sacc. Syll. Fung. X : 622 ; Chupp, p. 301. On leaves of *Melilotus parvifiora,* Pasrur (Zain).

C. dolichi Ell. & Ev.; Sacc. Syll. Fung. X : 622 ; Chupp, p. 303 ; Malik & Khan, p. 525. On leaves of *Dolichos lablab,* Hazara (S. A. Malik).

C. dubia (Riess) Wint.; Sacc. Syll. Fung. IV : 456 ; Ahmad & Lodhi, p. 269 ; Chupp, p. 112. On leaves of *Chenopodium album,* Lahore ; Sangla Hill.

C. gossypina Cke.; Sacc. Syll. Fung. IV : 441 ; Chupp, p. 371. On leaves of *Gossypium* sp., Lyallpur ; Hazara (S. A. Malik).

C. heliotropii-bocconii Scalia ; Sydow & Ahmad, p. 446 ; Chupp, p. 93. On leaves of *Heliotropium eichwaldii,* Pakpattan ; Sangla Hill.

C. jasminicola Muell. & Chupp ; Chupp, p. 416. On leaves of *Jasminum* sp., Lahore.

C. koepkei Krueger ; Sacc. Syll. Fung. X : 656 ; Chupp, p. 248 ; Butler & Bisby, p. 142 as C. *longipes* But!. On leaves of *Saccharum officinarum,* Sialkot.

C. medicaginis Ell. & Ev.; Sacc. Syll. Fung. X : 622 ; Chupp, p. 319. On leaves of *Medicago denticulata,* Lahore.

C. meliae. Ell. & Ev.; Sacc. Syll. Fung. X : 639 ; Chupp, p. 385.- Syn.
     *C. leucosticta* Ell. & Ev.    On leaves of *Melia azedarach*, Karachi.

C. nebulosa Sacc.; Sacc. Syll. Fung. IV : 441; Chupp, p. 375. On leaves of
     *Althaea rosea*, Lahore.

C. neriella Sacc.; Sacc. Syll. Fung. IV : 473 ;. Chupp, p. 48.   On leaves of
     *Nerium odorum*, Lahore.

C. nicotianae Ell. & Ev.; Sacc. Syll. Fung. XI : 628 ; Chttpp, p. 545. On
     leaves of *Nicotiana tabacum*, Sialkot ; Sangla Hill.

C. rosicola Passer.; Sacc. Syll. Fung. IV : 460 ; Chupp, p. 486. On leaves
     of *Rosa centifolia* , Tarnab Farm, Peshawar ; Jalalpur Jattan ; of *R.
     damascena*, Akbarpore, Peshawar.

C. sissoo Syd. in Annal. Mycol. 31 : 92, l935 ; Sydow & Ahmad , p. 446 ;
     Chupp, p. 352. Oh leaves of *Dalbergia sissoo* , Ladhar, Sheikhupura
     Dist.; Sargodha. This *is* the imperfect stage of *Mycosphaerella dal-
     bergiae.*

C. solani Sacc.; Sacc. Syll. Fung. IV : 449 ;. Chupp, p. 550 ; Petrak & ·
     Ahmad, Sydowia 8 : 185 as *C. nigrescens* Wint. On leaves of *Solanum
     nigrum*, Lahore. ·

C. subsessi.lis H. & P. Sydow; Sacc. Syll. Fung. XXV: 911 as *Cercosporina ;*
     Chupp, p. 386 ; Malik & Khan, p. 525. On leaves of *Melia azedarach*,
     Hazara (S.A. Malik).

C. traversiana Sacc.; Sacc. Syll. Fung. XVIII : 600 ; Chupp, p. 338. On
     leaves of *Trigonella Joenum-graecum*, Lahore.

C. viticola (Ces.) Sacc.; Sacc. Syll. Fung. IV : 458 ; Malik & Khan, p.
     525.- Syn. *Pseudocercospora vitis* (Lev.) Speg.; Chupp, p. 605. On
     leaves of Vitis *vinifera* , Hazara (S. A. Malik). This is the imperfect
     stage of *Mycosphaerella personata* Higgins.

C. withaniae Syd.; Sacc. Syll. Fung. *XXV* : 891 ; Mundkur & Ahmad, p.
     10 ; Chupp, p. 553. On leaves of *Withania somnifera* , Lahore ;
     Ladhar, Sheikhupura Dist.

Circinotrichum Nees

C. maculiforme Nees ; Sacc. Syll. Fung. IV : 314.    On fallen leaves of
     *Cordia obliqua*, Lahore.

C. microspermum v. Hoehn.; Sacc. Syll. Fung. XXII : 1360. On dead
     branches of *Capparis aphylla*, Lahore.

Cladosporium Schw.

C. carpophilum Thuem.; Sacc. Syll. Fung. IV : 353 ; Malik & Khan, p.
     525.    On fruits of *Prunus persica* , Quetta ; Peshawar (S. A. Malik).

C. cucumerinum Ell. & Arth.;, $acc. Sy!!. Fung. X: 601; Petrak & Ahmad, p. 185. On living lea,ves of *Cucurbita pepo*, Ladhar, Sheikhupura Dis.

C. herbarum (Pers.) Link ; Sacc. Syll. Fung. IV : 350 ; Malik & Khan, p. 525. On withering green parts of plants ; common everywhere.

—**var.** citricola Fawcett & Berger; Sacc. Syll. Fung. XXV: 796; Chaudhuri, J. Agr. Sci. Ind. 8 : 96. On leaves of *Citrus* sp., Panjab.

C. typharum Desm.; Sacc. Syll. Fung. IV : 366. On leaves of *Typha angustata*, Lahore.

C. zizyphi Karst. & Roum.; Sacc. Syll. Fung. X : 604. On living leaves of *Zizyphus jujuba*, Lahore'; Changa Manga.

### Clasterosporium Schw.

C. mori Syd.; Sacc. Syll. Fung. XVI : 1060. On livihg leaves of *Marus alba*, Lahore ; Changa Manga ; Sangla Hill ; Sialkot.

### Coniothecium Corda

C. chomatosporum Corda ; Sacc. Syll. Fung. IV : 510 ; Malik & Khan, p. 525. On *Pyrus malus*, Peshawar (S. A. Malik).

### Curvularla Boidijn

C. lunata (Wakker) Boed.; Lodhi & Naeem, Brit. Myc. Soc. Trans. 38 : 241 ; Sacc. Syll. Fung. XIV : 1089 s *Acrothecium lunatum.* Isolated from seeds of *Spinacea oleracea*, Lahore.

C. penniseti (Mitra) Boed. ?; Lodhi & Naeem, p. 241 ; -Syn. *Acrothecium penniseti* Mitra.. Isolated from seeds of *Daucus carota*, Laho:re.

C. spicifera (Bain.) Boed.; Lodhi & Naeem, p. 241 ; Sacc. Syll. Fung. XXII : 1399 as *Brachycladium spiciferum.* Isblated from seeds of *Daucus carota* and *Setaria 'lutesceris*, Lahoe.

C. trifolii (Kauffm.) Boed.; Lodhi & Naeem, p. 241 ; Sacc. Syll. Fung. XXV : 835 as *Brachysporium trifolii.* Isolated from seeds of *Datura alba*, Lahore.

### Fusicla dium on.

F. dendriticum (Wall.) Fckl.; Sacc. Syll. Fung. IV : 345. On leaves and. fruits of *Pyrus* sp., Lahore ; Lyallpur. This is the imperfect stage of *Venturia inaequalis* (Cke.) Wint.

### Hadrotrichum Fuck.

H. phragmites Fuck.; Sacc. Syll. Fung. IV : 301 ; Sydow & Ahmad, p. 446. On leaves of *PhragT!lites lwrka*, Lahore ; Ladhar, Sheikhupura Dist.

## Helminthosporium Link ex Fr.

H. anoma:Ium Gilm. & Abbott ; Hukam Chand, Proc. Ind. Acad. Sci. 5 : 325.　Isolated from soil, Lahore.

H. avenae Eidam ; Sacc. Syll. Fu ng. XXII : 1393. On leaves of *Avena sativa*, Malir, Karachi ; Lahore ; Peshawar.

H. oryzae Breda de Hahn ; Sacc. Syll. Fung. XXII : 1394.　On leaves of *Oryza sativa*, Upper· Sind.

H. sativum Pammel, King & Bak k ; Malik & Khan, p. 525 ; Lodhi & Naeem, p. 251.　On leaves of *Triticum vul gare* and *H ord eum vul gare*, Peshawar (S. A. Malik). Isolated from seeds of *Bomba x malabaricum*, 'Lahore.

H. turcicum Pass.; Sacc. Syll. Fung. IV : 420. On leaves .and inflorescence of *Z ea mays* and on leaves of *Sor ghum vul gare.* Common.

## Heterosporium Klotszch ex Cooke

H. allii Ell. & Mart.; Sacc. Syll. Fung. IV : 480 ; Hukam Chand, p. 325. Isolated from soil, Lahore.

## Lacellina Sacc.

L. libyca Sacc. & Trott.; Sacc. Syll. Fung. XXV : 781. On lea ves of *Saccharum munja* , S. *spontaneum,* S. *officinarum* and sever al other grasses, Lahore ; Gujrat ; Sargodha ; Sangla Hill.

## Macrosporium　Fr.

M. parasiticum Thuem.; Sacc. Syll. Fung. IV : 537. On dead branches, etc., Murree ; Lahore ; Kagan Valley. This is the imperfect stage of *Pl eospora herbarum.*

## Nigrospora Zimm.

N. sphaerica (Sacc.) Mason ; Lodhi & Naeem, p. 242 ; Sacc. Syll. Fung. IV : 293 as *Trichosporium sphaericum.* Isolated from seeds of *H el i-chrysum* sp. (Compositae), Lahore.

## Periconia Tode ex Fr.

P. pycnospora Fres. ; Sacc. Syll. Fung. IV : 271.　On dead herbaceous branches, Lahore.

## Polythrincium Kze. & Schm. ex Fr.

P. trifolii Kze. ; Sacc. Syll. Fung. IV : 350.　On leaves of *Trifolium resupinatum,* Ladhar, Sheikhupura Dist. ; Sargodha; Lahore ; Chillianwala ; Montgomery ; of *T . repens,* Kagan Valley : Shogran. This is the imperfect stage of *M ycosphaerel la killiani* Petr.

## Spondylocladium Mart. ex Cda.

S. fumosum Mart. ; Sacc. Syll. Fung. IV : 483 ; Hukam Chand, p. 325. Isolated from soil, Lahore.

## Sporodesmium Link. ex Fr.

S. polymorphum Cda. ; Sacc. Syll. Fung. IV : 501. On dead wood, Lahore.

## Stmphyllium Wallr.

S. paradoxum (Cda.) Fckl. ; Sacc. Syll. Fung. IV : 520. On dead branches of *Betula utilis,* Swat :Kalam.

S. consortiale (Thuem.) Groves & Skolko ; Sacc. Syll. Fung. IV : 539 as *Macrosporium* ; Lodhi & Naeem, p. 242. Isolated from seeds of *Beta vulgaris,* Lahore.

## Stigmina Sacc.

S. platani (Fckl.) Sacc. ; Sacc. Syll. Fung. IV : 394 ; Malik & Khan, p. 526. On living leaves of *Platanus orientalis,* Abbottabad (A. H. Khan).

## Trichosporium Fr.

T. masseei Sacc. ; Sacc. Syll. Fung. XXII : 1356.- Syn. *T. aterrima* Mass. (non *T. aterrima* (Cda.) Sacc.). On the bark of *Moru alba,* Changa Manga.

## Family : STILBACEAE

## Coremiella Bubak & Krieger

C. cystopodoides Bub;ik & Krieg. ; Sacc. Syll. Fung.- XXV :927 ; Ginai, p. 280 (1936). On dung, Lahore.

## Den.drostilbella Hoehne}

D. byssina Alb. & Schw. ; Mahju, Ind. Bot. Soc. Jour. 12 : 162. On dung, Lahore.

## Isaria Pers. ex Fr.

I. brachiata (Batsch) Schum. ; Sacc. Syll. Fung. IV :589 ; Mahju, P·. 63. On dung, Lahore.

I. pulcherrima Berk. & Br. ; Sacc. Syll. Fung. IV :595. On petioles. '?. *Phoenix dactylifera,* Ladhar, Sheikhupura Dist.

## Graphium Corda

G. paradoxum Sacc. ; Sacc. Syll. Fung. XVI : 1087 ; Ginai, p. 280 (1936). On dung, Lahore.

## Stemmaria Preuss

S. terrestris Chaudhuri & Sachar in Annal. Mycol. 32 : 100, 1934. Isolated from humus soil, Lahore.

## Stysamis Corda

S. stemonites (Pers.) Corda ; Snee. Syll. Fung. IV : 621 ; Mahjll, p. 162. On dung, Lahore.

### Family : TUBERCULARIACEAE

## Cerebella Ces.

C. antidotale Subram. in Jour. & Proc. Asiatic Soc. Bengal N. S. 17 : 206, 1921. Growing saprophytically on the *Sphacelia-stage* of *Claviceps* on *Panicum antidotale*, Sangla Hill (G. S. Cheema).

C. cenchroides Subram. in Jour. & Proc. Asiatic Soc. Bengal. N. S. 17 : 206. Growing saprophytically on the *Sphacelia-stage* of *Claviceps* on *Cenchrus pennisetiformis* & *C. setigerus*, Lahore (G. S. Cheerna).

## Cryptocoryneum Fuck.

C. obovatum Oud. ; Sacc. Syll. Fung. XXI : 1062 ; Ahmad & Lodhi, p. 299. On pieces of dead wood, Murree.

## Epicoccum Link ex Wallr.

E. nigrum Link ; Sacc. Syll. Fung. IV : 736 ; Lodhi & Naeem, p. 242. Isolated from seeds of *Paa annua*, Lahore.

## Fusarium Link ex Fr.

F. orthoceros App. & Woll. ; Sacc. Syll. Fung. XXII : 1477 ; Malik & Khan, p. 525. On *Cicer arietinum*, Peshawar (S. A. Malik).

F. pannosum Mass. ; Sacc. Syll. Fung. XVI': 1098. On trunks of trees, Murree.

F. semitectum Berk. & Rav. ; Snee. Syll. Fung. IV : 718 ; Lodhi & Naeem, p. 242. Isolated from seeds of *Bombax malabaricum*, Lahore.

F. udum Butl. ; Snee. Syll. Fung. XXII : 1479 ; Malik & Khan, p. 525. On *Crotolaria juncea*, Peshawar (S. A. Malik).

F. vasinfectum Atk. ; Sacc. Syll. Fung. XXII : 1481. On roots and stems of *Gossypium* sp.

## Myrothecium Tode ax Fr.

M. roridum Tode ex Fr. ; Sacc. Syll. Fung. IV : 750. On dead branches *etc.,* Lahore ; Sangla Hill.

## Papularia Fr

P. sphaerosperma (Pers.) v. Hoehn. ; Ahmad & Lod hi, p. 269 ; Sacc.
Syll. Fung. III : 759 as *Melanconium sphaerospermum* (Pers.) Link.
On culms of *Bambusa bambos,* Changa Manga.

## Pucciniopsis Speg.

P. quercina Wakef. ; Malik & Khan, p. 525. On *Quercus dilatata,* Hazara
(S. A. Malik).

## Tubercularia Tod e ex Fr.

T. vulgaris Tode ex Fr. ; Sacc. Syll. Fung. IV : 638. On dead branches
of *Prunus cornuta, Viburnum grand ijlorum* and *Berberis lycium ,*
Murree, Changla Gali ; Shogran ; Kalam. This is t he impefect
stgae of *N ectria cinabarina.*

## ADDENDA

On page 13, under the Order Pseudosphaeriales, add

### Ellisiodothis Theiss.

E. smilacis (de Not.) v. Arx & Mueller in Beitr. Kryptoga menf. Schw.
11 : 97, 1954 ; Sacc. Syll. Fu ng. II : 660 as *Myiocopron smilacis.* On
dead branches of *Smil ax parvifolia,* Murree.

On page 65, under the Family Thelephoraceae, add

### Solenia Pers. ex Fr.

S. candida Pers. ex Fr.; Sacc. Syll. Fung. VI : 424. On decayed leaves
of *Saccharum munja ,* Lahore ; Lad har, Sheikhupura Dist.

S. poriaeformis (DC.) Fr.; Sacc. Syll. Fung. VI : 428. On decayed wood ,
Kagan Valley : Kawai.

On page 90, u nder the Family Sphaeropsida ceae, add

### ?viyxofusicoccum Died.

M. prunicolum (S. R.) Died.; Sacc. Syll. Fung. III : 722 as *M yxos porium
prunicolum* Sacc. & Roum. On dead branches of *Prunus* sp., Kaga n
Valley : Shogran.

## REFERENCES

Ahmad, Sultan. Gasteromycetes of West Pakistan. Publ. Dep. Bot. Univ. Panjab, No. 11, pp. 1-92, 1952.

Ahmad, Sultan. Pezizales of West Pakistan. Biologia, 1(1) : 1-24, 1955.

Ahmad, Sultan. Uredinales of West Pakistan. Biologia, 2 (1) :29-101, 1956.

Ahmad, S. & Lodhi, S. A. Some new or unreported fungi of West Pakistan. Sydowia, 7 : 266-269, 1953.

Arthur, J. C. & Cummins, G. B. Rusts of North West Himalayas. Mycologia, 25 : 397-406, 1933.

Blumer, S. Die Erysiphaceen Mittleeuropas mit besonderer Beruksichtigung der Schweiz. Bcitrage zur Kryptogamenflora der Schweiz, 7 : 1-483, 1933.

Butler, E. J. & Bisby, G. R. The Fungi of India. Imp. Coun. of Agr. Res. India Sci. Mono. I., xviii+237 pp., Calcutta, 1931.

Chaudhuri, H. Diseases of Citrus in the Punjab. Ind. J. Agr. Sci., 6 : 72-109, 1936.

Chaudhuri, H. Molds of the Panjab-II. Proc. Ind. Acad. Sci. B., 8 : 93-99, 1938.

Chaudhuri, H. & Banerjee, M. L. Indian Water Moulds-IV. Proc. Ind. Acad. Sci. B., 15 :216-224, 1942.

Chaudhuri, H. & Kochhar, P. L. Indian Water Moulds-I. Proc. Ind. Acad. Sci. B., 2 : 137-154, 1935.

Chaudhuri, H. & Lotus, S. S. Indian Water Moulds-II. Proc. Ind. Acad. Sci. B., 3 :328-333, 1936.

Chaudhuri, H. & Sachar, G.S. A study of the fungous flora of the Punjab soils. Ann, Myc., 32 :90-100, 1934.

Chaudhuri, H. & Singh, J. Une nouvelle maladie du Grenadier. Bull. Soc. Mycol. France, Tome L. Fasc. 2, 1934.

Chaudhuri, H. & Singh, J. A disease of pomegranate ( *Punica granatum* Linn.) due to *Amphichaeta ptmicae* n. sp. Trans. Brit. Mycol. Soc., 19 : 139-144, 1934.

Chaudhuri, H. & Umar, M. Molds of the Panjab-I. The Aspergilli. Proc. Ind. Acad. Sci. **B., 8** : 79-92, 138.

Chaudhuri, H., Kochhar, P. **L.**, Lotus, S. S., Banerjee, M. **L.** & Khan, A. H. *A Handbook of Indian Water Moulds*, Part I. 70 pp., Lahore, 1947.

Chupp, Charles. *A Monograph of the Fungus Genus* Cercospora. 667 pp., New York, 1953.

Coker, W. C. *The Saprolegniaceae with notes on other water moulds.* iv+ 200 pp., 1923.

Cook, W. R. Ivimy. A monograph of the Plasmodiophorales. Arch. Pro-tistenk., **80** (2) : 179-254, 1933.

Cummins, G. B. Uredinales from the North West Himalayas. Mycologia, , 35 : 446-458, 1942.

Fischer, G. W. *Manual of the North American Smut Fungi.* 343 pp., New York, 1953.

Galloway, L. D. & Sen, R. R. An unusual rust fungus on tulip. Ind. **J.** Agric. Sci., **6** : 743-744, 1936.

Gaumann, E. Beitrage zu einer Monographie de Gattung *Peronospora* Corda. Beitrage zur Kryptogamenflora der Schweiz, **5** : 1-360, 1923.

Ginai, M. A. Further contribution to our knowledge of Indian coprophi-lous fungi. Jour. Ind. Bot. Soc., **15** : 269-284, 1936.

Ginai, M. Asghar. A species of *Phyllactinia* occurring on almond *(Prunus amygdalus).* Ind. **J.** Agr. Sci., **10** (1) : 96-97, 1940.

Ginai, M. Asghar. A note on *Botrytis-rot* of Grapes in the Quetta Valley. Ind. **J.** Agr. Sci., **9** (5) : 719-725, 1939.

Hamid, Abdul. Indian Water Moulds-III. Proc. Ind. Acad. Sci. B., **15** : 206-215, 1942.

Hukam Chand. A study of the fungus flora of the Lahore soils. Proc. Ind. Acad. Sci. B., **5** : 324-331, 1937.

Joerstad, Ivar. Parasitic Fungi, chiefly Uredineae from Tirich Mir in the State of Chitral, N. Pakistan. Nytt Mag. Bot., **1** (2) : 71-87, 1952.

Kheswala, K.F. Fruit diseases in Baluchistan. Agric. and Livestock in India, **6** : 204-215, 1936.

Lister, G. *A Monograph of the Mycetozoa.* xxxiii+296 pp., London, 1925.

Lodhi, S. A., Some Myxomycetes from West Pakistan. Sydowia. **5** : 375-383, 1951.

Lodhi, S. A. & Naeem, A.    Some seed-borne fungi from Pakistan. Trans. Brit. Mycol. Soc., 38 (3) : 240-242, 1955.

Mahju, N.A.    A contribution to our knowledge of Indian coprophilous fungi. J. Ind. Bot. Soc., **12** : 153-164, 1933.

Malik, S.A. & Khan, M.A.    Parasitic Fungi of the North West Frontier Province. Ind. ]. Agr. Sci., **13** : 522-527, 1944.

Martin, G.W.    Myxomycetes, in *North Amercian Flora*, **1** (1) : 1-151, 1949.

Mueller, E. & Ahmad, Sultan.    Ueber einige neue oder bemerkenswerte Ascomyceten aus Pakistans I. Sydowia, **9** : 233-245, 1955.

Mundkur, B.B.    Fungi of the Northwestern Himalayas : Ustilaginales. Mycologia; **36** : 286-292, 1944.

Mundkur, B.B. & Ahmad, Sultan.    Revisions of and additions to Indian fungi- II. Imp: Mycol. Inst., Mycol. Papers, **18** : 1-11, 1946.

Mundkur, B.B. & Thirumalachar, M.J.    *The Ustilaginales of India.* Mycol. Papers, C.M. I., pp. 1-83, 1952.

Petrak, F. & Ahmad, Sultan.    Beitrage zur Pilzftora Pakistans.    Sydowia, **8** : 162-185, 1954.

Raper, KeQneth B. & Thom, Charles.    *A Manual of the Penicillia:* ix+ 875 pp., Baltimore, 1949.

Seaver, Fred **J.**    *The North American Cup-Fungi (Operculates).*    248 pp., New York, 1928.

Seaver, Fred ].    *The North American Cup-Fungi (Inoperculates).*    428 pp., New York, 1951.

Sydow, H. & Ahmad,, Sultan.    Fungi Panjabensis. Ann. Myc., .37 : 439-447. 1939.

Thind, K.S.    The genus *Peronospora* in the Panjab. **J.** Ind. Bot. Soc. **21** : 197-215, 1942.

Thom, Charles & Raper, Kenneth B.    *A Manual of the Aspergilli.*    ix+ 373 pp., Baltimore, 1945.

Wehmeyer, L.E.    *The genus* Diaporthe *Nitschke and its segregates.*    x+ 349 pp., Ann Arbor, 1933.

Zundel, George **L.**    *The Ustilaginales of the World.*    410 pp., Pennsylvania, (Mimeographed).

Zycha, H.    Pilze II. Mucorineae in *Kryptogamenfiora der Mark Brandenburg.*    viii+264 pp., Leipzig, 1935.

# INDEX TO GENERA

| | | | | | |
|---|---|---|---|---|---|
| Acanthostigma | 21 | Ceratiomyxa | **1** | Dacryopinax | 40 |
| Achlya | *5* | Cercospora | 98 | Dactyl aria | **96** |
| Acladium | 95 | Cerebell a | 104 | Daedalea | 71 |
| Aecidium | SS | Cerotelium | 40 | Daldinia | 22 |
| Agaricus | 76 | Ceuthospora | 86 | Darluca | 86 |
| Ahmadia | 93 | Chaetocladium | 11 | Dasyscypha | 37 |
| Ahmadinula | 93 | Chaetomium | 21 | Dendrophoma | 87 |
| Albugo | 7 | Chrysomyxa | 40 | Dendrostilbella | 103 |
| Aleuria | 29 | Cintractia | S6 | Diachea | 2 |
| Aleurina | 29 | Circinotrichum | 100 | Diaporthe | *25* |
| Alternaria | 98 | Cistella | 37 | Diaport hopsis | *25* |
| Amanita | 76 | Cladosporium | 100 | Diatrype | 24 |
| Amaurochaete | 1 | Clasterosporium | 101 | Diatry pell a | 24 |
| Am phichaeta | 93 | Clavaria | 68 | Dichaena | 19 |
| Am phidid ymella | 12 | Clavariadel ph us | 68 | Dichomera | *81* |
| Amphisphaerella | 21 | Clavulina | 69 | Dicranophora | 11 |
| Amphisphaeria | 12 | Clav ulinopsis | 69 | Dictydi um | **1** |
| Ari.t hostomella | 21 | Clitopilus | 76 | Dictyophora | 84 |
| Arcyria | **1** | Coleophoma | 86 | Dictyoporthe. | 2S |
| Arth robotrys | 9S | Coleospori um | 40 | Diderma | 2 |
| Ascobolus | *29* | Colletotrich um | 93 | Didymella | 13 |
| Ascocalyx | 3S | Collettogloeum | 93 | Didymium | 1 |
| Ascochyta | 84 | Colpoma | 34 | Didymosphaeria | 13 |
| Ascodesmis | 30 | Comatricha | 4 | Dilophospora | 87 |
| Ascophanus | 30 | Coniochaeta | 22 | Dinemasporium | 92 |
| Ascot richa | 20 | Coniophora | 63 | Diorchidium | 41 |
| Aspergillus | 9S | Coniothecium | 101 | Diplodia | 87 |
| Asterophora | 76 | Coniothyrium | 86 | Diplodiella | 88 |
| Auricul aria | 38 | Coprinus | 76 | Diplodina | 88 |
| Auriscalpium- | 67 | Coremiella | 103 | Discosia | 92 |
| Badhamia | 2 | Corticium | 63 | Disceseda | 80 |
| Battarrea | 82 | Coryneum | 94 | Ditangium | 39 |
| Beauveria | 96 | Craterium | 2 | Doassansia | 61 |
| Bol bitius | 76 | Cribraria | 1 | Dothidea | **13** |
| Bolet us | 71 | Cronartium | 40 | Dothiorella | 88 |
| Bombardia | 21 | Crucibulum | 84 | Duportella | 63 |
| Bot ryodiplodia | SS | Cryptocoryneum | 104 | Durella | 36 |
| Botryosphaeria | 12 | Cryptostictis | 94 | Ellisiodothis | 10S |
| Botrytis | 96 | Cucurbitaria | 13 | Empusa | **11** |
| I3ovista | 80 | Cunninghamella | **11** | Endogone | **11** |
| I3remia | 7 | Curvularia | 101 | Endophyllum | 42 |
| Broomella | 26' | Cyathicula | 36 | Enteridium | 4 |
| Calocera | 39 | Cyathus | 84 | Entomophthora | **11** |
| Calvatia | **SO** | Cytospora | 86 | Entyloma | 61 |
| Cama rosporiu m | SS | Cytosporella | 86 | Epichloe | 2S |
| Cephalospori·.im | 96 | Dacrymyces | 39 | Epicoccum | 104 |

| | | | | | |
|---|---|---|---|---|---|
| Epithele | 63 | Hysterium | 19 | Mycoacia | 68 |
| Erysiphe | 27 | Irpex | 73 | Mycosphaerella | 15 |
| Euryachora | 13 | Isaria | 103 | Myrothecium | 104 |
| Eutypa | 24 | Isoachlya | 6 | Myxofusicoccum | 105 |
| Eutypella | 24 | Itajahya | 84 | Myxotrichum | 20 |
| Exidia | 39 | Karstenula | 14 | Naematoloma | 78 |
| Fistulina | 71 | Khekia | 19 | Nectria | 27 |
| Fornes | 71 | Lacellina | 102 | Neocosmospora | 27 |
| Fracchiaea | 29 | Lachnocladium | 69 | Neovossia | 62 |
| Fuligo | 3 | Lamproderma | 4 | Nigrospora | 102 |
| Fusarium | 104 | Lamprospora | 31 | Nitschkia | 29 |
| Fuscoporia | 72 | Lanopila | 80 | Nummularia | 22 |
| Fusicladium | 101 | Lasiobolus | 31 | Odontia | 68 |
| Fusicoccum | 88 | Lasiobotrys | 14 | Oedocephalum | 96 |
| Ganoderma | 72 | Lasiosphaeria | 14 | Ophiobolus | 16 |
| Gastrosporium | 79 | Lecanidion | 38 | Orbil'ia | 36 |
| Geastrum | 81 | Lenzites | 73 | Othia | 16 |
| Geoglossum | 37 | Leotia | 37 | Otidea | 32 |
| Geopyxis | 30 | Leptomassaria | 14 | Panaeolus | 78 |
| Gibberidea | 13 | Leptosphaeria | 14 | Papularia | 105 |
| Glomerel la | 26 | Leptostroma | 92 | Paxina | 32 |
| Gloniopsis | 19 | Leptothyrium | 92 | Pellicularia | 64 |
| Glonium | 19 | Leveillula | 28 | Penicillium | 96 |
| Gnomonia | 25 | Linospora | 26 | Peniophora | 64 |
| Gomphus | 77 | Lophiostoma | 20 | Penzigia | 23 |
| Grandinia | 67 | Lophodermium | 34 | Pericladium | 57 |
| Graphiola | 62 | Lycogala | 2 | Periconia | 102 |
| Graphium | 103 | Lycoperdon | 80 | Peridermium | 56 |
| Guignardia | 14 | Macrolepiota | 77 | Peronospora | 8 |
| Gymnoascus | 20 | Macrophoma | 89 | Pestalotia | 94 |
| Gymnosporangi um | 42 | Macrophomina | 90 | Pezicula | 35 |
| Hadrotrichum | 101 | Macrosporium | 102 | Peziza | 32 |
| Haematomyxa | 38 | Magnusia | 20 | Phakopsora | 41 |
| Haplosporella | 89 | Ma rasmius | 77 | Phallus | 84 |
| Helminthosporium | 102 | Massaria | 15 | Phellorina | 82 |
| Helotium | 36 | Massarina | 15 | Phleogena | 38 |
| Hel vella | 33 | Melampsora | 40 | Phlogiotis | 39 |
| Hemitrichia | 4 | Melanconiu m | 94 | Pholiota | 78 |
| Hendersonia | 89 | Melanogaster | 79 | Phoma | 90 |
| Hericium | 67 | Melanopsichi um | 57 | Phomopsis | 90 |
| Heterochaete | 39 | Melanospora | 21 | Phragmidium | 42 |
| Heterospori um | 102 | Merulius | 70 | Phyllachora | 24 |
| Hexagona | 73 | Metasphaeria | 15 | Phyllactinia | 28 |
| Hirrieola | 38 | Microdiplodia | 90 | Phy llosticta | 90 |
| Humaria | 30 | Microsphaera | 28 | Phyllostictina | 91 |
| Humarina | 31 | Microstroma | 94 | Physa rella | 3 |
| Hyalopsora | 40 | Mollisia | 35 | Physarum | 3 |
| Hydnum | 67 | Monosporidium | 56 | Physoderma | 5 |
| Hymenochaete | 63 | Montagnites | 77 | Phytophthora | 10 |
| Hypocrea | 26 | Morchella | 33 | Pilobolus | 10 |
| Hypomyces | 26 | Mortierella | 11 | Piptocephalis | 11 |
| Hy poxylon | 22 | Mucor | 10 | Piricularia | 97 |
| Hysterographium | 19 | Mycenastrum | 81 | Plasmopara | 9 |

| | | | | | |
|---|---|---|---|---|---|
| Platystomum | 20 | Saccobolus | 33 | Teichospora | 18 |
| Plectania | 32 | Saprolegnia | 6 | Terfezia | 34 |
| Plenozythia | 92 | Schizophyllum | 78 | Termitomyces | 78 |
| Pleospora | 16 | Schizostoma | 82 | Tetramyxa | 5 |
| Pleuroplaconema | 91 | Schizoxylon | 34 | Thecaphora | 59 |
| Pleurotus | 78 | Scleroderma | 79 | Thelephora | 66 |
| Plowrightia | 17 | Scleroderris | 36 | Therrya | 35 |
| Podaxis | 82 | Sclerospora | 9 | Thielavia | 20 |
| Podocrea | 27 | Secotium | 79 | Thyridium | 18 |
| Podosphaera | 28 | Sepedonium | 97 | Thyrsidium | 95 |
| Polyporus | 73 | Septogloeum | 94 | Tilletia | 62 |
| Polystictus | 75 | Septoria | 91 | Tolyposporium | 59 |
| Polystigma | 27 | Sepultaria | 33 | Trabutia | 18 |
| Polystigmina | 92 | Simblum | 83 | Trachyspora. | 52 |
| Polythrincium | 102 | Sirodesmium | 103 | Trametes | 76 |
| Poria | 76 | Sirodiplospora | 91 | Tremella | 39 |
| Poronia | 23 | Sirothyrium | 92 | Trichoderma | 98 |
| Pringsheimia | 17 | Solenia | 105 | Trichoglossum | 37 |
| Protoachly;i | 6 | Sordaria | 23 | Trichoscyphella | 37 |
| Protomyces | 12 | Sorosphaera | 4 | Trichosporium | 103 |
| Protubera | 79 | Sorosporium | 57 | Trichothecium | 98 |
| Pseudoperonospora | 9 | Sparassis | 65 | Tubifera | 4 |
| Pseudopeziza | 35 | Sphacelotheca | 57 | Tubercularia | 105 |
| Puccinia | 43 | Sphaerobolus | 84 | Tulostoma | 82 |
| Pucciniastrum | 41 | Sphaerotheca | 28 | Tympanis | 36 |
| Pucciniopsis | 105 | Spicaria | 97 | Tympanopsis | 29 |
| Pucciniostele | 51 | Spondylocladium | 103 | Uncinula | 28 |
| Pyrenopeziza | 35 | Sporodesmium | 103 | Uredo | 56 |
| Pyronema | 32 | Sporormia | 17 | Urocystis | 62 |
| Pythiogeton | 10 | Stemmaria | 104 | Uromyces | 52 |
| Pythiopsis | 6 | Stemonitis | 4 | Ustilago | 59 |
| Pythium | 10 | Stemphyllium | 103 | Valsa | 26 |
| Ramaria | 69 | Stephanoma | 97 | Valsaria | 18 |
| Ramularia | 97 | Stereum | 65 | Valsella | 26 |
| Ravenelia | 52 | Stictis | 34 | Velutaria | 37 |
| Rechingeriella | 17 | Stigmina | 103 | Venturia | 18 |
| Reticularia | 4 | Strobilomyces | 71 | Verpa | 34 |
| Rhizidiomyces | 5 | Stropharia | 78 | Volvariella | 78 |
| Rhizopogon | 79 | Stysanus | 104 | Xerocomus | 71 |
| Rhizopus | 10 | Syncephalus | 11 | Xylaria | 23 |
| Rhyparobius | 32 | Synchytrium | 5 | Xylosphaeria | 19 |
| Rhytisma | 35 | Tapesia | 36 | Zignoella | 24 |
| Rosellinia | 23 | Taphrina | 12 | Zythia | 92 |

# HOST INDEX

The hosts are indicated in italics. For hosts other than vascular plants, see the last page of the index.

*Abies pind row*
 Ascocalyx abieties
 I)itangiurn cerasi
 Fornes pini
 F. pinicola
 Gibberidea pithyophila
 Peniophora gigantea
 Scleroderris sollaeana
 Trichoscy phella calycina
 Tyrnpanis abietina
 Valsa abieties
*Abelia triflora*
 Septoria ahmadii
*Abutilon indicum*
 Pleospora scroph ulariae
*Acacia arabica*
 Cytosporella lignicola
 Fornes badius
 Pleospora herbarurn
 Polyporus ostreiforrnis
 Polystict us hirsu tus
 Septogloeurn acaciae
*Acacia f arnesiana*
 Botryodiplodia acacigena
 Haplosporella bakeriana
*Acacia modesta*
 Cucurbita ria pakistanica
 Fornes badius
 Ganoderrna applanat um
 Haernatornyxa pakistani
 Ravenelia taslirnii
*Acer oblongum*
 Rhy tisrna punctatum
*Acer pictum*
 Gnornonia cerastis ·
 Rhytisrna acerinum
*Ac hyranthes aspera*
 Cercospora achyranthis
*Aconitum l aeve*
 lJromyces lycoct oni
*Acrachne racemosa*
 Tilletia eleusines

*Aesculus indicus*
 Fornes fomentarius
*Agave americana*
 Microdiplodia agaves
*Agrimonia eupatorium*
 Pucciniastrum agrimoniae
*Agropyron semicostatum*
 Puccinia grarninis
*A grostis munroana*
 Puccinia grarninis
 P. poae-nemoralis
 P. pygrnaea
*Agrostis pilosula*
 Puccinia coronata
*Albizzia lebbek*
 Colletotrichu m lebbek
 Ravenelia sessilis
 Teichospora patellarioides
*Al hagi maurorum*
 Septoria alhagiae
*All ium cepa*
 Puccinia allii
*, Al l ium rubell um*
 lJrocystis magica
*Althaea rosea*
 Cercospora nebulosa
*Amarantus bl itum*
 Albugo bliti
*Amarantus paniculatus*
 Albugo bliti
*And rachne cord ifol ia*
 Monosporidium andrachnis
*Anemone obtusil oba*
 Puccinia pu lsatillae
 U rocystis anemones
*An gelica gl auca*
 Puccinia angelicae
*Apl ud a aristat a*
 Sphacelotheca apludae
*A plud a mutica*
 lJromyces apludae

112

*Aquilegia fragrans*
  Puccinia melasmioides
*Aquilegia vulgaris*          .
  Mycosphaerella thasslana
  Pleospora permunda
*Aquilegia pubifiora*
  Puccinia melasmioides
  P. rubigo-vera
*Argemone mexicana*       ..
  Peronospora gaeumannu
*Aristida adscencionis*
  Puccinia aristidae
*Artemisia* sp.
  Leptosphaeria artemisiae
  Pleospora hispida
  Pleospora permunda
*Artemisia parvifiora*
  Puccinia absinthii
*Artemisia persica*
  Puccinia absinthii
*Arthraxon serrulatus*
  Colletotrichum arthraxonis
*Asparagus* sp.
  Cercospora asparagi
  Fusicoccum asparagi
*Asparagus gracilis*
  Puccinia phyllocladiae
*Asphodelus tenuifolius*
  Phyllostictina   solierii
  Puccinia   barberi
*Aster bellidioides*
  Hendersonia astericola
*Astragalus* sp.
  Cucurbitaria astragali
  Hendersonia astragalina
  Microsphaera astragali
  Pleospora polyasca
  Uromyces lapponicus
*Astragalus coluteocarpus*
  Uromyces   phacae-frigidae
*Astragalus maddenianus*
  Uromyces lapponicus
*Astilbe rivularis*
  Pucciniostele clarkiana
*Astragalus tribuloides*
  Peronospora astragalina
*Atriplex laciniata*
  Peronospora littoralis
  Phoma changna
*Atriplex crassifolia*
  (=A. *laciniata*)
*Avena sativa*
  Helminthosporium   avenae

  Puccinia   coronata
  Ustilago avenae
  U. kolleri
*Bambusa* sp.
  Ganoderma colossus
*Bambusa bambos*
  Papularia sphaerosperma
*Berberis* sp.
  Amphididymella ahmadii
  Aecidium montanum
  Camarosporium berberidis
  Diatrype berberidis
  Didymella cadubriae
  Lecanidion tetrasporum
  Lophiostoma macrostomoides
  Nectria coccinea
  Othia lisae
  Pleospora herbarum
  Plowrightia berberidis
*Berberis ceratophylla*
  Aecidium montanum
*Berberis lycium*
  Aecidium montanum
  Cucurbitaria berberidis
  Dichomera macrospora
  Tubercularia vulgaris
*Berberis petiolaris*
  Aecidium montanum
*Berberis vulgaris*
  Pleospora orbicularis
*Beta vulgaris*
  Cercospora beticola
  Stemphyllium consortiale
*Betula utilis*
  Polystictus cinnabarinus
  Stemphyllium paradoxum
*Bignonia* sp.
  Schizoxylon insignis
*Blumea membranacea*
  Cercospora blumeae
*Boerhaavia diffusa*
  Albugo platensis
  Phoma nyctaginea var. boerhaaviae
  Pleospora permunda
*Bombax malabaricum*
  Diplodia bombacina
  Fusarium   semitectum
  Helminthosporium sativum
*Bothriochloa intermedia*
  Puccinia duthiae
*Bothriochloa ischaemum*
  Sphacelotheca andropogonis

'Bothriochloa pertusa
  Puccinia duthiae
  Sphacelotheca tenuis
Brachypodium sylvaticum
  Epichloe typhina
Brassica campestris
  Albugo candida
  Alternaria brassicae
  Peronospora brassicae
Brassica juncea
  Peronospora brassicae
Brassica napus
  Peronospora brassicae
Bromus japonicus
  Puccinia graminis
Bulbostylis barbata
  Puccinia liberta
Bunium sp.
  Erysiphe umbelliferarum
Calamagrostis pseudo-phragmites
  Dilophospora alopecuri
Calamintha clinopodium
  Puccinia menthae
Calamintha umbrosa
  Leptosphaeria doliolum
  Puccinia menthae
Calendula officinalis
  i\lternaria dianthi
Calotropis procera
  Cercospora calotropidis
  Diplodia asclepiadea
Caltha palustris
  Puccinia calthae
Campanula canescens
  Coleosporium campanulae
Campanula colorata
  Coleosporium campanulae
Campanula evolvulacea
  Coleosporium campanulae
Cannabis sativa
  Cercospora cannabina
  Peronospora cannabina
Capparis aphylla
  Botryodiplodia ambigua
  Camarosporium capparidis
  Circinotrichum microspermum
  Diatrypella barleriae
  Dinemasporium herbarum
  Diplodina capparidincola
  Hypoxylon latissimum
  Karstenula capparidis
  Leptomassaria capparidis
  Leptosphaeria capparidicola

Penzigia capparidis
Capsella bursa-pastoris
  Albugo candida
Capsicum annuum
  Colletotrichum capsici
  Pythium aphanidermatum
Carduus nutans
  Puccinia carduorum
Carex sp.
  Thecaphora atterrima
Carex wendelboi
  Cintractia caricis
Carthamus oxyacantha
  Puccinia carthami
Carthamu tinctorius
  Puccinia carthami
Cassia occidentalis
  Phoma cassiae
Cedrela serrata
  Fornes conchatus
Cedrus deodara
  Botryodiplodia deodarae
  Hericium caput-ursi
  Merulius lacrymans
  Nectria sanguinea
  Valsa pini
Celtis australis
  Uncinula polychaeta
Celtis eriocarpa
  Uncinula polychaeta
Cenchrus ciliaris
  (=C. pennisetiformis )
Cenchrus setigerus
  Cerebella cenchroides
  Poronia indica
  Sphacelotheca punjabensis
Cenchrus pennisetiformis
  Cerebella cenchroides
  Sorosporium penniseti
Centauraea calcitrapa
  Puccinia calcitrapae
Centauraea phyllocephala
  Puccinia calcitrapae
Cheiranthus cheiri
  Chaetomium gangligerum
Chenopodium album
  Cercospora dubia
  Dothiorella chenopodii
  Leptosphaeria gallicola
  Metasphaeria ambigua
  Peronospora effusa
  Peronospora variabilis
  Phoma herd;irum

115

*Chenopodium botrys*
  Erysiphe polygoni
*Chenopodium ambrosioides*
  Cercospora beticola
*Chenopodium murale*
  Peronospora muralis
*Chrysanthemum griffithi*
  Puccinia tanaceti
*Chrysopogon* sp.
  Phyllachora fallax
  Sorosporium tumefaciens
*Cicer arietinum*
  Ascochyta rabiei
  Fusarium orthoceros
  Neocosmospora vasinfecta
  Uromyces ciceris-arietinis
*Circaea alpina*
  Puccinia circaeae
*Citrullus colocynthis*
  Puccinia citrulli
*Citrullus vulgaris*
  Puccinia citrulli
*Citrus aurantium*
  Botryodiplodia lecanidion
  Colletotrichum gloeosporioides
  Daldinia eschscholzii
  Diplodia aurantii
  Eutypa lundibunda
  Fuscoporia laevigata
  Hypoxylon glomeratum
*Citrus* sp.
  Acrothecium lunatum
  Alternaria citri ,
  Cladosporium herbarum var.
                          citricola
  Eutypa lundibunda
  Haplosporella hesperidica
  Hypoxylon glomeratum
  Pleospora herbarum
*Citrus medica*
  Colletotrichum gloeosporioides
*Citrus sinensis*
  Alternaria citri
*Clematis grata*
  Aecidium orbiculare
  Puccinia clavata
  Puccinia wattiana
*Clematis montana*
  Coleosporium clematidis
*Clematis orientalis*
  Puccinia rubigo-vera
*Clematis* sp.
  J\ecidium clematidis

Aecidium orbiculare
Ahmadinula excelsa
Broomella montaniensis
Puccinia clavata
*Cleome viscosa*
  Albugo candida
*Clerodendron inerme*
  Colletotrichum clerodendri
*Cnicus argyracanthus*
  Ophiobolus penicillus
  Puccinia cirsii
*Cnicus arvensis*
  Albugo tragopogi
  Puccinia punctiformis
*Cnicus wallichii*
  Puccinia cirsii
*Colchicum luteum*
  Aecidium colchici
  Urocystis colchici

  maculiforme Cytosporella
  corticola Duportella velutina
  Lecanidion atratum
  L. clavisporum
  Polyporus grammocephalus
*Coriandrum sativum*
  Protomyces macrosporus
*Cornus macrophylla*
  Fornes scruposus
*Cotoneaster bacillaris*
  Gymnosporangium distortum
  Phyllactinia mespili
*Cotoneaster integerrima*
  Gymnosporangium clavariaeforme
*Cotoneaster nummularia*
  Gymnosporangium clavariaeforme
*Cotoneaster vulgaris*
  Gymnosporangium confusum
*Cousinia* sp.
  Puccinia cousiniae
*Cousinia minuta*
  Albugo tragopogi
*Crataegus oxyacantha*
  Gymnosporangium confusum
*Cressa cretica*
  Puccinia tuyutensis
*Crotolaria juncea*
  Fusarium udum

*Commelina benghalensis*
Ustilago commelinae
*Convolvulus arvensis*
Erysiphe convolvuli
*Cordia obliqua*
Circinotrichum
maculiforme

Uromyces decoratus
*Cucumis melo*
  Pseudoperonospora cubensis
*Cucurbita pepo*
  Cladosporium cucumerinum
  Sphaerotheca fuliginea
*Cycas revoluta*
  Phyllosticta cytadina
*Cymbopogon jwarancus4*
  Sorosporium ladharense
  Sphacelotheca lanigeri
*Cymbopogon schoenarithtts*
  Sphacelotheca lanigeri
*Cynanchum* sp.
  Diaporthe arctii
*Cynodon dactylon*
  Dinemasporium graminum
  Dothiorella graminicola
  Massarina graminicola
  Phyllachora cynodontis
  Puccinia cynodontis
  P. graminis
  Ustilago cynodontis
*Cynoglossum wallichii*
  Erysiphe horridula
*Cyperus dijformis*
  Puccinia romagnoliana
  Sphacelotheca cypericola
*Cyperus rotundus*
  Cintractia limitata
  Puccinia philippinensis
*Cystopterus fragilis*
  Hyalopsora polypodii
*Dactylis glomerata*
  Puccinia rubigo-vera
*Dactyloctenium aegyptium*
  Tilletia eleusines
  Ustilago sparsa
*Dactyloctenium scindicum*
  Ustilago idonea
*Dalbergia sissoo*
  Cercospora sissoo
  Collettogloeum dalbergiae
  Daldinia eschscholzii
  Daedalea flavida
  Diplodia dalbergiae
  Ganoderma lucidum
  Haplosporella dalbergiae
  Hysterographium dalbergiae
  Hypoxylon hypomiltum
  Irpex flavus
  Lecanidion atratum
  Mycosphaerella dalbergiae

Nectria sanguinea
Odontia corrugata
0. queletii
Phyllactinia subspiralis
Polystictus proteus
P. pubescens
Rosellinia aquila
Thyridium americanum
Uredo sissoo
Xylosphaeria ahmadii
*Datura alba*
  Curvularia trifolii
*Daucus carota*
  Curvularia penniseti
  C. spicifera
*Desmodium tiliaefolium*
  Aecidium callianthum
  Phyllachora desmodii
  Platystomum compressum
  Uromyces capitatus
*Desmostachya bipinnata*
  Stereum pusillum
  Uromyces eragrostidis
*Dianthus angulatus*
  Ustilago violacea
*Dicanthium annulatum*
  Puccinia duthiae
  P. propinqua
  Sphacelotheca andropogonis-annulati
  Uromyces andropogonis-annulati
*Digera arvensis*
  Albugo bliti
*Digitaria bicornis*
  Diorchidium digitariae
*Digitaria cruciata*
  Ustilago rabenhorstiana
*Digitaria royleana*
  Ustilago royleana
*Dolichos lablab*
  Cercospora dolichi
  Uromyces appendiculatus
*Dubyaea oligocephala*
  Puccinia major
*Echinochloa colonum*
  Ustilago trichophora
*Echinochloa frumentacea*
  Ustilago panici-frumentacei
  U. paradoxa
*Echinops* sp.
  Leptosphaeria doliolum
  Ophiobolus acuminatus
  O. ogilviensis
*Echinops cornigerus*

Puccinia echinopsis
*Echinops echinatus*
Puccinia pulvinata
*Eleusine fia gellifera*
Dinemasporium graminum
Massarina graminicola
Phoma graminis
*Enneapogon* sp.
Sphacelotheca pappophon
*Epil asia ammophil a*
Albugo tragopogī
*Eragrostis dipl achnoid es*
Ustilago egenula
*Eragrostis ja ponica*
(=E. *diplachnoides*)
*Eragrostis poaeoid es*
Sphacelotheca montamens 1s
Ustilago spermophora
*Eremurus himalaicus*
Puccinia eremu ri
*Eremurus persicus*
Puccinia eremuri
*Erianthus ravennae*
Sphacelot heca erianthi
Uredo ravennae
*Eruca sativa*
Albugo candida
Peronospora parasitica
*Eryngium coeruleum*
Colletotrichum.eryngii
*Erysimum hieracifolium*
Puccinia holboelli
*Eucladiu m syriacum*
Albugo candida
*Eulaliopsis binata*
Ustil ago indica
*Euphorbia* sp.
Uromyces tu berculatus
*Euphorbia cornigera*
Melampsora euphorbiae
Plenozythia euphorbiae
Pyrenopeziza mollisioides
*Eu phorbia d racunculoid es*
Melampsora euphorbiae
Ustilago euphorbiae
*Euphorbia* aff. *esul a*
Aecidium euphorbiae
Uromyces striolatus
*Euphorbia fal cata*
Melampsora euphorbiae-gerardi-
anae
*Eu phorbia helioscopia*
MP-lampsora eu phorbiae

*Euphorbia hispid a* .
Uromyces proemmens
*Euphorbia hypericifolia*
Uromyces proeminens
*Euphorbia k anaorica*
Melampsora euphorbiae
*Euphorbia thomsoniana* ,
Melampsora euphorbiae
*Ficu s* sp.
• Cercospora annulata
*Ficus benghalensis*
Auricularia nigricans
Septoria arcuata
*Ficus elastica*
Phyllosticta ficina
*Ficus palmata*
Cerotelium fici
Dothiorella ficina
Rosellinia aquila
*Ficus religiosa*
Xylosphaeria ahmadii
*Fimbrist ylis dichotoma*
Puccinia flavipes
*Fimbristylis schoenoid es*
Puccinia flavipes
*Fimbrist ylis tenera*
Cintractia axicola
*F ragaria indica*
Marsonina potentillae
*F ragaria vesca*
Marsonina potentillae
Mycosphaerella fragariae
*F rankenia pulverul enta*
Puccinia frankeniae
*F ritillaria royl ei*
Uromyces fritillariae
*Fumaria indica*
Peronospora affinis
*Galium* sp.
Erysiphe cichoracearum
Pseudopeziza repanda
*Galium aparine*
Peronospora aparines
Puccinia ambigua
*Gentiana kurroo*
Puccinia gentianae
*Geranium* sp.
Vent u ria geranii .
*Geranium aconitifolium*
Uromyces geranii
*Geranium collinum*
Puccinia leveillii

118

*Geranium collinum* var. *egl and ulosum*
Puccinia leveillii
*Geranium pratense*
Puccinia leveillii
*Geranium rectum*
Puccinia leveillii
P. polygoni-amphibii
*Geranium wallichianum*
Plasmopara pusilla
Puccinia polygoni-amphibii
*Gerbera lanuginosa*
Aecidium crypticu m
*Geum urbanum*
Sept oria gei
*Gleditschia triacanthos*
Leptothyrium gleditschiae
*Gol dbachia laevigata*
Peronospora brassicae
*Gossypium* sp.
Alternaria macrospora
Botryodiplodia gossypina
Cercospora gossypina
Didymosphaeria verrucispora
Fusarium vasinfectum
Haplosporella gossy pina
Hy poxylon latissimu m
Neocosmospora vasinfecta
Phoma gossypii
Trichot hecium inaequale
*Grewia vil l osa*
Pericladium grewiae
*Gueldenstaed tia* sp.
U romyces kondoi
*Gymnos poria royleana*       .
Dichomera gymnospona
*H aloxylon recurvum*
Uromyces heteromallus
*H edera nepalensis*
Aecidium hederae
Dot hidea tetraspora
Mycosphaerella hedericola
Thyrsidium hedericola
*H eleocharis palustris*
Pleospora heleocharidis
*H elianthus annuus*
Puccinia helianthi
*H el ichrysum* sp.
Nigrospora sphaerica
*H eliotropium eichwal dii*
Cercospora heliotropii-bocconii
*H emarthria compress a*
Sphacelotheca rottboelliae
Uredo rot tboelliae

*H eracleum candicans*
Aecidium stewartianum
Puccinia heraclei
*H eracl eum thomsoni* var. *glabiur*
Erysiphe umbelliferarum
Puccinia heracleicola
*H eteropogon contortus*
Puccinia duthiae
P. versicolor
Sphacelotheca monilifera
*H ibiscus cannabinus*
Cercospora abelmoschi
*H ibiscus esculentus*
Co!letotrich um hibisci
*H ibiscus tiliaceous*
Alternaria dianthi
*H ieracium vul gatum*
Puccinia hieracii
*H ordeum vul gare*
Helminthosporium sativum
Puccinia graminis
Ustilago hordei
U. nuda
*Impatiens* sp.
Puccinia koma rovi
*I mpatiens brachycentr a*
Puccinia argentata
*I mpatiens roylei*
Plasmopara obducens
*I mperata cyl indrica*
Puccinia rufipes
Sphacelotheca schweinfurthiana
*Ind igofera* sp.
Ophiobolus indigoferae
Pleospora scroph ulariae
Thyridium rousselianu m
*Indigofera linifolia*
Uromyces orientalis
*Ind igofera gerardiana*
Lophiostoma simillim um
*Ipomoea aquatica*
Albugo ipomoeae-pand uratae
*I pomoea hed eracea*
Albugo ipomoeae-pand uratae
*Iris germanica*
Puccinia iridis
*J asminum* sp.
Alternaria dianthi
Cercospora jasminicola
Hendersonia obtusa
*J asminum humile*
Septoria aitchisonii

119

*Jasminum sambac*
  Hendersonia obtusa
  Phomopsis jasmini
*Jugl ans regia*
  Fornes fomentarius
  F. scruposus
  .Melanconium juglandinum
  Microstroma juglandis
  Pleuxotus ostxeatus
  Poly porus squamosus
*Juncus* sp.
  Puccinia ju nci
*Juniperus macropod a*
  Fornes demidoffii
  Gymnosporangiu m confusum
*K obresia laxa*
  Cint ractia caricis
*Kochia ind ica*
  Peronospora kochiae
*Lactuca brunoniana*
  Puccinia prena nthes var.
                    himalensis
*Lactuca scariol a*
  Bremia lactucae
*La genaria vul garis*
  Colletotrichum lagenariae
  Curvularia affinis
*Lagerstroemia ind ica*
  Dothiorella lagerstroemiae
*Lamium rhomboideum*
  Puccinia phlomidis
*Lantana indica*
  Pleospora rudis
*Lathyrus aphaca*
  Uromyces fabae
*Lathyrus od oratus*
  Uromyces fabae
*Lathyrus sativus*
  Peronospora lathyri-palustris
*Launaea asplenifolia*
  Puccinia butleri
*Launaea nud icaulis*
  Bremia lactucae
  Puccinia butleri
*Lavatera kashmiriana*
  Endophyllum tuberculatum
  Pyrenopeziza lavaterae
*Lepid ium draba*
  Puccinia isiacae
  Septoria lepidii
*Lespedeza falconeri*
  Phyllachora lespedezae
*Les pedeza sericea*

  Uromyces lespedezae-sericeae
*Linum usitatissimum*
  Melampsora lini
*Lolium perenne*
  Puccinia rubigo-vera
  P. striaeformis
*Lonicera* sp.
  Amphisphaeria xylostei
  H:ysterium pulicare
  Lasiobot.rys lonicerae
  Metasphaeria helvetica
  Teichospora ignavis
*Lonicera quinquelocularis*
  Dasyscypha barbata
  Fornes ajazii
  Fuscoporia punctata
*Lonicera asperifolia*
  Lych nis apetala
  Ustilago violacea
  Puccinia longirostris
*Lycium europeum*
  Puccinia turgida
*Malcolmia africana*
  Albugo candida
  Peronospora brassicae
*Mangifera ind ica*
  Botryodiplodia mangiferae
  Coleophoma mangiferae
  Colletotrich um gloeosporioides
  Dothiorella ladharense
  Fracchiaea heterogenea
  Phoma mangiferae
  Phomopsis mangiferae
  Polystictus leoninus
*Marsd enia roylei*
  Cercospora ahmadii
*Marsilea minuta*
  Synchtrium marsiliae
*Medicago denticulata*
  Cercospora medicaginis
  Peronospora aestivalis
  Uromyces striatus
*Medicago lupulina*
  Pseudopeziza medicaginis
  Uromyces striatus
*Medica go sativa*
  Peronospora aestivalis
  Uromyces striat us
*Melia azed arach*
  Botryodiplodia azedarachta
  Cercospora meliae
  C. subsessilis
  Eutypa lundibunda

Polyporus ostreiformis
*Melilotus alba*
  Peronospora meliloti
*Melilotus parvijlora*
  Cercospora davisii
  Peronospora meliloti
*Mentha sylvestris*
  Puccinia menthae
*Merendera persica*
  Aecidium merenderae
*Mimosa himalayana*
  Ravenelia mimosae-himalayae
*Mirabilis jala pa*
  Colletotrichum mirabilis
*Morina* sp.
  Ustilago morinae
Morns *alba*
  Botryodiplodia anceps
  Botryosphaeria dothidea
  Clasterosporium mori
  Daldinia eschscholzii
  Diplodia mori
  Dothiorella berengeriana
  Fornes lividus
  Ganoderma lucidum
  Irpex flavus
  Haplosporella moricola
  Hypoxylon glomeratum
  Hypoxylon hxpomiltum
  Lenzites adusta
  Massaria epileuca
  Nectria sanguinea
  Polyporus adustus
  P. hispidus
  Polystictus proteus
  Phyllactinia corylea
  Rosellinia aquila
  Stereum schomburgkii
  Trametes lactinia
  Trichosporium masseei
  Valsella moricola
  Xylaria hypoxylon
*Musa paradisiaca*
  Colletotrichum musarum
*Nepeta* sp.
  Puccinia menthae
*Nerium odorum*
  Botryodiplodia nerii
  Cercospora neriella
  Haplosporella nerii
  Schizoxylon insignis
*Neslia paniculata*
  Albugo candida

*Nicotiana tabacum*
  Cercospora nicotianae
*Notoceros canariense*
  Albugo candida
*Oenanthe stolonifera*
  Puccinia oenanthes
*Olea cusptdata*
  Camarosporium oleae
  Ceuthospora oleae
  Coleophoma oleae
  Didymella olearum
  Fuscoporia punctata
  Haematomyxa pakistani
  Hysterographium fraxini
  Teichospora oleicola
  Schizoxylon insignis
  Metasphaeria scalaris
*Origanum vulgare*
  Camarosporium origani
  Puccinia menthae
*Oryza sativa*
  Helminthosporium oryzae
  Neovossia horrida
  Piricularia oryzae
*Oryzopsis lateralis*
  Epichloe typhina
*Otostegia limbata*
  Pleospora herbarum
  Uredo otostegiae
*Oxytropis sp.*
  Microsphaera astragali
  Uromyces punctatus
*Paeonia emodi*
  Euryachora paeoniae
  Lophodermium paeoniae
*Panicum antidotale*
  Cerebella antidotale
  Diplodina panici
  Tilletia tumefaciens
  Uromyces superfluus
*Papaver rhoeas*
  Entyloma fuscum
  Peronospora arborescens
*Papaver somniferum*
  Peronospora arborescens
*Paspalum distichum*
  Tolyposporium evernium
*Pastinacea sativa*
  Chaetomium globosum
*Peganum harmala*
  Camarosporium pegani
  Leveillula taurica
  Pleospora pegani

*Pennisetum flaccidum*
   Neovossia barclayana
   Sphacelotheca stewartii
*Pennisetum orientale*
   Phyllachora penniseti
*Pennisetum typhoides*
   Curvularia penniseti
   Sclerospora graminicqla
   Tolyposporium penicilla riae
*Pentatropis cynanchoides*
   Ahmadia pentatropidis
*Peristrophe bicalyculata*
   Pleospora scrophulariae
*Peucedanum aucheri*
   Puccinia bullata
*Peucedanum graveolens*
   Dothiorella peucedani
*Phalaris minor*
   Puccinia striaeformis
*Phaseolus mungo* var. *radiatus*
   Cercospora cruenta
*Phoenix dactylifera*
   Diplodia sicula
   Graphiola phoenicis
   lsaria pulcherrima
   Pesta lotia phoenicis
   Poria ravenalae
*Phragmites karka*
   Hadrotrichum phragmitis
   Puccinia invenusta
   P. isiacae
*Phytolacca acinosa*
   Leptosphaeria doliolum
   Phomopsis phytolaccae
   Phyllosticta phytolaccae
*Picea morinda*
   Chrysomyxa deformans
   Peridermium thomsoni
   Polyporus stipticus
   P. tephroleucus
   Pucciniastrum areolatum
*Pimpinella diversifolia*
   Puccinia pimpinellae
*Pinus excelsa*
   Auriscalpium vulgare
   Fornes borneonensis
   F. fastuosus
   F. pini
   -var. abieties f. rnicropora
   Hyrnenochaete leonina
   Hysteriurn macrospora
   Leptostrorna ahrnadii
   Lophodermiurn pini-excelsae

   Merulius aureus
   Odontia arguta
   Podocrea cordiceps
   Polyporus dryaedeus
   Stereurn chailletii
   S. purpureurn
   Therrya cembrae
*Pistacia khinjuk*
   Polyporus tinctorius
*Pisum sativum*
   Erysiphe pisi
   Uromyces fabae
*Plantago amplexicaulis*
   Peronospora alta
*Plantago lanceolata*
   Puccinia cynodontis
*Plantago ovata*
   Erysiphe cichoracearum
*Platanus orientalis*
   Stigrnina platani
*Plectranthus rugosus*
   Didyrnosphaeria brunneola
*Pleurospermum stylosum*
   Puccinia chitralensis
*Poa annua*
   Epicoccurn nigrurn
   Puccinia poarurn
*Poa bulbosa*
   Phyllachora poae
*Poinsettia pulcherrima*
   Colletotrichurn poinsettiae
   Fusicoccurn euphorbiae
*Polygonum* sp.
   Puccinia solrnii
*Polygonum amplexicaule* var. *speciosurn*
   Puccinia barclayii
*Polygonum aviculare*
   Erysiphe polygoni
   Uromyces polygoni-aviculariae
*Polygonum barbatum*
   Ustilago cordai
   U. utriculosa
*Polygonum glabrum*
   Melanopsichiurn pennsylvanicurn
   Ustilago utriculosa
*Polygonum nepalensis*
   Ustilago nepalensis
*Polygonum persicaria*
   Sphacelotheca hydropiperis
*Polygonum pterocarpum*
   Puccinia polygoni-arnphibii
*Polygonum viviparum*
   Uromyces polygoni-aviculariae

*Populus alba*
 Melarnpsora populnea
*Populus ciliata*
 Linospora populina
 Melarnpsora ciliata
 Taphrina aurea
 Uncinula salicis
*Portulaca oleracea*
 Albugo portulacae
*Potentilla argentea*
 Phragrnidiurn potentillae
*Potentilla argyrophylla*
 Phragrnidiurn laceianurn
*Potentilla kleiniana*
 Phragrnidiurn potentillae
*Potentilla nepalensis*
 Phragrnidiurn nepalensis
 P. papillaturn
 P. potentillae
*Prosopis julifiora*
 Haplosporella prosopidina
 H. prosopidincola
 Nectria sanguinea
 Valsa ceratosperrna
*Prunus amygdalus*
 Phyllactinia salmonii
*Prunus cornuta*
 Diaporthe decorticans
 Exidia glandulosa
 Gloniurn clavisporurn
 Lenzites betulina
 Polystigrna ochraceurn
 Polystigrnina pallescens
 Tyrnpanis rnalicola
 Tubercularia vulgaris
*Prunus eburnea*
 Taphrina deforrnans
*Prunus padus*
 Taphrina pruni
*Prunus persica*
 Cladosporiurn carpophilurn·
 Polyporus ostreiforrnis
 Puccinia pruni-spinosae
 Taphrina deforrnans
*Psidium guava*
 Phorna psidii
*Punica granatum*
 Arnphichaeta punicae
 Dendrophorna punicina
 Pleuroplaconerna punicae
 Schizoxylon insignis
 Zythia versoniana
*Pyrus* sp.

 Botryosphaeria dothidea
 Fusicladiurn dendriticurn
 Valsaria insitiva
 Venturia inaequalis
 Zignoella herbana
*Pyrus communis*
 Phyllosticta pirina
*Pyrus malus*
 Coniotheciurn chornatosporurn
 Podosphaera leucotricha
 Trichotheciurn roseurn
*Pyrus pashia*
 Fuscoporia laevigata
 Marsonia rnali
*Quercus* sp.
 Coryneurn umbonaturn
 Daedalea gollanii
*Quercus dilatata*
 Arnphisphaeria fallax
 Auricularia rnesenterica
 Colporna quercina
 Dasyscypha indica
 Dichaena quercina
 Discosia artocreas
 Fistulina hepatica
 Fornes torulosus
 Hericiurn coralloides
 Hyrnenochaete cinnarnornea
 Nurnrnularia bulliardi
 Penzigia quercurn
 Polyporus cuticularis
 P. sulphureus
 Pucciniopsis quercina
 Stereurn purpureurn
 Trabutia quercina
*Quercus incana*
 Auricularia rnesenterica
 Fornes fastuosus
 Nurnrnularia bulliardi
*Ranunculus* sp.
 Entylorna ranunculi
*Ranunculus faleatus*

 Puccinia ranunculi-falcatae
*Rananculus hirtellus*
 Aecidiurn ranunculacearurn
*Rhamnus dahuricus*
 Puccinia coronata
*Rhamnus virgatus*
 Puccinia coronata
*Raphanus sativus*
 Peronospora brassicae
*Ribes rubrum*
 Cronartiurn rubrurn

Puccinia ribis
*Ricinus communis*
  Botryodiplodia ricini
*Rosa sp.*
  Coniothyrium fuckelii
  Cryptostictis caudata
  Cytospora ambiens
  Dasyscypha bicolor
  Diplodia rosarum
  Exidia glandulosa
  Fornes ribis f. rosae
  Pezicula brenckleana
  Phragmidium butleri
  P. mucronatum
  Tapesia rosae
  Velutaria rufo-olivacea
*Rosa centifolia*
  Cercospora rosicola
  Phragmidium rosae-moschatae
*Rosa damascena*
  Cercospora rosicola
*Rosa macrophylla*
  Phragmidium butleri
*Rosa moschata*
  Cytospora rosarum
  Phragmidium rosae-moschatae
*Rosa webbiana* '
  Phragmidium kamtschatke
  P. rosae-moschatae
  P. tuberculatum
*Rottboellia exaltata*
  Sphacelotheca ophiuri
*Rubia cordifolia*
  Puccinia collettiana
*Rubus sp*
  Coniothyrium fuckelii
  Cytospora ambiens
  Leptosphaeria sepincola
  Phragmidium shogranense
  Pringsheimia sepincola
*Rubus fruticosus*
  Cytospora ambiens
  Hendersonia rubi
*Rubus lasiocarpus*
  Phragmidium barclayi
*Rubus niveus*
  Phragmidium shogranense
  P. mysorense
*Rumex dentatus*
  Ramularia decipiens
  Uromyces rumicis
*Rumex hastatus*
  Lophiostoma insidiosum

*Rumex nepalensis*
  Puccinia nepalensis
  Venturia rumicis
*Rumex orientalis*
  Puccinia acetosae
*Rumex vesicarius*
  Uromyces thallungi
*Saccharum sp.*
  Sphacelotheca erianthi
*Saccharum officinarum*
  Cephalosporium sacchari
  Cercospora koepkei
  Colletotrichum graminicola
  Coniochaeta pulveracea
  Lacellina lybica
  Ustilago scitaminea var.
            sacchari-barberi
*Saccharum munja*
  Coniochaeta pulveracea
  Epithele typhae
  Daldinia albozonata
  Grandinia mutabilis
  Lacellina lybica
  Leptosphaeria spegazinii
  Lophiostoma msidiosum
  Pleospora vulgaris
  Poronia kurziana
  Puccinia kuehnii
  Sphacelotheca sacchari
*Saccharum spontaneum*
  Glomerella tucumanensis
  Lacellina lybica
  Ophiobolus spirosporus
  Phyllachora sacchari-spontanei
  Pleospora lecanora
  Puccinia kuehnii
*Sagittaria guayanensis*
  Doassansis sagittariae
*Salix sp.*
  Cytospora ambiens
  C. salicis
  Fornes igniarius
  Melampsora epitea
  Uncinula salicis
*Salix acmophylla*
  Melampsora salicis-albae
*Salix hastata*
  Melampsora epitea
*Salix tetrasperma*
  Phyllactinia suffulta
*Salvadora oleoides*
  Camarosporium capparidis
  Cytosporella verrucosa

Diplodia salvadoriqa
Guignardia bidwelli
Haplosporella salvadorae
Nitschkia salvadorae
Polyporus calcuttensis
Valsaria salvadorina
*Saluia plebeia*
Peronospora swinglei
*Salvia hydrangea*
Puccinia bithynica
*Sarcococca saligna*
Doth1dea collecta
Stictis radiata
*Saxifraga ciliata*
Puccinia saxifragae-ciliatae
*Saxifraga stracheyi*
Puccinia saxifragae-cilia tae
*Schismus arabicus*
Ustilago schismi
*Scirpus* sp.
Physoderma schroeteri
*Scirpus littoralis*
Puccinia scirpi
*Scirpus maritimus*
Uromyces lineolatus
*Scrophularia* sp.
Leptosphaeria modesta
Ophiobolus tenellus
*Sedum heterodontum*
Puccinia umbilici
*Selinum papyraceum*
Puccinia ligustica
*Senecio chrysanthemoides*
Leptosphaeria dearsa
**L.** dolioloides
**L.** nitschkei
**L.** ogilviensis
*Serratula pallida*
Albu go tragopogi
Puccinia schirajewskii
*Setaria glauca (= S. lutescens)*
*Setaria italica*
Ustilago crameri
*Setaria lutescens*
Curvularia spicifera
Uromyces setariae-italicae
Ustilago neglecta
*Setaria verticillata*
Tilletia setaricola
*Silene moorcroftiana*
Sorosporium saponariae
*Sisymbrium irio*
Albugo candida

Peronospora sisymbrii-officinalis
*Skimmia laureola*
Nectria cinnabarina
Helotium virgultoru m
*Smilax parvifolia*
Amphididymella ahmadii
Ellisiodothis smilacis
*Solanum nigrum*
Cercospora solani
*Solanum tuberosum*
Alternaria solani
Phytophthota infestans
*Solidago virga-aurea*
Puccinia extensicola
*Sor1chus arvensis*
Puccinia sonchi
*Sonchus oleraceus*
Bremia sonchi
*Sorghum halepense*
Puccinia purpurea
Sphacelotheca cruenta
S. sorghi
*Sorghum vulgare*
Colletotrichu m graminicolu m
Helminthosporium tu rcicum
Puccinia pu rpurea
Sphacelotheca reiliaha
S. sorghi
Tolyposporium ehrenbergii
*Spinacea oleracea* •
Cercospora beticola
Chaetomium brasiliense
C. indicum
Curvularia lunata
Melanospora theleboloides
*Spiraea* sp:\
Dictyoporthe ahmadii
*Spiraea lindleyana*
Diaporthopsis spiraeae
*Sporobolum marginatus*
Uromyces ignobilis
*Stellaria media*
Ustilago violacea
*Stipa sibirica*
Urocystis stipae
*Strobilanthes dalhousianus*
Puccinia polliniae
*Suaeda Jruticosa*
Eutypella stellulata
Uromyces chenopodii
Xy losphaeria ahmadii
*Swertia petiolata*
Puccinia swertiae

*Swertia speciosa*
  Puccinia swertiae
*Tamarix articulata*
  Polyporus ca,lcuttensis
  P. hispid us
  Sirodiplospora tamaricis
  Valsaria tamaricis
*Taraxacum· officinal e*
  Protomyces pachydermus
  Puccinia silvatica
  P. taraxaci
  Sphaerotheca fuliginea
*Taxus baccat a*
  Pestalotia funerea
  Sirothyrium taxi
*Themed a anathera*
  Sphacelotheca vrybu rgii
*Thevetia neriifolia*
  Fusicocum lahoreanum
*Tragopogon* sp.
  Puccinia hysterium
*Tricholaena teneri.ffae*
  Sphacelotheca tricholaenae
*Tricholepis stewartii*
  Pleospora planispora
  Puccinia tricholepidis
*Trifolium pratense*
  Pseud opeziza trifolii
*Trifolium repens*
  Polythrincium trifolii
  Uromyces nerviphilus
  U. trifolii-repentis
*Trifolium resupinatum*
  Mycosphaerella killiani
  Peronospora trifolii-repentis
  Physoderma trifolii
  Polythrincium trifolii
  Uromyces *minor*
  U. trifolii
*Trigonell a foenum- graecum*
  Cercospora traversia na
  Peronospora trigonellae
*Trigone lla gracilis*
  Uromyces anthyllidis
*Trigonell a incisa*
  Uromyces anthyllidis
  Peronospora trigonellae
*Trigonel la polycerata ( =T. incisa)*
*Triticum vul gare*
  Erysiphe graminis
  Helminthosporium sativum
  Macrophoma triticina
  Neovossia indica

  Puccinia graminis ,
  P. rubigo-vera
  P. striaeformis
  Septoria tritici
  Tilletia caries
  T. foetida
  Ustilago tritici
  Urocystis tritici
*Tul ipa stel lata*
  Puccinia prostii
*Typha angustata*
  Clad osporium typharum
  Phyllosticta typhina
  Puccinia typhae
*Urtica* sp.
  Puccinia caricis
  P. urticae
  Ramularia urticae
*Valeriana wallichii*
  Uromyces valerianae-walliChii
*Verbena* sp.
  Chaetomium gangligerum
*Vernonia elaeagnifol ia*
  D\Jportella velutina
*Veronica agrestis*
  Sorosphaera veronicae
*Viburnum grand if lorum*
  Botryosphaeria quercum
  Dasyscypha corticalis
  Diatrype stigma,
  Dothiorella advena
  Eutypa lata
  Exidia glandulosa
  Fornes glandulosa
  Hypomyces hyalinus
  Hypoxylof\ hypomiltum
  H. rubiginos1,1m
  Khekia m utabilis
  Merulius corium
  Nitschkia cupularis
  Tympanopsis euomphala
  Tubercularia vulgaris
*Vicatia coniifolia*
  Uredo vicatiae
*Vicia faba*
  Alternaria brassicae var. phaseoli
  Uromyces fabae
*Vicia hirsuta*
  Physoderma alfalfae
*Vicia sativa*
  Peronospora viciae-sativae
  Uromyces fabae

*Viola bi.flora*
  Puccinia violae
*Viola caespitosa*
  Puccinia violae
*Viola canescens*
  Puccinia violae
  8eptoria violae
*Viola odorata*
  Thielavia basicola
*Viola serpens*   ..'
  Puccinia violae
*Vitis viniJera* ·
  Cercospora vitis
  Diplodia viticola
*Withania somnifera*
  Cercospora withaniae
  Coniothyrium withaniae
  Diplodia withaniae
*Zan.r.iiche.llia palustris* var.
       *ped icellata*
  Tetramyxa parasitica
*Zea mays*
  Diplodia zeae
  Helminthosporium turcicum
  Physoderma maydis
  Puccinia maydis
  Sphaerotheca reiliana
  Ustilago maydis '
*Zizyphus jujuba*
  Auricularia peltata
  Cladosporiurri zizyphi
  Diplodia albozonata
  Diplodiella mllleri
  Eutypella zizyphi
  Ganoderm'!- applanatu m
  Ganoderma lucidum
  Humarina zizyphi

Phakopsora zizyphi vulgaris
Phoma zizyphina
Phyllosticta zizyphi
Polyporus• hispidus
Rosellinia. aquila
Xylaria hypoxylon
Xylosphaeria ahmadii
*Zizyphus nummuiaria*
  Phakopsora zizyphi-vulgaris
*Zizyphus oxyphylla*
  Valsaria insitiva

ANIMALS AS HOSTS
*Aphis* sp.
  Entomophthora aphidis
*Belone cancinula* ·
  Saprolegnia parasitica var. kochhari
*Hypera variabilis*
  Beauveria bassina
*Musca domestica*
  Empusa muscae

FUNGI AS HOSTS
*Boletus* sp.
  Hypomyces chrysosper;mum
*Daedalea flavida*
  Grandinia mutabilis
*Humaria hemisphaeric.a*
  Stephanoma strigosum
*Leptostroma .ahma.dii*
  Hendersonia leptostrornatis
*Mucor* sp.
  Chaetocladium jonesii
  Piptocephalis freseniana
  Syncephah.1s sphaerica
*Uredo rottboelliae*
  ·Darluca filum

Priniecf and published, by Dr Sultan Ahmad
Lahore

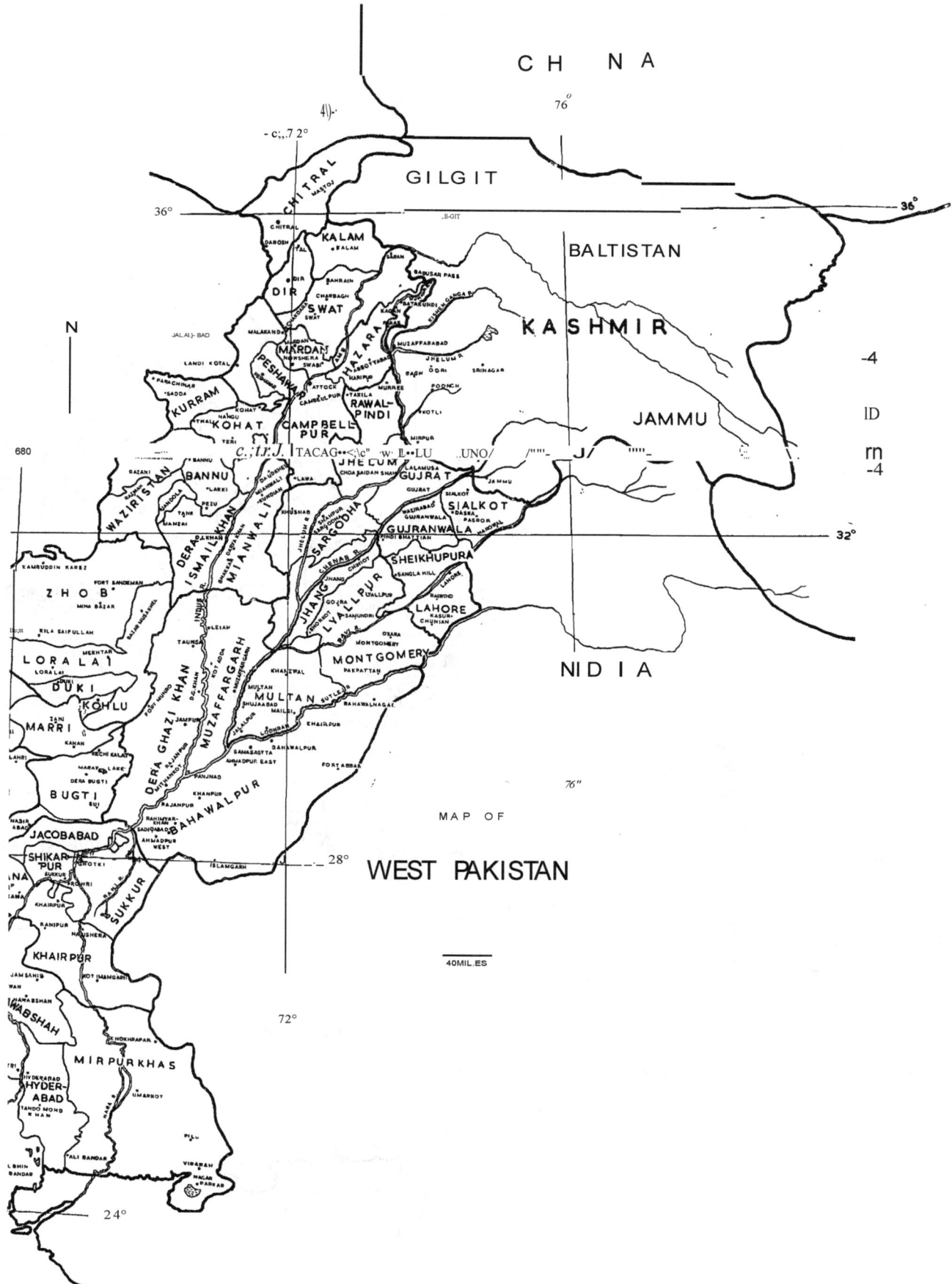

CH NA

GILGIT

76°

BALTISTAN

36°

KASHMIR

CHITRAL

KALAM

DIR

SWAT

MARDAN

JAMMU

-4

ID

rn

-4

PESHAWAR

KURRAM

KOHAT

CAMPBELL PUR

RAWAL-PINDI

JHELUM

GUJRAT

SIALKOT

GUJRANWALA

680

WAZIRISTAN

BANNU

DERA ISMAIL KHAN

MIANWALI

SARGODHA

JHANG

SHEIKHUPURA

32°

ZHOB

LORALAI

DUKI

KOHLU

MARRI

BUGTI

DERA GHAZI KHAN

MUZAFFARGARH

LYALLPUR

LAHORE

MONTGOMERY

MULTAN

BAHAWALPUR

JACOBABAD

SHIKAR-PUR

SUKKUR

KHAIRPUR

NAWABSHAH

28°

NIDIA

MAP OF

76"

WEST PAKISTAN

40 MILES

MIRPURKHAS

HYDER-ABAD

72°

24°

N

AFGHANISTAN

GILGIT

CHITRAL

KALAM

DIR

SWAT

MARDAN

HAZARA

PESHAWAR

KURRAM

KOHAT

CAMPBELL PUR

RAWAL-PINDI

WAZIRISTAN

BANNU

JHELUM

GUJRAT

SIALKOT

ISMAIL KHAN

MIANWALI

SARGODHA

SHEIKHUPURA

ZHOB

DERA ISMAIL KHAN

JHANG

LYALLPUR

LAHORE

LORALAI

DUKI

KOHLU

MARRI

SIBI

QUETTA-PISHIN

MULTAN

MONTGOMERY

DERA GHAZI KHAN

MUZAFFARGARH

NUSHKI

SARADAN

KACCHI

BUGTI

BAHAWALPUR

CHAGAI

KHARAN

KALAT

LARKANA

JACOBABAD

SHIKARPUR

SUKKUR

KHAIRPUR

MAKRAN

LASBELA

DADU

NAWABSHAH

MIRPURKHAS

HYDERABAD

TATTA

KARACHI

IRAN

ARABIAN SEA

MAP OF

WEST PAK

40 MILES

N

72°    36°
68°    32n
64°    28°
        14°
72°
64°    68°    2.40

www.ingramcontent.com/pod-product-compliance
Lightning Source LLC
Chambersburg PA
CBHW081656270326
41933CB00017B/3192